The Irish regiments
in the Great War

The Irish regiments in the Great War

Discipline and morale

TIMOTHY BOWMAN

Manchester University Press

Manchester and New York

distributed exclusively in the USA by Palgrave

Published by Manchester University Press
Oxford Road, Manchester M13 9NR, UK
and Room 400, 175 Fifth Avenue, New York, NY 10010, USA
www.manchesteruniversitypress.co.uk

Distributed exclusively in the USA by
Palgrave, 175 Fifth Avenue, New York NY 10010, USA

Distributed exclusively in Canada by
UBC Press, University of British Columbia, 2029 West Mall,
Vancouver, BC, Canada V6T 1Z2

British Library Cataloguing-in-Publication Data
A catalogue record for this book is available from the British Library

Library of Congress Cataloging-in-Publication Data
A catalog record for this book is available from the Library of Congress

ISBN 10: 0 7190 6285 3

ISBN 13: 978 0 7190 6285 8

First published 2003 by Manchester University Press

First paperback edition published 2004 by Manchester University Press

First digital, on-demand edition produced by Lightning Source 2007

For my parents

Contents

Tables and figures

Tables

Figure

Acknowledgements

I have incurred a large number of debts in the writing of this book. I would particularly like to thank Professor Ian Beckett who supervised the original PhD thesis on which the book is based and was kind enough to comment on the revised manuscript. Professor Keith Jeffery, who examined the thesis, has provided me with useful advice and support.

I would also like to take this opportunity to thank a number of individuals. Professor Alvin Jackson encouraged me to pursue postgraduate research on Ireland and the First World War and later, along with Dr Enda Delaney and Dr Peter Hart became a supportive colleague. Professor Brian Bond provided me with many helpful ideas about how to transform my PhD thesis into a book and Dr John Bourne introduced me to the mysteries of historical databases. Eric Mercer shared with me his findings on Belfast recruitment, while Nick Perry discussed with me his views on discipline and morale in the 36th (Ulster) Division. Students at the Queen's University of Belfast who studied my undergraduate course, 'Ireland and the Great War' during 2000–1 provided me with many useful insights.

I would like to thank the staff at Manchester University Press, especially Jonathan Bevan and Alison Whittle, for their patience and assistance.

In terms of finance, I would like to thank the University of Luton for awarding me one of their postgraduate bursaries from 1995 to 1998 and the Scouloudi Foundation for a generous grant which enabled me to complete research in London. This book was completed while I was a research fellow at the Institute of Irish Studies, Queen's University, Belfast and I would like to thank Queen's University for providing me with this research opportunity.

In London, the staff at the Imperial War Museum, National Army Museum, British Library, Public Record Office, Liddell Hart Centre for Military Archives, House of Lords Record Office and the Guildhall Library dealt with my many requests with patience and courtesy. Likewise, I am grateful to the staff of the Public Record Office of Northern Ireland, Linenhall Library, Central Library and Queen's University Library, who all made my research in Belfast a pleasurable experience. In Dublin, the staff of the National Archives, National Library of Ireland and the Jesuit Archives (particularly Father Stephen Redmond, SJ) all facilitated my research. The curators and staff of the regimental museums in Northern Ireland also proved most helpful, especially Amanda Moreno of the Royal Irish Fusiliers Museum, Armagh. Mr Peter Liddle kindly enabled me to view his archives at the University of Leeds at short notice, while the staff of the Bodleian Library and Liverpool Record Office dealt with my numerous requests in a very professional manner.

A number of groups also deserve my gratitude. Professor Brian Bond's military seminar at the Institute of Historical research, University of London, the history departmental seminar at the University of Luton and the research group at the Centre for Social History, University of Warwick provided much constructive criticisim of my thoughts on discipline and morale in the British army during the Great War.

Finally, and most importantly, I would like to thank my parents. Without their constant advice, support and encouragement, this book could not have been written.

Abbreviations

AIF	Australian Imperial Force
ANZAC	Australian and New Zealand Army Corps
ASC	Army Service Corps
BEF	British Expeditionary Force
CEF	Canadian Expeditionary Force
CO	Commanding Officer
CSM	Company Sergeant Major
GHQ	General Headquarters
GOC	General Officer Commanding
GSO	General Staff Officer
INV	Irish National Volunteers
IPP	Irish Parliamentary Party
IRA	Irish Republican Army
IWM	Imperial War Museum
JAD	Jesuit Archives, Dublin
LOL	Loyal Orange Lodge
NAM	National Army Museum
NCO	Non-Commissioned Officer
NLI	National Library of Ireland
ORs	Other Ranks
OTC	Officer Training Corps
POW	prisoner of war
PRO	Public Record Office, Kew
PRONI	Public Record Office of Northern Ireland
RIC	Royal Irish Constabulary
RSM	Regimental Sergeant Major

SR   Special Reserve
TF   Territorial Force
UVF   Ulster Volunteer Force
YMCA   Young Men's Christian Association

Abbreviations used in tables and figure

CR   Connaught Rangers
DORA   Defence of the Realm Act
FP   Field Punishment
IG   Irish Guards
InnsDrags   Inniskilling Dragoons
NIH   North Irish Horse
RDF   Royal Dublin Fusiliers
RIDG   Royal Irish Dragoon Guards
RInnsF   Royal Inniskilling Fusiliers
RIRegt   Royal Irish Regiment
RIrF   Royal Irish Fusiliers
RIRifs   Royal Irish Rifles
RMF   Royal Munster Fusiliers
SIH   South Irish Horse

Introduction

During the past fifteen years, research into the British army during the Great War has expanded enormously. There has been a decisive move away from the stale debates of the 1920s and 1930s (themselves revisited in the 1960s) over British generalship during the conflict, and the war and society school of military history has been firmly embraced by many able historians. Issues such as the expansion of the army, officer training, the role of the Territorial Force (TF) and recruitment have now received detailed consideration.

With regard to Irish regiments, historians have been well served. The disbandment of the Southern Irish regiments in 1922 created an impetus for the histories of these units to be written and many were completed by officers who had served in these units during the Great War, and as such provide an abundance of primary material.[1]

While, as recently as 1992, Keith Jeffery felt moved to describe Ireland's role in the Great War as 'an historical no man's land',[2] this has become increasingly less true. Certainly we know less about the home front in Ireland than in the rest of the United Kingdom, but in recent years the Irish regiments during the period 1914 to 1918 have received considerable attention. Terence Denman has completed an excellent study of the 16th (Irish) Division, demonstrating some of the political problems associated with the formation of this unit, its recruiting difficulties and its battle experience, particularly during the German Spring Offensive of 1918.[3] Meanwhile, Philip Orr and Nicholas

Perry have examined, in some detail, the formation and early combat experience of the 36th (Ulster) Division, although it should be stressed that Perry's article does demonstrate a number of the problems which this formation experienced, when it first arrived on the Western Front, which were ignored by Orr.[4] The wartime service of the Royal Munster Fusiliers has been considered, in detail, by Martin Staunton,[5] while the whole issue of Irish recruitment has received detailed attention from Patrick Callan, T. P. Dooley, David Fitzpatrick, Eric Mercer and Nicholas Perry.[6] Keith Jeffery has written on the Irish military contribution to the British Empire,[7] and, more recently, has provided an excellent survey of Ireland and the Great War, concentrating particularly on recruitment and the commemoration of the war.[8] The interesting and detailed work of these historians means that we probably know more about Irish units in the Great War than most of their English, Scottish or Welsh counterparts.

Discipline and morale have, however, remained two under-researched issues, both in the British army as a whole and in the Irish regiments in particular. Partly, this was due to the closure of archives – before 1995 only those prepared to make speculative assumptions based on incomplete court martial records or medical statistics were brave or foolish enough to tackle this complex subject.

In general terms, there has also been a tendency to concentrate on headline cases. This has, not surprisingly, been encouraged by the public campaign to gain pardons for British soldiers executed during the Great War, led by Andrew Mackinlay, MP. Following a government review of the relevant court martial records, Dr John Reid, then Minister for the Armed Forces, stated in July 1998 that the granting of pardons was impracticable due to the lack of surviving evidence but expressed a 'deep sense of regret' for the loss of life. However, those seeking pardons are currently continuing their campaign, now turning to local authorities for support.[9] What Ian Beckett has described as, 'the relatively minor matter of 312 wartime executions'[10] has therefore received enormous attention, given that a total of 5,704,416 men served in the British army between August 1914 and November 1918.[11] Indeed, even the eminent historian David Englander was prepared to make sweeping and questionable comments on morale and discipline in the British army based on the court martial records of Private Robert Young of the 11th Worcestershire Regiment, executed in September 1918.[12] Similarly, based on the tiny and highly unscientific sample of surviving capital courts martial transcripts, Gerard Oram has suggested that the High Command was lenient with conscripts and especially harsh with Irish soldiers.[13] Significantly, this is not a view with which Julian Putkowski concurs. Indeed, Putkowski suggests that Irish soldiers were not over-represented in the numbers of men executed following courts martial.[14]

Similarly, mutinies have received considerable attention, especially those at Blargies, Etaples and Marseilles.[15] However, these studies have generally ignored some fundamental facts. As will be developed further in this work, most mutinies did not result in executions and, as Peter Simkins has pointed out, the military authorities were prepared to dismiss what were, technically, mutinies as 'disturbances' in the New Armies while they were training in the United Kingdom.[16]

With reference to the Irish regiments, there has been a tendency to concentrate on well-defined episodes, namely Irish soldiers' reactions to the Easter Rising of 1916 and the alleged poor performance of the 16th (Irish) Division during the German Spring Offensive of March 1918. That is not to say that these matters have been exhaustively considered but they have been treated in isolation with regard to discipline and morale in Irish units throughout the war.

Studying disciplinary problems in the Irish regiments is also made difficult by the tendency of some historians to see Irish soldiers as very different to those in the rest of the British army. Gloden Dallas and Douglas Gill compared them, unconvincingly, to Czech troops in the Austro-Hungarian army,[17] while Terence Denman has drawn comparisons with French colonial troops.[18] Undoubtedly, discipline in Irish regiments was different to that in English units and this will be examined in more detail in chapter 1. However, in this matter Irish soldiers can much more meaningfully be compared with their counterparts in the Scottish highland regiments than with French colonial or Austro-Hungarian troops.[19] Equally, such generalisations can be based on a crude caricature of discipline in the British army. As

Gary Sheffield has shown, the manner in which disciplinary measures were employed differed markedly between units and discipline in a regular battalion took a very different form to that in a Territorial Force unit.[20]

The present work came about as an attempt to re-evaluate discipline and morale in the British army as a whole, based on courts martial records released at the Public Record Office, Kew in 1995.[21] However, it became clear at an early stage that a sample of units was required as the number of courts martial cases was so vast. It was decided to use the Irish regiments as a case study. Partly, this simply reflected my own research interests but on more scientific grounds the Irish units provided a mixture of regular and new army, and cavalry and infantry units serving in all the major theatres of the war. Equally, the political pressures placed on Irish soldiers by the rise of Sinn Fein would suggest that Irish soldiers were prone to demoralisation and it seemed logical to assume that, if serious problems were not occurring in the Irish regiments, then they would not be occurring elsewhere in the British army. A small sample of non-Irish units were also considered, so that some wider conclusions could be drawn about discipline in the British army.

Many of the conclusions reached by this study were to be expected. For example, men serving in Irish regiments clearly felt little sympathy for those involved in the Easter Rising. Indeed, the point is often forgotten that it was reserve battalions of the Irish regiments which initially contained the Rising. Similarly, Terence Denman's work on the 16th (Irish) Division in March 1918 appears fully justified – the Division did put up a firm defence and only collapsed when outflanked and outnumbered.

The 10th (Irish) Division was fortunate in that it was able to draw on large numbers of recently retired officers and other ranks and the pick of the Officer Training Corps (OTC). As a result its training was more extensive than that provided to either the 16th (Irish) or 36th (Ulster) Divisions. However, this formation suffered a high casualty rate at Gallipoli and its morale appears to have been low while serving at Salonika. Its 'Indianisation' in April 1918, whereby six of the Irish battalions were sent to France and their places taken by Indian units does, nevertheless, seem to have been due entirely to the manpower problems faced by the British army following the German Spring Offensive. There is nothing to suggest that this division was split up due to disciplinary problems.

Research into the 36th (Ulster) Division has also led the traditional assumption that the Ulster Volunteer Force (UVF) became the 36th (Ulster) Division to be questioned.[22] It is clear that, far from assimilating a large number of well trained paramilitary volunteers into the British army, this division had serious recruiting problems. Indeed, UVF links actually seem to have been damaging to this formation. They lumbered it with many senior officers, appointed for political reasons, who had retired long before 1914 and a number of junior officers whose only military experience was a brief dalliance with the UVF. Similarly, the division's political links prevented Catholics from joining it in large numbers, which provided serious recruiting difficulties in many rural areas. These problems only became apparent when this formation arrived on the Western Front.

The 16th (Irish) Division suffered from fewer problems, but like the 36th (Ulster) Division and many other New Army formations it suffered from a number of mutinies during its period of training in Ireland and England. Similarly, the division did end up with more than a few officers who were incompetent, superannuated or both. Like the 36th (Ulster) Division, the 16th (Irish) Division did have its own party political trappings, which may have damaged recruitment. However, during its formation, the division was ordered to send a large draft of men to the 10th (Irish) Division to complete it for overseas service. This meant that the 49th Brigade lost most of its trained and experienced men shortly before the 16th (Irish) Division embarked for overseas service and this may explain the poor discipline in this formation.

From 1916 the Irish regiments, especially those on the Western Front, began to suffer from serious manpower shortages. The result of this, as examined in chapter 5, is that many units were amalgamated and disbanded. When this took place in most British army formations the most junior battalion was simply disbanded, whereas in Irish formations other factors came into play. These certainly included assessments of the various units' discipline and morale and also reflected some political concerns.

While this work is very much a case study of the Irish regiments, some broader points can be made regarding discipline and morale in the British army as a whole. Direct comparisons with a sample of non-Irish units suggests that the numbers of courts martial tended to be much higher in Irish than non-Irish units. The possible reasons for this are posited in greater detail in chapter 1. It is also the case that courts martial were much more frequent in infantry than cavalry units. Officers were treated more leniently by the army's disciplinary system than were other ranks. This is particularly clear in the cases of Rifleman James Crozier and Second Lieutenant A. J. Annandale, examined in chapter 4. Both, effectively, deserted but while Crozier was executed following a trial by court martial, Annandale, much to the annoyance of his commanding officer, was allowed to resign his commission on health grounds. It is also clear that inefficient officers were frequently transferred to training units in the United Kingdom or to less demanding work behind the front line.

It is much more difficult to make any general points about discipline in regular, Special Reserve or New Army units. The experience of the Irish regiments suggests that each infantry battalion and cavalry regiment had its own unique courts martial record and it is certainly not the case that regular units consistently experienced more courts martial cases than New Army battalions. Equally, it is clear that while by 1917 regular and New Army battalions were obtaining drafts from exactly the same sources, differences did still exist between these battalions.

The whole question of the death penalty, as already noted, has received considerable attention elsewhere and it will not receive detailed consideration in this work. The only point which needs to be developed with reference to this issue is that, at least in the case of the 36th (Ulster) Division, it appears to have achieved its aims. The case of the 107th Infantry Brigade, which will be examined in more detail in chapter 4, demonstrates that the execution of three men in this formation instilled discipline and enabled this brigade to enter front-line service. It is also clear, in this context, that the death penalty was not used lightly. Only when other methods (including the replacement of the Brigade Commander and temporary transfer to a regular division) had failed, was the death penalty resorted to.

Some issues do remain something of an enigma. Apart from the courts martial summaries little material has been uncovered regarding mutinies in Irish regiments during the Great War. Possible causes of the largest mutiny which occurred in April 1918 and involved 116 men of the 16th (Irish) Division are considered in chapter 6. Other findings during this research were more surprising. Soldiers serving in Irish regiments were court-martialled for their part in seven mutinies during the war, a fact which has been neglected in previous studies of the Irish regiments. Also, a number of events, which were properly 'mutinies' but for which no men were court-martialled, occurred in Irish New Army divisions during their training period in the United Kingdom and in the 6th Connaught Rangers during the winter of 1916/17.

The whole question of Sinn Fein infiltration or sympathy in the Irish regiments has proved difficult to gauge. As Sinn Fein ran a slick anti-recruitment campaign from well before the war, it seems unlikely that many Sinn Fein activists joined the British army. Nevertheless, some of those who joined the army, most notably Tom Barry, were clearly radicalised by their experiences and joined the Irish Republican Army (IRA) following their demobilisation.

An assessment of Sinn Fein activism is made more difficult by the unreliable reports furnished by senior officers. It seems likely, as examined in chapters 5 and 6, that incompetent officers, from Lieutenant Colonel Denys Reitz (a former Boer Commando leader), of the 7th Royal Irish Rifles to Lieutenant General Sir Hubert Gough, used supposed Sinn Fein infiltration of units under their command to explain their own shortcomings as commanding officers.

However, this study has tended overall to confirm John Bourne's view of the British army as a collection of self-contained battalions, rather than an army in the continental sense.[23] It is clear that each battalion in the Irish regiments had its own separate and unique disciplinary record and random sampling of other British Expeditionary Force (BEF) units suggests that this was a trend which persisted throughout the entire army.

Notes

1 An excellent example of this is H. F. N. Jourdain, *The Connaught Rangers* (Royal United Services Institution, London, 1924–28).

2 K. Jeffery, foreword in T. Denman, *Ireland's Unknown Soldiers: The 16th (Irish) Division in the Great War, 1914–18* (Irish Academic Press, Dublin, 1992).

3 Denman, *Ireland's Unknown Soldiers*.

4 P. Orr, *The Road to the Somme: Men of the Ulster Division Tell Their Story* (Blackstaff Press, Belfast, 1987); and N. Perry, 'Politics and Command: General Nugent, the Ulster Division and Relations with Ulster Unionism, 1915–17', in B. Bond (ed.), *'Look to your Front': Studies in the First World War* (Spellmount, Staplehurst, 1999).

5 M. Staunton, 'The Royal Munster Fusiliers in the Great War, 1914–19', unpublished MA thesis, University College Dublin, 1986.

6 P. Callan, 'Voluntary Recruiting for the British Army in Ireland during the First World War', unpublished PhD thesis, University College Dublin, 1984; T. P. Dooley, *Irishmen or English Soldiers? The Times and World of a Southern Catholic Irish Man (1876–1916) Enlisting in the British Army during the First World War* (Liverpool University Press, Liverpool, 1995); D. Fitzpatrick, 'The Logic of Collective Sacrifice: Ireland and the British Army, 1914–1918', *Historical Journal*, XXXVIII, 4, 1995; E. Mercer, 'For King, Country and a Shilling a Day: Recruitment in Belfast During the Great War, 1914–18', unpublished MA dissertation, Queen's University of Belfast, 1998; N. Perry, 'Nationality in the Irish Infantry Regiments in the First World War', *War and Society*, XII, 1, 1994; and N. Perry, 'Maintaining Regimental Identity in the Great War: The Case of the Irish Infantry Regiments', *Stand To*, 52, 1998.

7 K. Jeffery, 'The Irish Military Tradition and the British Empire', in K. Jeffery (ed.), *'An Irish Empire'? Aspects of Ireland and the British Empire* (Manchester University Press, 1996).

8 K. Jeffery, *Ireland and the Great War* (Cambridge University Press, 2000).

9 On this issue see, J. Peaty, 'Capital Courts-Martial during the Great War', in B. Bond (ed.), *'Look to Your Front'*, pp. 89–91 and 101–4, *Guardian*, 25 July 1998 and *Daily Telegraph*, 25 July 1998.

10 I. Beckett, 'Facing Armageddon: A Select Bibliography', in H. Cecil and P. H. Liddle (eds.), *Facing Armageddon: The First World War Experienced* (Leo Cooper, London, 1996), p. 893.

11 P. Simkins, 'The Four Armies 1914–1918', in D. Chandler and I. F. W. Beckett, *The Oxford Illustrated History of the British Army* (Oxford University Press, 1994), p. 241.

12 D. Englander, 'Discipline and morale in the British army, 1917–1918', in J. Horne (ed.), *State, Society and Mobilization in Europe during the First World War* (Cambridge University Press, 1997), pp. 128–9.

13 G. Oram, *Worthless Men: Race, Eugenics and the Death Penalty in the British Army during the First World War* (Francis Boutle Publishers, London, 1998), pp. 42, 59 and 119.

14 J. Putkowski, 'Shot at Dawn: Irish "Cowards" in the First World War', unpublished paper presented at a research seminar in the School of Politics, The Queen's University of Belfast, 10 December 1998.

15 A. Babington, *For the Sake of Example: Capital Courts Martial 1914–18 The Truth* (Leo Cooper, London, 1983); G. Dallas and D. Gill, *The Unknown Army: Mutinies in the British Army in World War I* (Verso, London, 1985); G. Dallas and D. Gill, 'Mutiny at Etaples Base in 1917', *Past and Present*, 69, 1975; L. James, *Mutiny in the British and Commonwealth Forces, 1791–1956* (Buchan and Enright Publishers, London, 1987); J. Putkowski, *British Army Mutineers, 1914–1922* (Francis Boutle Publishers, London, 1998) .

16 P. Simkins, *Kitchener's Army: The Raising of the New Armies, 1914–16* (Manchester University Press, 1998), pp. 200–1, 238–9 and 243–4.

17 Dallas and Gill, *The Unknown Army*, p. 47. For a more balanced account of disciplinary problems in Czech units during the Great War see, M. Cornwall, 'Morale and Patriotism in the Austro-Hungarian Army, 1914–1918', in J. Horne (ed.), *State, Society and Mobilization in Europe*.

18 T. Denman, 'The Catholic–Irish Soldier in the First World War: The "Racial Environment"', *Irish Historical Studies*, XXVII, 108, 1991.

19 D. M. Henderson, *Highland Soldier, A Social Study of the Highland Regiments, 1820–1920* (John Donald Publishers Ltd., Edinburgh, 1989), pp. 267–78.

20 G. D. Sheffield, *Leadership in the Trenches, Officer–Man Relations, Morale and Discipline in the British Army in the Era of the First World War* (Macmillan, London, 2000), pp. 13–28.

21 Public Record Office, Kew (hereafter PRO), WO86/62–85, Ledger books of District Courts Martial, October 1913 to December 1918 (WO86/80 is missing from this series), WO90/6 and WO90/8, Registers of General Courts Martial, 1900–1947, WO92/3–4, Registers of General Courts Martial overseas, 1899–1945 and WO213/1–24, Ledger Books of Field General Courts Martial, August 1914 to November 1918.

22 For a more detailed consideration of this issue see my 'The Ulster Volunteer Force and the Formation of the 36th (Ulster) Division', *Irish Historical Studies*, XXXII, 128, 2001.

23 J. M. Bourne, *Britain and the Great War 1914–18* (Edward Arnold, London, 1989), pp. 154–5.

1

Measuring discipline and morale

This chapter will consider a number of methodological issues which are of relevance in developing this study. The differences between discipline in Irish and other British regiments and comparisons between civil and military law will then be considered. Finally, some consideration will be given to one issue surrounding discipline and morale which can be meaningfully considered in a thematic form: namely the attempts made to maintain high morale in the Irish regiments during the Great War.

In this study, I have decided to stay with basic definitions, concluding generally that morale is the force which comes from within which makes a soldier carry out his duty but which can be influenced by external factors such as regimental loyalty, efficient administration, good leadership and patriotism. Meanwhile discipline is an external force which carries out the same function.[1] This is for two main reasons. Firstly, while discipline and morale have been the subject of modern sociological studies, it is impossible to use such models given the nature of the source material which survives for the Great War.[2] Secondly, it is unclear how exactly the British army measured discipline and morale during this period. The censorship of soldiers' letters was certainly being used to assess morale in early 1918 and detailed statistics regarding cases of trench foot, shell shock and courts martial were kept, although it is unclear what conclusions were drawn from these.[3] Traditional and unquantifiable issues such as the dress and cleanliness of troops, the frequency of saluting and chats with battalion commanders, of varying degress of formality, were used to assess both discipline and morale.[4]

This book differs from previous studies of discipline and morale as it is based on a systematic study of courts martial records. A database of all 5,645 soldiers tried by courts martial, serving in Irish units on the Western Front between August 1914 and 11 November 1918, was compiled from courts martial papers held at the Public Record Office.[5] In addition separate databases used sample numbers of Irish battalions, serving at Gallipoli and in the Middle East, Salonika and in the United Kingdom during this period and considered the courts martial held in all Irish units based in the United Kingdom between 1 August 1913 and 31 July 1914. This means that it is now possible to assess how courts martial verdicts varied in the different theatres of war and between peace and wartime. A database was also compiled of courts martial in a small number of non-Irish units, which enables a comparison to be made between the treatment of Irish and English, Scots, Welsh and Australian troops by court martial.

The use of these records has created some problems, which is far from surprising given the difficulties which historians have found in dealing with modern British crime statistics.[6] Only in the case of courts martial, which resulted in the death penalty being utilised, have case transcripts been properly preserved (although, during research for this work some courts martial papers have been found attached to officers' personal files[7]). For most cases, the only surviving material is a brief entry, stating the accused's name and unit, the date and place of trial, the charge brought against him, the sentence passed, and whether this was amended by higher authority. Therefore, in the vast majority of cases, it is unclear what factors influenced the severity of the sentence passed.

The abbreviations used in the Judge Advocate General's records can also be confusing and prevented a thematic study of disciplinary problems. Frequently, soldiers were charged, not with a specific offence, but under a section of the Army Act. These are difficult to interpret, especially in the case of Section 40 of the Act, which is a universal charge, with no precedent in civil law – 'Every person subject to military law who commits any of the following offences; that is to say, is guilty of any act, conduct, disorder or neglect, to the prejudice of good order and military discipline'[8] – was in breach of this section. In cases where officers were charged under Section 40 of the Act, the actual charge was specified and these range from ownership of a camera on active service to homosexual activities.[9] Section 10 of the Army Act is similar in nature, covering a wide variety of offences – 'Every person subject to military law who commits any of the following offences; that is to say (1) Being concerned in any quarrel, fray or disorder, refuses to obey any officer (though of inferior rank) who orders him into arrest, or strikes, or uses or offers violence to, any such officer; or (2) Strikes, or uses or offers violence to any persons, whether subject to military law or not, in whose custody he is placed, and whether he is or is not his superior officer; or (3) Resists an escort whose duty it is to apprehend him or to have him in charge; or (4) Being a soldier breaks out of barracks, camp, or quarters'[10] – infringed this section.

The use of these charges on such an extensive number of offences makes it, at times, very difficult to assess what exactly were emerging as specific disciplinary problems in the Irish regiments and accounts for the large number of miscellaneous offences, noted in subsequent chapters. Equally problematic is the fact that a number of offences were multiple. It seems that many harassed adjutants would charge men with, for example, drunkenness, absence and Section 40 of the Army Act, presumably to insure that all possible charges had been made against the accused.

It seems that the usefulness of this source material demands some defence. Anthony Babington, Julian Putkowski and Julian Sykes have all held that capital courts martial cases were badly handled during the Great War and that many trials served 'for the sake of example' rather than to dispense any recognisable form of justice. To a large extent, these authors are correct in these assumptions; the role of military law was and is, primarily to maintain discipline in units. A number of serious allegations made against the British court martial system during the Great War appear much less serious when military law is compared with contemporary civil law. As previous authors have noted, 'prisoner's friends', officers appointed to conduct the defence of accused soldiers, rarely played an active part in proceedings.[11] However, they have ignored the fact that in civil courts, few working-class defendants could afford legal representation and that the system of legal aid was in its infancy.[12]

The position of 'prisoner's friends' was, as has often been ignored, rather different to that of a defence counsel in a civil court and this is typified in the writings of Captain E. A. Godson of the 9th Royal Irish Fusiliers. On 17 December 1916, Godson noted that he was

> Busy looking into the defence of Private Edgar who is charged with 'desertion' & looks as if he will suffer the extreme penalty. This is a stigma for the Batt[alio]n. & if possible to be avoided. On looking into the case it strikes one as being very pathetic as he gave a false age on enlistment in order to be able to join up & is now only 18½ & has been in the Army 2 years. He got a dose of gonorrhoea in Ireland & it has weakened him physically & morally. On the night before he fell out of the ranks on the way up to the trenches he undoubtedly was done up & did not realise what his action would bring him in for. If he were 12 years older his action would be unpardonable but I think it will be hard for the youngster to be shot.[13]

Godson felt that the court martial of Edgar was carried out fairly.[14] Nevertheless, he was disappointed by the outcome stating, 'P[riva]te. Edgar's sentence was published today – 6 months imprisonment, this is too light, not good for the B[attalio]n. but it is something of a personal triumph.'[15]

Much has been made of the 'class bias' supposedly evident at courts martial between middle-class officers and working-class other ranks.[16] This is of course a crude stereotype of the British army in the Great War; the massive expansion of the army and the horrific casualty rates meant that many working-class men received commissions as the war progressed.[17] More importantly, this stereotypical image of British officers ignores the fact that even after the removal of the property qualification for Justices of the Peace in 1906, the magistracy remained firmly middle and upper class in its composition in this period.[18] It should also be noted that trial by jury was not common in Edwardian civil courts. By 1900, less than one-eighth of trials in Ireland were by jury.[19] David Johnson further noted that jury trial 'was supposed to represent judgement by one's peers, although, in nineteenth-century Britain, given the property qualification for jurors, there was frequently a wide social gulf between those in the jury box and those in the dock.'[20]

Furthermore, while Putkowski and Sykes have stated that 'commanders reviewing capital cases frequently seemed reluctant to commute death sentences',[21] the truth is that just 10.82 per cent of British soldiers sentenced to death by courts martial during the Great War were actually executed.[22] As a comparison with civil law it should be noted that between 1914 and 1918 of the 97 people sentenced to death by civil courts in the United Kingdom, 40 were executed, 43 had their sentence commuted to penal servitude and only 3 had their convictions quashed by the Court of Criminal Appeal.[23] Strictly speaking, of course there was no appeals structure available to those found guilty by courts martial.[24] However, in a very real sense the Judge Advocate General's office did act as an appeal court and large numbers of cases were either quashed or amended, as discussed later in this chapter. In some ways, this system was fairer than the civilian appeals procedure; all court martial cases were subject to scrutiny to insure that proper procedures had been followed. An interesting comparison with civil courts is that between 1909 and 1912 the Court of Criminal Appeal heard an average of only 450 applications to appeal and 170 actual appeals, per annum.[25]

Some reservations regarding the reliance on court martial records as the measure of a unit's record of discipline and morale must be made. Commanding Officers (COs) held considerable personal powers to discipline the men under their command. They were entitled to detain a soldier and stop his pay for up to twenty-eight days on their own authority, without recourse to any form of court martial. Company officers could also impose lesser punishments (normally consisting of extra drill) on soldiers who had been involved in minor military offences, for example, being late for parade.[26] These provisions meant that, in some cases commanding officers could cover up serious disciplinary breaches, for fear that they would reflect badly on their own ability to command. The 14th Royal Irish Rifles, for example, had a very small number of courts martial during their period of training in Ireland, as the Battalion's adjutant refused to refer absence without leave cases to courts martial.[27] However, if the accused requested a court martial this had to be held and the available evidence suggests that a reasonably large number of soldiers, throughout the war, were aware of this right and made use of it.[28]

Full details of cases tried by COs or company commanders were never kept in a systematic, centralised fashion, and few actual case details have survived. However, it would seem fairly clear that, in most cases, the CO acted in a reasonably impartial fashion. The then Private Robert McKay, attending an orderly room parade in the 109th Field Ambulance in May 1915 noted,

> One man, Joe McMinn, was charged by the Sergeant-Major with refusing to obey an order, and the sequel was rather interesting. After the charge was read out by the S[er]g[ean]t. Major, McMinn asked the Commanding Officer could he cross question the S[er]g[ean]t. Major. Given permission, McMinn began by asking the S[er]g[ean]t. Major, 'When I was doing extra drill, were there not a number of other men also undergoing punishment?' The S[er]g[ean]t. Major admitted this was so. McMinn: 'You gave me an order to quick march, and I obeyed; now I was at the far end of the parade ground and my back was toward you. When you gave the order "About Turn" did you name me?' S[er]g[ean]t. Major: 'No, I did not.' McMinn, 'How, then, was I to know the order "About Turn" was for me?' The result was the case was dismissed. And, after we came out of the orderly room the S[er]g[ean]t. Major came up to McMinn and said 'Congratulations, McMinn, you got out of that well.'[29]

However, not all hearings by company officers were conducted within the requirements of the Army Act. Second Lieutenant Percy McElwaine on joining the 19th Royal Irish Rifles at Newcastle, Co. Down in August 1916, remembered,

> I had to take company orderly room and I had a case in which a man was charged with refusing to go into the sea on a bathing parade. The only evidence provided was a note written by the sergeant in charge of the party. I refused to accept this and as no witness was produced to prove either that the order had been given or that it was disobeyed I dismissed the case. This got round like wildfire and the cases in the other companies were dismissed too. The company commanders did not like my 'technicalities'.[30]

In terms of assessing discipline, the point must also be made that a number of officers seem to have dealt with disciplinary problems in an entirely illegal matter, using what could be termed 'informal discipline'. At its most extreme this involved shooting retreating troops[31] but it could take much more subtle forms and seems to have been practised fairly widely in Irish regular and New Army battalions. Captain Montgomery of the 9th Royal Irish Rifles gives an example of 'informal discipline' at work,

> I got a draft the other day. Undesirables from the 3rd. Batt[alion]. in Dublin – mostly old soldiers – tried some of the old tricks on the young fellow that couldn't know anything, I don't but nice and quietly I said 'Serg[ean]t. Major please arrange to have these people well beaten after parade, I don't want to be bothered writing things on their conduct sheets. I don't like writing. If one beating isn't enough you needn't bother me about it. Just have 'em beaten everyday at reveille for as long as it takes to lick 'em into <u>our</u> shape. When we get 'em in the trenches we can see if any of them are likely to come up to our standards or not.'[32]

The attitude of Captain Gerald Achilles Burgoyne is even more interesting as he had served in the 3rd Dragoon Guards during the Boer War of 1899–1902 and in the 3rd Royal Irish Rifles (Special Reserve) before joining the 2nd Royal Irish Rifles, and was therefore possibly reflecting a normal practice in regular and Special Reserve units. He recalled that the 'worst man' in his company had forgotten to draw ammunition before coming up to the line: 'I kicked him as far as I could and then hammered him over the back with my stick ... I think I'd have shot him had I had my revolver on me at the time.'[33] Burgoyne justified this by noting that this man had put the entire company at risk.

Conversely, a point which is not acknowledged by Babington, Putkowski and Sykes is that courts martial were reviewed by the Judge Advocate General's office, in considerable depth and many soldiers escaped severe sentences due to technicalities. A number of problems arose at courts martial, which saw the sentence passed quashed or amended. For example, in the case of soldiers serving on the Western Front, in Irish regiments, of 5,645 tried by courts martial between the arrival of their units in France and the Armistice, 1,917 (or 34 per cent) had their sentence altered in some way, following the submission of the case transcript to the Judge Advocate General.

Of these cases, 161 were quashed.[34] In most of these cases courts were wrongly constituted, mainly as members of the court did not hold sufficient commissioned service to be sitting in judgement. However, the sentences against Privates J. Doyle and J. Dunne of the 6th Royal Dublin Fusiliers and Private F. Lahiff, 7th Royal Munster Fusiliers were quashed purely as 'a Captain of the 6th. B[attalio]n., Royal Dublin Fusiliers and a Lieutenant of the 7th. B[attalio]n., Royal Munster Fusiliers served on the court in each case in place of a Captain of the 6th. B[attalio]n., Royal Munster Fusiliers and a Captain of the 7th. B[attalio]n. Royal Munster Fusiliers as appointed by the Convening Order; and the Courts therefore had no jurisdiction.'[35]

Another breach of regulations was carried out by Major General Powell, the GOC, 36th (Ulster) Division, who frequently held Field General Courts Martial in his division when it was based in Britain, although these could only legally be held overseas.[36] Another problem was with wrongly completed paperwork. An extreme, if not untypical example, of this was in the case of Private Francis Dillon of the 6th Connaught Rangers. The Judge Advocate General's Office noted that no less than five seperate forms had either been wrongly completed or were missing from the case notes.[37]

Taken together this catalogue of mistakes demonstrates that many officers, especially in New Army units, were almost completely unfamiliar with the intricacies of court martial proceedings, and this enabled a considerable number of men to escape on technicalities. Writing on his own legal training, Captain Montgomery, a New Army officer in the 36th (Ulster) Division noted,

> I have had to make up a lot of law, both military and civil and also, of course get a real good practical working knowledge of the rules of evidence. It is like everything else, I have had to pick it up by doing it in real earnest. No fancy courses or other luxury of that kind – just go and do it and may the Lord have mercy on you if you make a mess of it. I have been lucky enough up to now. I haven't even had a case returned to me. It is largely a matter of luck however.[38]

Partly to balance this, there does seem to be some evidence to suggest that higher command moved successful 'prisoner's friends' to other duties. Lieutenant Percy McElwaine of the 14th Royal Irish Rifles, who had practised as a barrister in both Ireland and Canada before the war, believed that he was transferred to Amiens, as a divisional purchasing officer, because he successfully defended three men.[39]

Therefore, it must be acknowledged that courts martial statistics are not a completely reliable guide to disciplinary problems in a unit. Officers could deal with military crimes, either formally or informally, without passing it to higher authority to protect their own position or the standing of their unit. Similarly, overzealous officers, involved in preparing defence cases, could be assigned to other duties to insure that the correct verdict (at least in disciplinary terms) was reached. However, to counterbalance this, it is clear that the Judge Advocate General's office extensively reviewed cases and altered or dismissed a number of verdicts due to legal technicalities. Similarly, some officers taking over command of a unit may have opted to have a large number of men court-martialled to stamp their own authority on the unit. This does seem to have been the approach adopted by Brigadier General W. M. Withycombe when he took command of the 107th Brigade, 36th (Ulster) Division in late 1915. Interpreting courts martial records is, clearly, a complicated issue; however, it does appear that the statistics used in this study are much more reliable than the indiscriminate use of statistics relating to health problems or reliance on a few random courts martial reports which were found in war diaries, which have been used by some previous authors.[40]

As previously mentioned, it is clear that discipline in Irish regiments was seen as different to that in English units and this is an important issue when assessing disciplinary problems in the Irish regiments. For example, Brigadier W. Carden Roe, who served as a lieutenant with the 1st Royal Irish Fusiliers during the Great War stated, 'The Irish soldier is undoubtedly a pleasant fellow to deal with. He gives a certain amount of trouble at times, but there is no malice behind it: it rather resembles the behaviour of a naughty child.'[41] Likewise, Captain P. L. Sulman, serving in the 11th Hampshire Regiment (the pioneer battalion of the 16th (Irish) Division) wrote,

Have got some tame Irishmen with me again. They're so nice; have you ever noticed how very polite the working class Irishman is. They work like mad if you push around with them, but the minute you go away they all sit round the fire and play toss halfpenny or something so as not to get bored ... Still they're an awfully good lot if you know [how] to treat them. Cursing is absolutely no use. They only think you're a fool to get so excited over nothing. Treat everything as a joke and with a little bit of blarney and everything goes swimmingly.[42]

Sir Francis Vane made similar comments with reference to his time as a major with the 9th Royal Munster Fusiliers, 'the Irish have to be treated – if the best is to be obtained from them – in quite another manner to English or Scots soldiers ... A kindly familiarity which might injure discipline in a British regiment, will never be presumed on by the Irish – and if you have to correct them for minor irregularities it is better to do it with a smile than a frown.'[43]

While seen as 'child-like' or 'colonial' by British officers, Irish soldiers were also, somewhat perversely, seen as more politically motivated than their English, Scottish or Welsh counterparts. This, of course, was not without reason: during the 1798 rebellion some Irish units had not shown particularly good discipline,[44] while Fenian infiltration of Irish regiments had caused concern in the 1860s.[45] More recently, during the Third Home Rule Crisis indiscipline was evident amongst many officers, most noticeably amongst serving and reserve officers who were actively involved in the UVF; while other ranks in the Special Reserve battalions of the Royal Inniskilling Fusiliers, Royal Irish Rifles and Royal Irish Fusiliers and in the North Irish Horse, exhibited strong UVF sympathies.[46] Finally, the rise of Sinn Fein, post 1916, appears to have led to some concern about discipline in Irish regiments. These fears over Irish discipline do seem to have led to a situation where many incidents, written off in English, Welsh or Scots units as 'strikes' led to prosecutions for mutiny in Irish units. This is particularly clear in the period when the 16th (Irish) Division was training in Ireland.

Such stereotypes are to be expected, given the portrayal of Irishmen in contemporary popular culture. As L. P. Curtis has commented, there was a,

widespread belief in Victorian England that Englishmen and
Irishmen were separated by clear-cut ethnic or racial as well as
religious and cultural barriers was reinforced continually by
political events in both countries. Intermittent rebellions and
chronic agrarian unrest in Ireland, combined with the disorderly
behaviour of some Irishmen in Britain, seemed to confirm the
notion that Irish Celts were a sub-race or people with habits anti-
thetically opposed to English norms of thought and behaviour.[47]

In terms of crime rates, there were clear differences between
English, Scots, Welsh and Irish crime patterns, which demonstrate that this view, outlined by Curtis, did have some basis in
fact. In his study of crime amongst Irish immigrants in Great
Britain in the nineteenth century, Roger Swift noted that the
Irish born were five times as likely to be committed to prison as
their English counterparts, between 1861 and 1901.[48] Swift
emphasises that, 'Irish criminality was highly concentrated in
the often inter-related categories of drunkenness, disorderly
behaviour and assault (including assaults on the police) and, to
a lesser extent, petty theft and vagrancy.'[49]

These high crime rates were not confined to Irish immigrants
living in Britain. J. V. O'Brien has shown that, by 1911, of the
major English cities, only Liverpool and London had higher
numbers of people proceeded against for indictable or non-
indictable offences than Dublin.[50] In rural Ireland the situation
was little better; Waterford and Limerick had higher arrest
records for drunkenness than Dublin and faction fights were
regular events, not only in Belfast, but in much of the Irish coun-
tryside.[51]

These high crime rates amongst the Irish in the Victorian and
Edwardian periods obviously had an impact on the number of
men from Irish units tried by courts martial. Firstly, it should
come as no surprise that offences such as drunkenness, which
were common in Irish civil society, were also common in Irish
regiments. Secondly, the stereotypical image of the Irishman in
early twentieth-century Britain, may have meant that officers
were prepared to have men serving in Irish regiments tried by
courts martial for crimes such as drunkenness, much more
readily than their counterparts in English, Scottish or Welsh
regiments. This stereotypical view of Irish soldiers may account
for the relatively high number of courts martial in Irish units,

even from 1916 to 1918, when many contained large numbers of non-Irish personnel. A similar stereotypical image of Australian troops may account for the very high numbers of courts martial in the Australian Imperial Force (AIF), for example in the Fourth Army in December 1916 of 182 cases of absence without leave, 130 involved Australians.[52]

As already noted, the manner in which courts martial records are kept prevents a fully thematic study of this issue, and, indeed, disciplinary problems are best considered in a chrono-logical context. However, the attempts made to maintain high morale and good discipline in the Irish regiments, and indeed, the British army as a whole, do lend themselves to a thematic assessment.

During the Second World War the maintenance of morale was an issue of great importance to the armed forces. J. A. Crang, David French and S. P. Mackenzie have shown the devel-opment of such diverse morale-boosting measures as the army bureau of current affairs, army education, the Army Catering Corps and post-war planning schemes. Similarly, psychological testing was carried out in units after 1942 to try and remove the mentally unstable from front-line units.[53] However, during the Great War there were very few initiatives taken at the High Command level to foster morale; instead, regimental officers were largely left to use their own initiative.

The regimental system did possess many positive benefits in fostering morale. Organised sports had existed long before the war and these continued to be carried out throughout the period of hostilities. Socially exclusive sports, such as polo, rugby and hockey remained largely the preserve of officers,[54] but not surprisingly, soccer was the most popular event. In April 1916 the 9th Royal Irish Fusiliers and 10th Royal Inniskilling Fusiliers played a match against each other, apparently as part of a Divisional Cup game. Meanwhile, in December 1915, the 14th Royal Irish Rifles had inter-company and officers against sergeants matches, prior to a match with the 11th Royal Inniskilling Fusiliers, and officers were keen to maintain a supply of footballs for men in the 5th Lancers.[55] Equestrian events also remained popular. In May 1916, the officers of 'D' Squadron, 5th Lancers, organised a steeplechase, which consisted of two races and on which a sweepstake was held.

Less ambitiously there was a mule race organised in the 36th (Ulster) Division in April 1916.[56]

Regimental holidays were also useful in maintaining morale, the most important for Irish regiments being St Patrick's Day, although some units did have their own special holidays, for example, the 1st Royal Irish Fusiliers celebrated Barrosa Day on 5 March 1915 with an extra dinner for other ranks and officers.[57] Regimental comforts funds, also operated in this period. By late October 1914 a comforts fund, established by the wife of Lieutenant Colonel Churcher of the 1st Royal Irish Fusiliers, and operating in the Armagh area, had already dispatched forty 11-pound packages to the Battalion. These packages included electric torches, tobacco and daily newspapers.[58] Meanwhile, in March 1915 the 1st Connaught Rangers received an ambulance from 'The People of Galway'.[59] More elaborate comforts funds were formed for the benefit of 36th (Ulster) Division. The Ulster Women's Unionist Council established the Ulster Gift Fund based in Belfast while in London, Sir Edward Carson's wife, Ruby, set up the Comforts for the Ulster Division Fund.[60]

The regimental system also helped to foster paternalism in officer–man relations in the Irish regiments. It seems to have been relatively common for officers, at least in regular units, to obtain gifts, in the forms of clothing, foodstuffs, cigarettes or sporting equipment from either regimental funds, private companies or from their own resources. Mrs Nightingale sent out razors to men in the 2nd Royal Munster Fusiliers following a request by Captain Filgate, a friend of her son's.[61] Meanwhile, by March 1915, 'D' Company of the 2nd Royal Irish Rifles had received a football from the employees of Mackie and Sons Foundry, Belfast.[62] Lieutenant J. A. T. Rice obtained cigarettes, footballs and clothing for men in his troop of the 5th Lancers, from his parents.[63]

Such measures helped to make the regiment more than simply an administrative organisation and there is considerable evidence to show that men did develop real loyalty to their individual regiment or battalion. J. H. M. Staniforth, in hospital with scabies in August 1916 commented, 'they have started a poisonous system of pooling all drafts at the Base and sending them to the unit that needs them most; so although its not often done with officers, it's quite on the cards that I might find myself packed off to the West Rutlandshire Militia instead of the 7th. (S[ervice]) B[attalio]n., P.[rince] O.[f] W.[ales] Leinster Regiment.'[64] This was not a fear confined to officers, as some men of the 10th Royal Inniskilling Fusiliers, wounded on 1 July 1916, were posted to the 1st Royal Inniskilling Fusiliers in August 1916. As one veteran remembered, 'Every day we used to report to the Commanding Officer of the 1st Battalion and requested to be sent back to our Battalion, but again and again we were refused.'[65]

While the regimental system clearly did help to build morale, and meant that new drafts were mixed with experienced veterans, the system did lead to a number of problems during the war. As Hew Strachan notes, 'Logically, the experience of the First World War should have destroyed the regimental system. The mechanics of the Cardwell/Childers arrangements were redundant in 1914–18.'[66] A mixture of poor recruiting during the war and a regimental system which had failed to keep pace with demographic changes in Ireland since the 1880s meant that from a very early stage in the war the regimental structure of the Irish regiments virtually collapsed. This meant that cross-posting of men to other units became increasingly necessary. As early as November 1914, for example, 3 officers of the Royal Munster Fusiliers, 5 of the Royal Dublin Fusiliers, 1 of the Connaught Rangers and 1 of the North Staffordshire Regiment arrived for duty with the 2nd Royal Irish Regiment.[67] Likewise, by April 1915, officers from Special Reserve battalions of the Royal Dublin Fusiliers and Royal Inniskilling Fusiliers were serving in the 2nd Royal Irish Fusiliers.[68] As the war progressed, the cross-posting of men became increasingly necessary and it seems that this was an issue which caused particular problems in the Irish units. When Captain W. T. Colyer rejoined the 2nd Royal Dublin Fusiliers from a school of instruction, in April 1917, he noted,

> when I got there, what a change! In the first flush of disappointment I felt as if I might just as well have been sent to the 8th. Battalion, not to mention the 18th. Manchesters or the 118th. Cheshires! There was a new C.O., Colonel Jeffries [Jeffreys], also a new Adjutant, Captain Mallory-Scott, and two-thirds of the other officers I had never met before. As for the rank-and-file, not only did nearly all their faces seem to be new, but about half of them made no pretence of having come from Ireland at all. Two

large drafts of Londoners had been sent to the battalion; and, Londoner as I was myself, I resented their intrusion as keenly as if I had been born and bred on the banks of the Liffey.[69]

The importance of the regimental system in cementing drafts together should not be overestimated. The British regimental system had been designed to assimilate small numbers of recruits into regular military life, not to rebuild units after the level of casualties suffered during the Great War. Commenting on the 2nd Royal Irish Rifles, brought up to strength in November 1914 after being reduced to just over forty men in the Retreat from Mons, John Lucy (then a sergeant) stated, 'The new battalion was shiftless, half-baked in every way, and the non-commissioned officers were very poor stuff ... The old army was finished.'[70]

The Irish regimental system did survive the Great War, but Nicholas Perry's view that 'Irish units and formations did retain their Irish identities, and at any given stage of the war were likely to be at least as representative in terms of regional identity as most other units in the British army',[71] is highly debatable. A system which had been designed to meet the requirements of Imperial policing in the 1880s was not appropriate to the battlefields of the Great War. Irish regular battalions survived only by cannibalising their more junior Service battalions and this was an unpopular measure, influenced by diverse political factors, which will be examined in more depth in chapter 5.

Another important element in maintaining morale were the visits of important personages to the Irish regiments. Field Marshal Lord Roberts was an early visitor to the 2nd Leinster Regiment in November 1914, although, perhaps not surprisingly given his stand over the Home Rule issue, his welcome does not appear to have been effusive.[72] Political visitors to the Irish regiments did not arrive until much later. On 1 September 1915, Second Lieutenant Hitchcock of the 2nd Leinster Regiment noted, 'The O'Mahoney came to visit us with some members of the Irish League, who were visiting the Front. He gave us a long speech about Ireland, and congratulated the C.O. on having such a fine Battalion with such an excellent fighting record. The men cheered him like blazes, as they had a second payment that morning, and had spent some time in an estaminet hard by!'[73]

Similarly, in February 1916 Colonel Jamieson-Davis, of the INV received a warm reception when he visited the 9th Royal Munster Fusiliers.[74] However, by far the most popular political visitor to the Irish regular units was John Redmond, MP. Father Henry Gill described Redmond's address to the 2nd Royal Irish Rifles in November 1915, in which the leader of the Irish Parliamentary Party (IPP) stated that,

> He was glad to meet a regiment which contained men of every creed from different places in Ireland, especially the North. They were brothers in arms and he was sure their harmony and unity in the great cause in which they were fighting was a happy omen of the relationship which would exist between all Ireland after the war, etc. The C.O. called for three cheers and someone said, 'and an Irish one'... Seeing that the regiment is in a great part from the North of Ireland and containing many Protestants the reception of Mr. Redmond was very remarkable.[75]

Redmond's visit to the 2nd Royal Munster Fusiliers was similarly appreciated.[76] Redmond, himself, certainly enjoyed these occasions; thanking Field Marshal Sir John French for his kindness, he added, 'I feel my visit has done good – at any rate to me.'[77] Politicians' visits to units were normally sneered at, as in the case of Hitchcock's comments above, as the politicians were mostly Nationalist and the officers Unionist in political allegiance.

The visits of senior officers to Irish regiments seem to have meritted little excitement. However, Major General Oliver Nugent, related, with obvious relish, one incident when the then General Officer Commanding (GOC) of Third Army visited the 16th Royal Irish Rifles and his inspection degenerated into high farce,

> I hear Gen.[eral] Allenby inspected the Pioneer battalion of my Division [16th Royal Irish Rifles] unexpectedly the other day while they were at work. He was not expected and only the Orderly Officer was there. When he saw Allenby coming he was so frightened that he tried to run away + fell into a barbed wire fence and there was so terrified that he could not remember what regiment he belonged to. Then Allenby got into a trench and used such language that the guide climbed out of the trench + did run away. Allenby then slipped + sat down very hard on the point of a brick and his language was such that the men took refuge in

dugouts. Finally he stepped on to the roof of a dug out which was unfinished and fell through and ended his inspection by saying, 'So you're the kind of men we have got to expect from the New Armies, are you'. As a matter of fact they are very intelligent men in my Pioneers and more nearly gentlemen ... than A.[llenby] himself.[78]

At the divisional level other ideas were developed to maintain morale. A lack of primary source material means that it is unclear what measures were introduced in the 10th (Irish) and 16th (Irish) Divisions.[79] In the 36th (Ulster) Division, Major General Oliver Nugent introduced a concert troupe and cinema. In May 1916 Major Lord Farnham formed the 36th (Ulster) Division's follies, improbably named 'The Merry Mauve Melody Makers'.[80] The artistic merits and effect on morale of their performances are debatable; by June, one officer felt that their performance was a 'fair show only'.[81]

Major General Nugent purchased a cinema outfit, at a cost of £200, out of divisional funds, for the 36th (Ulster) Division. However, as he mentioned to his wife, 'I had to send a committee to inspect the first lot of films as the French Comic Films might not always be good for these innocent Ulster men.'[82] At a more mundane level, a staff officer of the 16th (Irish) Division, noted that the divisional baths were thoroughly enjoyed by the men.[83] Interestingly, trench newspapers, which J. G. Fuller considers to have been important in maintaining morale in the BEF as a whole,[84] were almost non-existent in the Irish regiments. The 14th Royal Irish Rifles, an exclusive, middle-class unit, which seems to have included a number of journalists and printers from the Belfast newspapers in its ranks, produced a journal entitled *The Incinerator*. However, this work was only produced in May and June 1916; the original editorial team presumably suffered heavy casualties in the Somme offensive of July 1916.

Outside the regiment and division two organisations were important in maintaining morale: the Army Chaplain's Department and the Young Men's Christian Association (YMCA). The YMCA provided a canteens system both for units overseas and in the UK itself. Major General Powell, GOC of the 36th (Ulster) Division, was so impressed with the work of the latter that he wrote to Mr Black, the YMCA organiser in

Belfast, 'I cannot tell you how greatly the Ulster Division is indebted to you and your Association for the excellent work you have carried out in the several Camps of this Division. You have been the means of cheering the men up many an evening during the monotony of their lives in camp; you have kept many a man away from drink and evil living, and no one realises this more than do the men who have benefited.'[85]

Many officers in Irish regiments, at least at the beginning of the war, were thankful that their units received Catholic chaplains. As Jane Leonard points out, 'the Catholic chaplain could accompany his men right up to the firing-line, whereas the Anglican chaplain was not officially permitted to go beyond base camp. This rule was relaxed in 1916, but the troops continued to label Anglican chaplains as cowards.'[86] As a result, Catholic chaplains were praised for their work in raising morale and maintaining discipline. As Father Gill noted, 'the Brigade Major speaking of the R.[oyal] I.[rish] Rif[le]s. said they were a 100% a better battalion than a month before. He apparently connected it with the presence of the Chaplain for he said "When you came the regiment was at it's worst" i.e. It had lost most of its original men, and had got a lot of very poor reserve men to fill up its ranks.'[87] Likewise, Captain Filgate was most complimentary about the chaplain appointed to the 2nd Royal Munster Fusiliers, 'I hope the 1st. Batt.[alion] have got a man like him, as you can't realise what a difference it makes to the men + Everyone for the matter of that whatever religion he may be.'[88] Such support for the chaplains did not only come from officers; Father F. M. Browne, appointed Chaplain to the 1st Irish Guards in March 1916, noted that men of the Battalion voluntarily found and cleared out a room in an old barracks and furnished it with salvaged furniture, to serve as his chapel.[89]

Some chaplains also carried out duties which, while not strictly speaking spiritual, did help to maintain morale. For example, Father Gill obtained a 'parlour cinematograph' from Messrs Butlers of Dublin and showed six different films each week to men of the 2nd Royal Irish Rifles, until the resumption of open warfare in 1918.[90] Gill also gave a demonstration of 'muscular Christianity', when he accompanied his battalion in an attack on a German trench. Following his part in this action, Gill was recommended for a Distinguished Service Order.[91]

In the mainly Protestant 36th (Ulster) Division, chaplains and religion in general were seen as important in maintaining morale, but some problems were encountered. When the 16th Royal Irish Rifles first went on active service, Reverend Gibson from Lurgan was the Battalion's Presbyterian chaplain. When it was found that most men in the Battalion were members of the Church of Ireland, he was replaced by an Anglican chaplain. Lieutenant Colonel Leader, finding his new chaplain 'useless' re-applied for Gibson's services.[92] Major W. B. Spender, GSO2, 36th (Ulster) Division, commented on the religious observance of the men, noting the surprise of the GOC 4th Division that so many Ulstermen read their bibles while in billets.[93]

Political imagery was seen as important in maintaining morale in the 16th (Irish) and 36th (Ulster) Divisions. Major General W. B. Hickie introduced a Divisional Parchment award, surmounted by a shamrock, which carried the heading 'The Irish Brigade'.[94] A similar award was produced for use in the 36th (Ulster) Division, but it seems to have been given out much more sparingly.[95]

Orange imagery in the 36th (Ulster) Division was used in a much more unofficial fashion. There remains controversy over the presence of Orange sashes on 1 July (the original anniversary of the Battle of the Boyne in the old-style calendar).[96] However, a number of battalions in the Division did have their own Orange lodges; certainly there was one in the 9th Royal Inniskilling Fusiliers from 1915 to 1919, which came under the jurisdiction of the Ballymena District in County Antrim; Loyal Orange Lodge (LOL) 865 was formed in the 16th Royal Irish Rifles and LOL 862 existed in the 14th Royal Irish Rifles.[97] As there was clear 'Orange' activity in the 12th Royal Irish Rifles and 11th Royal Inniskilling Fusiliers it would be logical to assume that they, too, had formed Orange lodges.[98] Certainly they enthusiastically celebrated 'Lundy Day' (the Orange festival in which an effigy of Colonel Robert Lundy, who advocated the surrender of Londonderry in 1689, is burnt) at least in 1915. As Second Lieutenant Young related,

> the 18th. of December [1915] being lundy [sic] day it was cele-
> brated by some Derry men and other Ulster boys ... Two Lundys
> had been prepared one large and the other small some of the

inhabitants suggested they were father + son the father was about 11 feet long stuffed with straw and rockets put in unexpected places with large wooded [sic] feet and wire knees head filled with gunpowder and surrounded by a large yellow trimmed admirals [sic] hat. On his chest was a large placard with 'Lundy the traitor' on it. The procession headed by torchlights and the band marched through the village playing no surrender, Derry Walls and the Boyne Water. Then Lundy was let down on a wire rope from the tree where he had been strung up and set fire to amid great cheering + boohing – he was well soaked with petrole [sic] + burnt well every now + then they gave him a shake and his knees wobbled in a most realistic fashion. bombs [sic] made of jam tins were thrown into a pond just beside him, there [sic] burst and of course broke all the windows of houses round. The procession then reformed + marched up to the top of the village where Lundy junior was burnt with like ceremony.[99]

While this was a well-attended and popular event, apparently organised by Non-Commissioned Officers (NCO)s of the 10th Royal Inniskilling Fusiliers, morale in this unit must have fallen when the men were told that they would have to pay for the windows broken in Gorenflos.[100] The role of Orange lodges in maintaining morale is almost impossible to assess, given the lack of material available relating to them. If lodges contained a significant number of men, then it may have increased unit cohesion and loyalty, and also maintained important links with events at home. Conversely, if lodges contained only a dozen or so men, as had been the case with military lodges in 1830,[101] then their influence would have been negligible. Finally, it should be noted that Orange lodges could actually have compromised discipline. If an NCO was the master of a lodge and officers members (as was the case in the 16th Royal Irish Rifles, where Regimental Sergeant Major (RSM) Gordon was the Worshipful Master and Major Gardiner, Captains Allen and Shepperd and Lieutenants Dickson and White, members[102]), then this would create a difficult situation, with problems of partiality in applying the army's disciplinary code.

A final mechanism used to raise morale in this period, and the most controversial, was the trench raid. Trench raids were not solely designed to raise morale; they were, more practically, used to gather intelligence on opposing forces and, arguably, to reinforce divisional control over battalions.[103] In the Irish units a number of units built up reputations as efficient trench raiders. Perhaps, as Denman believes, this was as trench raiding fitted in with officers' pre-conceived views of Irish soldiers as 'shock troops'.[104] Lieutenant Colonel F. P. Crozier, built up an unenviable reputation in the 36th (Ulster) Division, due to his advocacy of trench raiding. The then Second Lieutenant Stewart-Moore noted of trench raids, 'Their object was supposed to be the maintenance of an offensive spirit but so far as I could see they never achieved anything on our part of the front. Colonel Crozier who commanded the 9th. [Royal Irish] Rifles was particularly keen on sending out such patrols all to no purpose except to show off. He had the reputation of being a callous and overbearing martinet.'[105]

In the 16th (Irish) Division, trench raiding was carried out with more enthusiasm. The Division practised raids while in reserve[106] and Brigadier General Pereria was a particularly forceful exponent of this policy.[107] However, despite 'dummy runs', raids carried out by the 16th (Irish) Division were often poorly organised and led to heavy losses.[108] As Denman concludes, 'Whether the constant raiding did much harm to the Germans is debatable. Nearly all the big raids cost the 16th Division heavy casualties, disproportionately high among junior and non-commissioned officers. Far from sharpening the fighting edge of the division it seems likely that the constant raiding blunted its effectiveness by depriving it of many outstanding leaders.'[109]

Regular battalions were rarely more successful in trench raids than their New Army counterparts. One of the more successful raids launched by the 2nd Royal Irish Rifles resulted in the capture of 11 Germans, but also led to the deaths of 2 officers and 11 other ranks, and wounding of a further 2 officers and 37 other ranks in the Battalion.[110] A raid by the 1st Royal Dublin Fusiliers on 28/29 June 1916 led to 3 deaths, 2 officers and 7 other ranks wounded and 13 other ranks missing. The raiding party did not even reach the enemy front line.[111] Indeed, the only occasion on which an Irish unit captured a significant number of German troops during this period, apart from during major battles, was when two officers and 125 men surrendered to the 2nd Royal Irish Rifles, after being bombarded with rifle grenades. As Father H. V. Gill remarked, 'This success acted like a tonic on the men, who seemed to come to life again.'[112]

To some extent trench raids were necessary operations, to probe defences and ascertain the strength of the opposing forces. There seems to be little evidence, however, that trench raids did anything to raise morale. In terms of discipline, it is noticeable that units which actively engaged in trench raids, such as the 9th Royal Irish Rifles, often had poor disciplinary records. This would seem to confirm Denman's view that such actions deprived battalions of effective junior officers and NCOs, who, in normal circumstances, had a key role in maintaining discipline.

What is most surprising about the British army during the Great War is its apparent ability to somehow muddle through. Unlike continental armies which had prepared for large scale, if not long wars, the British army was not adequately prepared for its massive increase in 1914. The regimental system, very different to that in use in other European armies, was not well designed to cope with this massive expansion. However, this system does appear to have held a number of advantages in terms of maintaining morale: allowing experienced and inexperienced troops to serve together, inculcating a spirit of paternalism into officers and providing established regimental holidays and sporting fixtures. At divisional level, British officers showed imagination and both the 16th (Irish) and 36th (Ulster) divisions possessed their own concert troupes and cinemas. Indeed, the success of many of these measures in building morale is shown by the fact that many of the same methods were developed for use in the Second World War.

Notes

1 For an excellent brief discussion of discipline and morale in this period see I. F. W. Beckett, *The Great War 1914–18* (Longman, London, 2001), pp. 220–30.

2 An excellent synthesis is E. Dinter, *Hero or Coward: Pressures Facing the Soldier in Battle* (Frank Cass, London, 1985).

3 D. Englander, 'Discipline and Morale in the British Army, 1917–1918', in J. Horne (ed.), *State, Society and Mobilization in Europe*

during the First World War (Cambridge University Press, 1997), p. 133; J. Brent Wilson, 'The Morale and Discipline of the British Expeditionary Force, 1914–1918', unpublished MA thesis, University of New Brunswick, Canada, 1978, p. 101; and PRO, WO106/401, censor's report on morale, c. January 1918(?).

4 Englander, 'Discipline and Morale in the British Army, 1917–1918', p. 128; and WO154/73, war diary of APM, 63rd (Royal Naval) Division, entry for 6 June 1916.

5 The files used were PRO, registers of Field General Courts Martial, 1914–18, WO213/1–24; registers of District Courts Martial, 1914–18, WO86/62–85; and registers of General Courts Martial, 1900–47, WO90/6 and 8.

6 For examples of this see V. A. C. Gatrell, 'The Decline of Theft and Violence in Victorian and Edwardian England', in V. A. C. Gatrell, B. Lenman and G. Parker (eds.), *Crime and the Law: The Social History of Crime in Western Europe since 1500* (Europa Publications Ltd., London, 1980), pp. 279–84; D. Taylor, *Crime, Policing and Punishment in England, 1750–1914* (Macmillan, London, 1998), pp. 13–19; and J. J. Tobias, *Crime and Industrial Society in the Nineteenth Century* (B. T. Batsford Ltd., London, 1967), pp. 14–21.

7 See, for example, PRO, WO339/17067, personal file of Major C. H. Stainforth, MC, 7/8th Royal Inniskilling Fusiliers, tried on the 5 January 1918 for drunkenness; and WO339/14160 personal file of Second Lieutenant A. J. Annandale, 9th Royal Irish Rifles, tried on 1 February 1916 for 'Conduct to the prejudice of good order and military discipline.'

8 War Office, *Manual of Military Law* (HMSO, London, 1914), p. 412.

9 For an example of the former see PRO, WO90/6, General Courts Martial Register, the case of Temporary Lieutenant G. B. M. Reed, 14th Company, Machine Gun Corps, tried in the field on 10 April 1917 for 'S.40 (ownership of a camera)', p. 114. For the latter see WP90/6, General Courts Martial Register, the trial of Lieutenant H. Pope Hennessy, 49th Battalion, Canadian Expeditionary Force, tried on the 10 March 1917 for 'S40 (getting into bed with a private soldier)', p. 109.

10 War Office, *Manual of Military Law*, p. 388.

11 C. Pugsley, *On the Fringe of Hell: New Zealanders and Military Discipline in the First World War* (Hodder and Stoughton, Auckland, 1991), pp. 63–4; J. Putkowski and J. Sykes, *Shot at Dawn: Executions in World War One by Authority of the British Army Act* (Leo Cooper, London, 1993), pp. 14–15; and A. Babington, *For the Sake of Example: Capital Courts Martial 1914–18, The Truth* (Leo Cooper, London, 1983), pp. 12–14.

12 A. H. Manchester, *A Modern Legal History of England and Wales, 1750–1950* (Butterworths, London, 1980), p. 100.

13 Imperial War Museum (hereafter IWM), P.446, Captain E. A. Godson diary, entry for 17 December 1916.

14 *Ibid.*, entries for 23 December 1916 and 1 January 1917.

15 *Ibid.*, entry for 9 January 1917.

16 Putkowski and Sykes, *Shot at Dawn*, pp. 11 and 16.

17 G. D. Sheffield, *Leadership in the Trenches: Officer–Man Relations, Morale and Discipline in the British army in the Era of the First World War* (Macmillan, London, 2000), pp. 35–40; and K. Simpson, 'The Officers', in I. F. W. Beckett and K. Simpson (eds.), *A Nation in Arms: A Social Study of the British Army in the First World War* (Manchester University Press, 1985), pp. 81–5.

18 T. Skyrme, *History of the Justices of the Peace* (Barry Rose Publishers, Chichester, 1994), p. 686.

19 D. Johnson, 'Trial by Jury in Ireland, 1860–1914', *Legal History*, XVII, 3, 1996, p. 271.

20 *Ibid.*, p. 289.

21 Putkowski and Sykes, *Shot at Dawn*, p. 17.

22 PRO, WO93/49, p. 73.

23 Figures compiled from *The Report of the Royal Commission on Capital Punishment, 1949–53*, Cmd. 8932 (1953), pp. 298–9.

24 War Office, *Manual of Military Law*, p. 120. In September 1918 a Mrs Barff appealed to the Privy Council in an attempt to have her husband's court martial verdict overturned. The Judge Advocate General's view was that, 'In the event of any miscarriage of justice the only Appeal is by way of memorial to the Crown acting through the Secretary of State. It is the usual practice to refer the matter to the J.[udge] A.[dvocate] G.[eneral] and if need be to the Law Officers of the Crown for report, that no innocent man may suffer from error in the tribunal' (letter, Judge Advocate General to the Secretary, Privy Council Office, 11 September 1918, Judge Advocate General's letterbook, PRO, WO83/32).

25 W. R. Cornish, *Law and Society in England 1750–1950* (Sweet and Maxwell, London, 1989), p. 620.

26 War Office, *Manual of Military Law*, p. 27.

27 Royal Ulster Rifles Museum, Anon., 'Service with the 14th Battalion, Royal Irish Rifles. (Young Citizen Volunteers), 1914–18 War', p. 61.

28 See PRO, WO213/1–28, Field General Courts Martial Registers, 1914–18, for examples of this.

29 IWM, diary of Sergeant Robert McKay, 109th Field Ambulance, entry for 10 May 1915.

30 IWM, 92/35/1, Sir Percy McElwaine papers, p. 71.
31 See F. P. Crozier, *The Men I Killed* (Michael Joseph, London, 1937), p. 86; and letter from Major T. H. Westmacott to his wife, March 1918, Westmacott papers, IWM, 87/13/1, for examples of this.
32 Public Record Office of Northern Ireland (hereafter PRONI), D.2794/1/1/13, Major W. A. Montgomery papers, letter of 24 July 1916 from Montgomery to his parents.
33 C. Davison (ed.), *The Burgoyne Diaries* (Thomas Harmsworth Publishing, London, 1985), p. 60.
34 These figures have been calculated using the author's court martial database.
35 PRO, WO83/20, Judge Advocate General's letter book, p. 246.
36 PRO, WO81/144, Judge Advocate General's Office letter books, p. 504 for letter, 22 April 1915, from the Judge Advocate GOC, 36th Division, relating to the cases of Privates J. Hoey, W. Jordan, J. Burns and J. Love, 9th Royal Inniskilling Fusiliers, who were all tried by Field General Courts Martial.
37 PRO, WO81/144, Judge Advocate General's letter book, p. 47, entry for 26 February 1915.
38 PRONI, D.2794/1/1/21, letter from Montgomery to his parents, 30 January 1917.
39 IWM, 92/35/1, Sir Percy McElwaine papers, p. 81.
40 See, for examples of this approach, Brent Wilson, 'The Morale and Discipline of the British Expeditionary Force'; and L. S. Lemisko, 'Politics, Performance and Morale: The 16th (Irish) Division, 1914–18', unpublished MA thesis, University of Calgary, Canada, 1992.
41 IWM, 77/165/1, Brigadier W. Carden Roe, 'Memoirs of World War I', p. 8.
42 IWM, 82/29/1, undated (but late 1914) letter, from Captain P. L. Sulman to (?).
43 F. Vane, *Agin the Governments* (Samson Low and Marston, London, 1928), p. 249.
44 T. Bartlett, 'Indiscipline in the Armed Forces in Ireland in the 1790s', in P. Corish, *Radicals, Rebels and Establishments* (Historical Studies XV, Appletree Press, Belfast, 1985).
45 A. J. Semple, 'The Fenian Infiltration of the British Army', *Journal of the Society of Army Historical Research*, 52, 1974.
46 PRO, WO141/26, extract from Inspector General's summary of Police Reports to 24 July 1913; and I. F. W. Beckett (ed.), *The Army and the Curragh Incident, 1914* (Bodley Head for the Army Record Society, London, 1986), pp. 336–7 and 418.

47 L. P. Curtis, *Apes and Angels: The Irishman in Victorian Caricature* (David & Charles Ltd, London, 1971), p. 21.

48 R. Swift, 'Crime and the Irish in Nineteenth Century Britain', in R. Swift and S. Gilley (eds.), *The Irish in Britain 1815–1939* (Pinter Publishers, London, 1989), p. 165.

49 *Ibid.*, p. 167.

50 J. V. O'Brien, *'Dear, Dirty Dublin': A City in Distress, 1899–1916* (University of California Press, London, 1982), pp. 184–6.

51 C. McCullagh, *Crime in Ireland, A Sociological Introduction* (Cork University Press, 1996), p. 34; and C. Townsend, *Political Violence in Ireland, Government and Resistance since 1848* (Clarendon Press, Oxford, 1983), pp. 1–46.

52 J. Beaumont, 'The Anzac Legend', in J. Beaumont (ed.) *Australia's War, 1914–18* (Allen & Unwin Ltd, St Leonards, 1995), pp. 159–160. To date, there is no detailed study of Australian troop discipline during the Great War.

53 J. A. Crang, 'The British Soldier on the Home Front: Army Morale Reports, 1940–45', in P. Addison and A. Calder (eds.), *Time To Kill: The Soldier's Experience of War in the West 1939–1945* (Pimlico, London, 1997), pp. 60–76; D. French, *Raising Churchill's Army: The British Army and the War against Germany 1919–1945* (Oxford University Press, 2000), pp. 122–55; and S. P. Mackenzie, *Politics and Military Morale: Current Affairs and Citizenship Education in the British Army 1914–1950* (Clarendon Press, Oxford, 1992), pp. 57–173.

54 See, for example, National Army Museum (hereafter NAM), 7511–80–109 letter, Lieutenant J. A. T. Rice, 5th Royal Irish Lancers, to his father, 22 July 1915 (on polo); and PRO, WO95/1279, war diary of the 2nd Royal Munster Fusiliers, entries for the 11–20 June 1915 (on relay races and boxing tournaments).

55 IWM, P.446, Captain E. A. Godson Papers, p. 4, *The Incinerator*, May 1916, p. 11 and NAM, 7511–80–140, letter, Captain J. A. T. Rice to his mother, 21 October 1915.

56 NAM, 7511–80–204, letter, Captain J. A. T. Rice to his father, 21 May 1916; IWM, P.446, E. A. Godson papers, p. 4; and Liddle Collection, University of Leeds (hereafter LC), L. B. Brierly, unpublished manuscript entitled 'A Civilian's Military Career', p. 4.

57 IWM, 67/41/1, J. H. M. Staniforth, 'Kitchener's Soldier', p. 144; and PRO, WO95/1482, war diary of the 1st Royal Irish Fusiliers, entry for 5–6 March 1915.

58 Royal Irish Fusiliers Museum, Armagh, *Armagh Guardian*, 23 October 1914, extract in folder entitled 'War Cuttings 1914'.

59 PRO, WO95/3923, war diary of the 1st Connaught Rangers, entry for 19 March 1915.

60 D. Urquhart, *Women in Ulster Politics 1890–1940* (Irish Academic Press, Dublin, 2000), p. 66.
61 PRO, PRO30/71/3, Major Guy Nightingale papers, letter, Captain F. W. Filgate, 2nd Royal Munster Fusiliers, to Mrs Nightingale, 4 March 1915.
62 Davison (ed.), *The Burgoyne Diaries*, p. 143.
63 NAM, 7511–80/15 and 20, letter, J. A. T. Price to his mother, 10 October 1914 and to his father, 3 November 1914.
64 IWM, 67/41/1, letter, Staniforth to his parents, 28 August 1916, cited in J. H. M. Staniforth, 'Kitchener's Soldier', p. 180.
65 G. Mitchell, *'Three Cheers for the Derrys!': A History of the 10th Royal Inniskilling Fusiliers in the 1914–18 War* (Yes! Publications, Derry, 1991), p. 126.
66 H. Strachan, *The Politics of the British Army* (Clarendon Press, Oxford, 1997), p. 208.
67 PRO, WO95/1421, war diary of the 2nd Royal Irish Regiment, summary for November 1914.
68 PRO, WO95/2266, war diary of the 2nd Royal Irish Fusiliers, appendix to April 1915.
69 IWM, 76/51/1, W. T. Colyer, 'War Impressions of a Temporary Soldier', unpublished manuscript, unpaginated.
70 J. F. Lucy, *There's a Devil in the Drum* (Faber and Faber, London, 1938. Reprinted by the Naval and Military Press, London, 1992), p. 293.
71 N. Perry, 'Nationality in the Irish Infantry Regiments in the First World War', *War and Society*, XII, 1, 1994, p. 89.
72 F. E. Whitton, *The History of the Prince of Wales' Leinster Regiment (Royal Canadians)*, vol. II (Gale and Polden Ltd, London, n.d. (1926?)) p. 73.
73 Hitchcock, *'Stand to', A Diary of the Trenches, 1915–18* (Hurst and Blackett, London, 1937. Reprinted by Gliddon Books, London, 1988), p. 86. The United Irish League was somewhat similar to a constituency association for the Irish Parliamentary Party.
74 T. P. Dooley, *Irishmen or English Soldiers? The Times and World of a Southern Catholic Irish Man (1876–1916) Enlisting in the British Army during the First World War* (Liverpool University Press, 1995), p. 200.
75 Jesuit Archives, Dublin (hereafter JAD), H. V. Gill, 'As seen by a Chaplain', p. 63; and C. Falls, *The History of the First Seven Battalions, The Royal Irish Rifles (Now the Royal Ulster Rifles) in the Great War* (Gale and Polden, Aldershot, 1925), vol. II, pp. 48–9.
76 S. McCance, *The History of the Royal Munster Fusiliers, vol. II, From 1861 to 1922 (Disbandment)* (Gale and Polden, Aldershot, 1927) p. 132.

77 IWM, PP/MCR/C33/806, Field Marshal Sir John French papers, letter, Redmond to French, 25 November 15.

78 PRONI, D.3835/E/2/6/24A, Farren Connell papers, letter, Major General Oliver Nugent to his wife, 30 November 15.

79 J. G. Fuller notes that the 16th (Irish) Division had a divisional concert party and cinema from September 1915, see J. G. Fuller, *Troop Morale and Popular Culture in the British and Dominion Armies, 1914–18* (Clarendon Press, Oxford, 1990), p. 186.

80 Royal Ulster Rifles' Museum, Anon., 'Service with the 14th Battalion, Royal Irish Rifles', p. 138.

81 IWM, P.446, E. A. Godson diaries, p. 7.

82 PRONI, D.3835/E/2/6/10A and D.3835/E/2/6/31, letters, Nugent to his wife, 12 November 1915 and 7 December 1915.

83 WO95/1957, 16th (Irish) Division, Adjutant General and Quarter Master General's war diary, entry for 15 February 1916.

84 Fuller, *Troop Morale and Popular Culture*, pp. 7–20.

85 Letter (undated, but c. July 1915), Powell to Black, cited, W. E. Dornan, *1850–1950, One Hundred Eventful Years, An outline history of the City of Belfast Y.M.C.A.* (Nicholson & Bass Ltd, Belfast, 1950), p. 44.

86 J. Leonard, 'The Catholic Chaplaincy', in D. Fitzpatrick (ed.), *Ireland and the First World War* (Lilliput Press and Trinity History Workshop, Dublin, 1988), p. 10.

87 JAD, letter, Father Gill to Father Provincial, 2 March 1915.

88 PRO, PRO30/71/3, letter, Filgate to Mrs Nightingale.

89 Same to same, 15 April 1916.

90 JAD, H. V. Gill, 'As Seen by a Chaplain', pp. 57–8.

91 National Library of Ireland (hereafter NLI), Ms.15,229 (1), John Redmond papers, letter, Redmond to H. J. Tennant, 11 April 1916 and letter, Tennant to Redmond, 17 April 1916.

92 S. N. White, *The Terrors: 16th (Pioneer) Battalion, Royal Irish Rifles, 1914–19* (The Somme Association, Belfast, 1996), p. 75. For Nugent's problems in balancing Church of Ireland and Presbyterian chaplains in his division see PRONI, D.3835/E/2/6/6, letter from Nugent to his wife, 7 November 1915.

93 PRONI, D.1295/2/1A–9, manuscript, 'History of the U.V.F. and 36th (Ulster) Division', by W. B. Spender, p. 29.

94 A photograph of the certificate awarded to Lieutenant Colonel G. A. M. Buckley is reproduced in T. Denman, *Ireland's Unknown Soldiers: The 16th (Irish) Division in the Great War, 1914–18* (Irish Academic Press, Dublin, 1992), p. 94.

95 The only known example of this is that awarded to Sergeant R. McCarter. It is inscribed, 'For King, Home and Country' and

includes illustrations of Ulster Volunteers of 1800 and 1914. See Royal Inniskilling Fusiliers Museum, Box 35.

 96 For a discussion of this issue see M. Dungan, *Irish Voices from the Great War* (Irish Academic Press, Dublin, 1995), p. 109.

 97 J. Brown, *Orangeism Around Ballymena* (Mid Antrim Historical Group, Ballymena, 1990), p. 9; and White, *The Terrors: 16th (Pioneer) Battalion, Royal Irish Rifles*, p. 67. I would like to thank Mr Derek Harkness for allowing me to see a photograph in his possession of LOL 862 of the 14th Royal Irish Rifles. It shows 118 men of the Battalion wearing orange sashes.

 98 PRONI, T.3217, J. H. Stewart-Moore, 'Random Recollections', p. 2 and PRONI, D/3045/6/11, the diary of Lieutenant Guy Owen Lawrence Young, pp. 66–7.

 99 PRONI, D/3045/6/11, the diary of Lieutenant Guy Owen Lawrence Young, pp. 67–8. For a similar account see Anon. (A. P. I. S. and D. G. S.), *With the Ulster Division in France: A Story of the 11th Battalion Royal Irish Rifles (South Antrim Volunteers) from Bordon to Thiepval* (William Mullan & Son, Belfast, n.d.), p. 34.

100 Mitchell, *'Three Cheers for the Derrys!'*, p. 49.

101 T. Gray, *The Orange Order* (The Bodley Head, London, 1972), p. 131.

102 White, *The Terrors, 16th (Pioneer) Battalion, Royal Irish Rifles*, p. 67.

103 The whole issue of trench raids is well covered in T. Ashworth, *Trench Warfare, 1914–1918: The Live and Let Live System* (Macmillan, London, 1980), pp. 176–203.

104 T. Denman, 'The Catholic Irish Soldier in the First World War: The "Racial Environment"', *Irish Historical Studies*, XXVII, 108, 1991, p. 356.

105 PRONI, T.3217, J. L. Stewart-Moore, 'Random Recollections', p. 26.

106 Denman, *Ireland's Unknown Soldiers*, p. 72.

107 *Ibid.*, p. 75.

108 See, for example PRO, WO95/1955, war diary of 16th (Irish) Division General Staff, report by Pereria on a raid by the 7th Leinster Regiment on the 3/4 June 1916 and Denman, *Ireland's Unknown Soldiers*, p. 72.

109 Denman, *Ireland's Unknown Soldiers*, p. 76.

110 Falls, *The History of the First Seven Battalions, Royal Irish Rifles*, vol. II, p. 61.

111 H. C. Wylly, *Neill's 'Blue Caps', The History of the First Battalion, Royal Dublin Fusiliers, vol. III, 1914–22* (Gale and Polden, Aldershot, 1925), p. 66.

112 JAD, Father H. V. Gill, 'As seen by a Chaplain', p. 98.

2

Regular regiments at war

The period from the landing of the British Expeditionary Force in France in August 1914 until the end of September 1915 saw a large number of strains put on the discipline and morale of the Irish regiments and the expeditionary force in general. Firstly, there was the transition from a peacetime to a wartime situation, which naturally saw many changes in the British army, not least in its disciplinary code. Offences, such as sleeping on duty and desertion, which would, in peacetime, have led to little more than a short term of imprisonment, became capital offences in wartime.

Secondly, the horrific losses incurred by the BEF led to serious problems. Men, who were either army reservists (who, in some cases had not been in the army since the end of the South African War in 1902) or special reservists (who, in many cases, had very rudimentary training) were required to bring units up to their establishment on the outbreak of war and keep them up to strength for the early part of the war. Many of these reservists were either too old or unfit for active service, and, in at least some cases, resented being commanded by NCOs who had less service than them. Time-expired men were another potential problem group as soldiers nearing the end of their 'colour service' in August 1914 resented being kept in the army for another year. Lastly, middle-class recruits who, in a few cases, had joined Kitchener units, but then been posted as drafts to regular battalions, found the habits and behaviour of their new colleagues unpalatable. High losses also led to serious

problems in the supply of officers. While the most decrepit
retired officers were used to train New Army battalions in
Britain, a number of officers who were unfit to command did see
service in France. The desperate need for officers saw the rapid
commissioning of men from, for example, the ranks of exclusive
London Territorial Force units, with only the most minimal
officer training.[1] The replacement of NCOs was even more difficult. The shortage of officers saw some of the most intelligent
NCOs being promoted to commissioned rank, while the supply
of suitable privates, capable of carrying out an NCO's duties,
soon dwindled. Within a short space of time many units were
thus reliant heavily on NCOs with little experience or those who
had been reservists on the outbreak of war.

Thirdly, the winter of 1914 to 1915 is seen by many historians
as a nadir in the morale of the BEF.[2] The unofficial 'Christmas
Truces' of 1914, some of which lasted into January 1915,
certainly caused concern amongst the High Command. This low
point in morale seems to have been a result both of the appalling
conditions in the trenches and the realisation that no early end
to the war was in sight.

In this chapter, an assessment of the disciplinary problems
facing the BEF will be made, based on the court martial records.
Attention will then be devoted to perceived disciplinary problems in the BEF during this period. With reference to Irish units,
Sir Roger Casement's attempt to form a German–Irish Brigade in
early 1915 will be considered as the failure of Casement's
scheme does suggest that even the relatively apolitical regular
soldier did maintain certain ideals and values which made him
actively anti-German, even when other factors which would
have retained his loyalty to the British Crown had vanished.
Consideration will then be given to the morale problems facing
the BEF in this period, especially the difficulties involved in
keeping the force supplied with both trained personnel and
essential equipment.

A consideration of the number of courts martial held in Irish
infantry battalions during the period from the arrival of units in
France until 30 September 1915 shows marked differences. While
the 2nd Royal Dublin Fusiliers had a staggering 150 courts
martial cases over this period, the 2nd Royal Irish Regiment had
a mere sixty-three. Surprisingly, given their high courts martial

record, of 145 cases, the 2nd Leinster Regiment, as part of the 6th Division, did not arrive in France until 8 September 1914,[3] and their disciplinary record thus appears to be very poor.

There appears to be no easy explanation as to this marked difference between battalions, in terms of courts martial. An urban/rural recruiting base may provide part of the explanation, as the 2nd Royal Irish Rifles (with a recruiting area centred on Belfast) and the 2nd Royal Dublin Fusiliers (with a recruiting area centred on Dublin City) both had a very high number of men tried by courts martial. As Belfast and Dublin both had heavily unionised workforces in this period one may reasonably have expected some of this class antagonism to spill over into the army. There does seem to be some evidence to support this view as, by April 1915, at least some members of the 2nd Royal Dublin Fusiliers had joined the Regiment after being dismissed during the 1913 strike in Dublin.[4] Nevertheless, in the case of the 2nd Royal Irish Rifles, the argument that the men were drawn from the heavily unionised Belfast workforce seems distinctly unconvincing. John Lucy, serving with this unit pre-war, stressed that many of the men came from outside the regimental recruiting area. Father Henry Gill made a similar observation when he joined the Battalion in late 1914, noting the unexpectedly high number of Catholics serving in this unit and Nicholas Perry's work confirms that the regular battalions of the Royal Irish Rifles obtained a large percentage of recruits from outside their recruiting area.[5]

Lastly, an obvious answer to high courts martial rates would lie in losses in action, units with high losses naturally having fewer courts martial cases. However, again this does not provide a solution. While the 2nd Royal Dublin Fusiliers had 627 deaths in 1914 to 1915 and 150 court martial cases over the same period, the 2nd Leinster Regiment, with a court martial record almost similar to the 2nd Royal Dublin Fusiliers had only 351 deaths, one of the lowest for Irish units on the Western Front.[6]

In Irish battalions during this period, 35 per cent of all crime was solely attributable to drunkenness and this is reflected in the sample number of units shown in table 2.1. As Brent Wilson points out, 'Of course, most drunkenness occurred in the rearward areas or during open warfare, drunkenness at the front was uncommon.'[7] Therefore, drunkenness rarely impeded the combat effectiveness of a unit, although there were notable exceptions to this. For example, following a particularly raucous St Patrick's Day in 1915, the 1st Royal Irish Fusiliers were unable to dig new communications trenches, due to widespread drunkenness in the unit.[8]

Drunkenness, in disciplinary terms, was much more serious in that it demonstrated the incapacity of some NCOs to adequately carry out their duties. Lieutenant Hitchcock of the 2nd Leinster Regiment noted that on 12 August 1915,

Table 2.1. Offences for which men serving in a sample of units were tried by courts martial, from the units' arrival in France to 30 September 1915

Offence	1IG	2RInnsF	2RIRifs	2RMF	2RDF	5Lancers	NIH
War Treason	0	0	0	0	0	0	0
DORA	0	0	0	0	0	0	0
Offence against an inhabitant	3	0	0	1	0	0	0
Mutiny	0	0	0	0	0	0	0
Cowardice	0	1	2	0	0	1	0
Desertion	3	21	3	1	14	0	0
Absence	3	1	1	0	2	0	0
Striking or violence	2	0	2	2	1	0	0
Insubordination	1	0	1	0	1	0	0
Disobedience	3	2	5	0	0	1	0
Quitting post	3	1	2	1	2	0	0
Drunkenness	32	36	36	31	83	12	7
Injuring property	0	0	0	0	0	0	0
Loss of property	0	0	1	0	0	1	0
Theft	1	1	2	1	1	1	0
Indecency	0	0	0	1	0	0	0
Resisting escort	0	0	0	0	0	0	0
Escaping confinement	0	0	0	0	0	0	0
Miscellaneous and multiple military offences	16	31	64	13	46	20	3
Miscellaneous civil offences	1	0	0	0	0	0	0
Self-inflicted wound	1	0	0	0	0	0	0
Fraudulent enlistment	0	0	0	0	0	0	0
Enlisting after discharge	0	0	0	0	0	0	0
False answer	0	0	0	0	0	0	0
Neglect	0	0	0	0	0	0	0
Fraud	0	0	0	0	0	0	0
Totals	69	94	119	51	150	36	10

At 'Stand to' an issue of rum, which had been sent up under cover of darkness, was dished out, and was thoroughly appreciated. Serg[ean]t. Shields, Piper's platoon sergeant, who was somewhat ancient and had felt the strain of the day more than younger men, took a double ration, and started firing up at the stars and shouting out about the Battle of Colenso![9]

Captain Burgoyne, commanding 'C' Company of the 2nd Royal Irish Rifles was determined to prevent drunkenness in his unit, particularly after the events of 27 December 1914, when one of his sergeants was shot while issuing the rum ration. Burgoyne, with the endorsement of his CO and Divisional GOC, ceased issuing rum to his company following this incident. However, in February 1915, when, following the distribution of pay, a number of NCOs in his company became inebriated, Burgoyne felt unable to take disciplinary action: 'No use running them up before the C.O.; they'd be tried by court martial, and I couldn't get other men to take their places.'[10]

Official figures suggest that disciplinary offences in the Irish regiments during this period were broadly in line with those of the British army as a whole. However, exact estimates are difficult, given the fluctuating strength of the BEF from August 1914 to September 1915. However, the figures for two non-Irish units considered in this period, the 1st Gloucestershire Regiment and the 1/14th London (Scottish) Regiment, with nineteen and no men tried respectively by court martial, suggest that Irish regiments had, on average, more disciplinary cases than their English counterparts.

There are other indications that Irish discipline was considered to be much worse than that of other British units. In January 1915 Major General Alymer Haldane visited the 2nd Royal Irish Rifles to 'give them hell' as they were the 'bad boy' of his division.[11] Meanwhile, when commenting in February 1915 on the death sentence passed on Private Thomas Hope of the 2nd Leinster Regiment, General Sir Horace Smith Dorrien, GOC, Second Army noted, 'The Brigade discipline is 2nd. worst + the Batt[alio]n. discipline also the 2nd. worst in the army.'[12] The 1st Royal Irish Rifles, in September 1915, was also deemed to have an unsatisfactory disciplinary record, although it was seen to be improving by this date.[13] Men, or at least officers, in the Irish regiments, were aware of their poor disciplinary records. Father McCrory, the chaplain to the 2nd Connaught Rangers, believed that there was a general anti-Irish feeling in the army, which led to harsher punishments for Irish troops.[14]

The comparatively small number of courts martial in Irish cavalry, as opposed to Irish infantry units, also deserves consideration. The Irish cavalry regiment with the worst courts martial record in this period was the 5th Lancers with 36 cases, while the 8th Hussars had only 14 cases. The small number of men tried in the North Irish Horse (10) and South Irish Horse (4) can be explained by the fact that neither of these units was at full strength during this period. Only two squadrons of the North Irish Horse and one of the South Irish Horse were serving in France during August 1914 to September 1915. The small number of men tried in these units, and in the 1/14th London (Scottish) Regiment, may also be explicable by an unwillingness on the part of the military authorities or unit COs to try part-time soldiers with the same rigour as their regular counterparts.[15] In general terms, it is not surprising that the number of courts martial carried out in Irish cavalry units generally compared favourably to those carried out in Irish infantry regiments, as the nominally 'Irish' regular cavalry units were composed of largely non-Irish personnel.[16]

Another possible explanation for the comparatively good courts martial record of the Irish cavalry regiments could be the better discipline seen in cavalry as opposed to infantry units in the BEF in general. Reporting on his experiences with cavalry on the Western Front, J. E. B. Seely stated, 'it has been the experience of both the French and the English Armies that the cavalryman in the trench is more valuable man for man than the infantryman. I have seen many French Generals and they all agree that this is so, the reason generally given being that the proportion of officers and Non Commissioned Officers with dismounted cavalry is much greater than in the case of infantry.'[17] The initially high ratio of officers and NCOs to men in cavalry units, combined with low casualty rates in comparison with front-line infantry would seem to explain how discipline was better maintained in the cavalry units of the BEF. Nevertheless, the disparities between Irish and non-Irish units courts martial records (and, indeed, between those of Irish battalions) in this period lack any simple explanation.

Courts martial records do not give us a complete picture of military crime in a unit. For example, in the case of self-inflicted wounds, courts martial were not always instituted. Certainly, in some cases, the maiming itself was seen as punishment enough. As Sergeant A. T. Mathews of the 1st Royal Irish Regiment recounted of an incident in late 1915,

> One of the men – he did not belong to my platoon – said, 'I am fed up to the teeth, I'd blow my toes off if I had the guts to do it.' We were all terribly fed up but what was the use of giving way to our feelings. One of the other chaps said, 'If you haven't got the guts to do it, I'll do it for you', 'Right', he said, 'carry on and do it.' 'Put your foot against the side of the trench', and the chap who wanted his toes shot off did as he was bid. Up to this point we thought they were joking. Then there was a terrific bang as he fired at the foot. But his mate had not hit him in the toes but in the ankle and smashed it to smithereens ... The shooter was placed under arrest. They both got what they wanted – they got out of the line – one to undergo punishment and the other to be maimed for life.[18]

Even if we assume that a number of men who committed self mutilation were not tried by court martial, this still leaves some serious discrepancies in the statistics. For example, Jeffrey Greenhut suggests that from the arrival of the Indian Corps in France in October 1914, until 14 August 1915 there were fifty-four cases of hand wounds in the 1st Connaught Rangers.[19] Greenhut's implication is that all of these wounds were self-inflicted.[20] However, the official records kept by the Medical Officer of the 1st Connaught Rangers record only one case of self-inflicted wounds and one case of probable suicide for this period.[21] Likewise, for the Indian Corps as a whole, the Deputy Judge Advocate General recorded just nine Indian and two British troops convicted for self-mutilation or mutilation of a comrade, over the period that this corps was stationed in France.[22]

It is clear that there was a massive variation between peace-time and wartime offences, which is evident when comparing tables 2.1 and 2.2. The first and most obvious point is that the number of men tried by courts martial increased greatly in wartime. For example, while only twenty-nine men of the 2nd Royal Dublin Fusiliers were tried by courts martial between

1 August 1913 and 31 July 1914, 150 were tried between the battalion's arrival in France in August 1914 and 30 September 1915. Secondly, the disciplinary system itself showed different priorities. Fraudulent enlistment, seen as a serious matter in peacetime, became of considerably less importance in a war situation. Lastly, and perhaps most importantly, the difference between peacetime and wartime crimes was not a large one. Absence without leave, drunkenness and miscellaneous offences, all serious problems in Irish units on home service during 1913 to 1914, remained the major disciplinary offences committed by Irish troops in France during 1914 to 1915. Most noticeably some opportunities to commit crime, afforded by active service (for example, looting) do not seem to have been exploited by many of the Irish or British soldiers serving in France during 1914 and 1915.

A general order to the army noted the difference between peacetime and wartime discipline,

> The Commander in Chief has had under consideration certain sentences recently awarded by Courts-Martial ... He wishes to point out that certain offences which in peace time are adequately met by a small sentence, assume, on active service, a gravity which wholly alters their character. This principle is fully recognised in Military Law; for instance in the case of desertion, the Army Act in time of peace, permits a maximum sentence of two year's duration only, whereas on active service a Court is allowed to award a sentence of death for the same offence ... The Commander in Chief wishes to impress upon all officers serving upon Courts-Martial that it is their duty to give weight to consideration of good character, inexperience and all other extenuating circumstances, but that, at the same time, they are seriously to consider the effect which the offence in question may have upon the discipline of the Army.[23]

Therefore it is not surprising that the severity of many sentences increased during wartime. No British soldier had been executed since the Boer War (even when thirty-seven men of the 13th Hussars mutinied in India in 1911[24]). However, from August 1914 to September 1915, fifty-one British soldiers, including four Irish, were executed.[25] Penal servitude, a sentence awarded to no man serving in an Irish unit on home service during 1913 to 1914, was awarded to fifty-five men serving in Irish units in

Table 2.2. Offences for which men serving in Irish units stationed in the United Kingdom were tried by courts martial, 1 August 1913 to 31 July 1914

Offence	1IG	2RInnsF	2RIRifs	2RMF	2RDF	5Lancers
Mutiny	0	0	0	0	0	0
Desertion	1	4	1	1	0	0
Absence	12	0	5	0	0	0
Striking or violence	4	0	2	0	3	0
Insubordination	4	0	0	1	2	1
Disobedience	0	0	0	0	0	0
Quitting post	0	0	0	0	0	0
Drunkenness	4	2	5	0	4	0
Injuring property	2	0	1	1	0	0
Loss of property	2	0	0	0	0	0
Theft	0	1	2	1	4	4
Indecency	0	0	0	0	0	0
Resisting escort	0	0	0	0	0	0
Escaping confinement	0	0	0	0	0	0
Miscellaneous and multiple military offences	25	3	21	7	14	11
Miscellaneous civil offences	1	0	0	0	0	0
Self-inflicted wound	0	0	0	0	0	0
Fraudulent enlistment	0	0	0	1	0	1
Enlisting after discharge with disgrace	2	0	0	0	0	3
False answer	1	0	1	0	1	0
Neglect	0	0	1	0	1	0
Fraud	1	0	0	0	0	0
Totals	59	10	39	12	29	20

the BEF from August 1914 to 30 September 1915. The sentence of hard labour was used more frequently in wartime. Most noticeably of all, detention, the sentence awarded most frequently in peacetime, was not used at all in the first thirteen months of the war. In wartime field punishment replaced detention as the most frequently awarded sentence. Field punishment was an unpopular sentence: a form of corporal punishment which meant that a man under sentence was tied to a wheel or stake for two hours each day.[26] From the point of view of the military authorities, it had the advantage that, while serving his sentence, a man could remain on active service with his unit.

It would be wrong to suggest that wartime saw the entire

apparatus of military law become more repressive. The number
of not guilty verdicts, at least in the Irish units used in this case
study, increased from 2.8 per cent in 1913–14 to 4.8 per cent in
1914–15. Likewise, the number of sentences quashed increased
from 1.4 per cent in 1913–14 to 5.2 per cent in 1914–15. This
suggests that army officers themselves, sitting on courts martial,
and the Judge Advocate General's office refused to sentence
men, the charges against whom were poorly framed, simply
because they were on active service. The death penalty was not
used excessively; despite the high desertion rate in the 2nd
Royal Inniskilling Fusiliers, shown in table 2.1, no man in this
unit was executed during this period. Also, the introduction of
the Suspended Sentences Act in 1915 meant that men who,
previously, would have faced death or long terms of imprisonment, continued to serve with their units and, by future good
behaviour or heroism in action, could have their sentence
reduced or removed altogether.

It is now necessary in evaluating the discipline and morale of
the BEF as a whole, and the Irish units in particular, during the
August 1914 to September 1915 period to examine three
instances where discipline was under a severe strain. The first is
the so-called 'Colonels' Surrender' at St Quentin in August 1914
when Lieutenant Colonel Mainwaring of the 2nd Royal Dublin
Fusiliers and Lieutenant Colonel Elkington of the 1st Royal
Warwickshire Regiment proposed to surrender themselves and
their men to the advancing German forces. The second is the
'Christmas Truce' of 1914 and the general crisis of morale faced
by the BEF in the winter of 1914/15. The last issue to be examined will be the formation of Sir Roger Casement's 'Irish
Brigade' from Irish prisoners of war, during 1914 and 1915.

The 'Colonels' Surrender' at St Quentin has already received
considerable attention elsewhere.[27] However, given the involvement of men of the 2nd Royal Dublin Fusiliers in this affair and
the fact that this was one of the few occasions on the Retreat
from Mons when discipline did break down, it merits some
discussion. On 27 August 1914 Lieutenant Colonels Mainwaring
and Elkington promised the Mayor of St Quentin that they
would not fight in the town. If they could not evacuate their men
before the arrival of the Germans they pledged to surrender.[28] It
is difficult to ascertain the colonels' motivation in taking this

extreme course of action. Mainwaring suggested that he faced a mutiny situation, with his men refusing to continue to retreat and this view is supported by the account of Colonel Tom Bridges, who commanded the rearguard unit, the 4th Royal Irish Dragoon Guards.[29] In contrast Captain Arthur Osburn, the medical officer of the 4th Royal Irish Dragoon Guards, believed that the surrender was justified by the poor military position in which the men found themselves.[30] Accounts also vary as to how Bridges did finally rally the men. Bridges himself suggested that it was partly by issuing threats, but also by the use of a hastily improvised musical band, which helped to raise the men's morale.[31] Osburn believed that some men of the 4th Royal Irish Dragoon Guards may have shot a few of the most truculent stragglers.[32]

It is worth noting that Lieutenant Colonel Mainwaring was the only member of his unit to be tried by court martial following this incident, suggesting either that references to a mutiny amongst the 2nd Royal Dublin Fusiliers are exaggerated or that the military authorities were sympathetic to the problems endured by the troops during the Retreat from Mons. Similarly, it must be stressed that this action was largely atypical of the actions of other Irish battalions during this period. Indeed, the 2nd Royal Munster Fusiliers and 2nd Royal Irish Rifles were seen as highly successful rearguard units. The 2nd Royal Munster Fusiliers, in their action at Etreux, were decimated, with only five officers and 196 other ranks surviving.[33] Nevertheless, the Battalion's action effectively prevented German pursuit of I Corps.[34] The high regard shown for the 2nd Royal Irish Rifles for its rearguard action was outlined by the unit's chaplain, Father Henry Gill, who observed, 'The Battalion had also the unique honour of being received by the Brigade at the close of their rearguard action during the Retreat from Mons by a special ovation. The road was spontaneously lined by troops from the other units who rushed out to shake hands with the officers and men.'[35]

The only other Irish unit over which any doubts concerning discipline and morale lay in this period was the 2nd Connaught Rangers. This unit was surrounded at Le Grand Fayt on the night of 26/27 August 1914 while serving as a rearguard. The regimental history suggests that most of the Battalion escaped

from the position, but that Lieutenant Colonel Abercrombie and
a number of others were either captured or killed.[36] However,
Father McCrory, the Battalion's chaplain stated that
Abercrombie surrendered to German soldiers, leaving his men
to their own devices.[37] This failure in leadership may partially
explain why the 1st and 2nd Connaught Rangers were amalgamated in December 1914, in what was the only permanent
amalgamation of regular British battalions during the entire
war, although this amalgamation is usually attributed solely to
the Regiment's recruiting problems.[38] However, the account
provided by Sergeant J. McIlwaine, regarding wider officer
problems in the Battalion may also have accounted for the amalgamation. On 30 September 1914 McIlwaine noted that
Lieutenant De Stacpoole was removed to hospital:

> He was in a bad way indeed as the only officer in the company
> those few days on the hill at Verneuil. He could not give an order
> without shouting at the men. Raucously he roared at me to 'Get
> these men together', and so on. He screamed hysterically. This
> habit of uncontrolled yelling I soon found to be infectious at times
> of stress and alarm. It was bad for discipline and I succeeded in
> resisting it. De S. was almost beyond control, and was sent away
> just in time ... Captain White came as commander of our
> company. I had known him many years before. He was one of
> these wealthy officers who come and go, serve for a year or two
> with the colours as it suits them, then retire on half pay. There are
> now only eight officers left in the battalion.[39]

A major 'crisis of morale' for the BEF during the Great War is
believed by many historians to have occured in the winter of
1914/15. As J. Brent Wilson notes, 'A study of the B.E.F. during
the first winter is essentially a portrait of a shaken peacetime
army attempting to cope with a war gone wrong.'[40] However,
the number of men tried by courts martial in Irish units during
1914 and 1915 suggests that the disciplinary record is an
extremely complex one, and certainly does not suggest that the
BEF was facing a 'crisis of discipline' in the winter of 1914/15.
The 1st Irish Guards, 1st Royal Irish Regiment and 2nd Royal
Dublin Fusiliers all had worse disciplinary records in the
summer months of 1915, than in the winter of 1914/15. By
contrast the 2nd Royal Irish Rifles had just over half of its total
number of court martial trials for this entire sixteen-month

period conducted during December 1914 and January and February 1915. The worst period, in terms of disciplinary offences, for the 2nd Royal Dublin Fusiliers was November 1914, and some of the Battalion's worst disciplinary offences appear to have been resolved by the onset of winter.

The unofficial Christmas truces of 1914 were serious breaches of military discipline, although no soldier in the BEF was actually court-martialled for his actions in arranging or participating in these festivities.[41] Reactions to the truce varied in the Irish regiments, as indeed they did in the BEF as a whole. Major Trefusis, the acting CO of the 1st Irish Guards noted in his diary for 27 December 1914, 'I hear that on Christmas day in one part of the line, some Officers were invited by the Germans to come and have a drink. They went and asked the Germans to come back. They refused but two or three hours afterwards, they came over and were taken prisoners. So complications may arise, and we have been told not to hold any sort of Armistice, but I don't suppose any sensible man would.'[42] In sharp contrast, the 1st Royal Irish Fusiliers were keen participants in the Christmas truce and, as late as 13 January 1915, Captain Burrows noted, 'No sniping, this has been the case since Christmas. Enemy seem to understand that we will not snipe them so long as they do not snipe us.'[43]

The 2nd Leinster Regiment took a more pragmatic view of the truce. While, on Christmas Eve, the Battalion refused overtures from the Germans (even shooting to pieces Chinese lanterns raised over the German trenches), on Christmas Day men of 'A', 'B' and 'C' companies fraternised with the Germans in no-man's land. Meanwhile 'D' Company refused to co-operate in the truce, continued to snipe at German units opposite it and generally used the truce to strengthen their defences.[44] Nevertheless, like the 1st Royal Irish Fusiliers, the 2nd Leinster Regiment maintained a truce until ordered to resume hostilities in mid-January 1915.[45]

There is a reasonably clear link between Irish battalions' disciplinary records and their involvement in the Christmas truce. The 2nd Royal Dublin Fusiliers, 1st Royal Irish Fusiliers, 1st Royal Irish Rifles and 2nd Leinster Regiment, participated in the truce[46] and had, respectively, 62, 26, 35 and 62 men tried by courts martial from their arrival in France until the end of

December 1914. This meant that units which participated in the truce had an average courts martial rate of forty-six cases over this entire period. By contrast, the Irish battalions in France which were not involved in the truce had an average figure of eighteen cases. Nevertheless, there is no absolute link between poor discipline ànd participation in the Christmas truce (the 2nd Royal Irish Rifles which did not take part in the truce had forty courts martial cases over this period) but units with good courts martial records were much less likely to participate in the armistice than units with bad or indifferent disciplinary records.

Political pressures were put on the discipline of Irish soldiers in the British army during 1914 and 1915 by the formation of Sir Roger Casement's 'Irish Brigade'. Casement had been in the USA when war broke out and travelled to Germany with the backing of Republican Irish–American groups. Initially his activities met with success; by the end of 1914 the German government had agreed to supply arms and ammunition to Irish Republicans, to recognise and support an independent Irish government and to authorise the formation of an Irish Brigade in the German army.[47] Casement's 'Brigade' was, of course, to be raised from Irish prisoners of war and firm reports of its existence did not reach MI5 until March 1916. However, it would seem appropriate to examine this brigade and its impact on Irish soldiers in this chapter as Casement's aim was to raise it from Irish regular soldiers, captured in 1914 and 1915.

The package offered by Casement and the German authorities to Irish prisoners of war prepared to join the Irish Brigade was a comprehensive and, indeed, a generous one. This was fully outlined in a circular distributed to prisoners at Limburg Camp on 9 May 1915, which promised men good pay and conditions, that they would serve only under Irish officers and that, at the end of the war, they would have the opportunity of emigrating to the USA.[48] Despite these generous terms and conditions, Casement's so-called 'Irish Brigade' did not approach company strength, at its height consisting of only around fifty men.[49] This sluggish recruitment suggests that, even when removed from the threat of disciplinary action (and the only action that the British army could take against members of the 'Irish Brigade' in Germany was to stop their pay and allowances to their families[50]) and measures which would enhance their morale (the regimental system, comforts from home, etc.), most Irish soldiers continued in their loyalty to the Crown. Indeed, many soldiers risked disciplinary action from the German authorities to show their opposition to the Brigade. When Irish prisoners of war (POWs) were moved to Limburg Camp, the senior NCOs present sent a message to the camp commandant stating that they wanted no special treatment as, 'in addition to being Irish Catholics, we have the honour to be British soldiers'.[51] When he visited Limburg Camp in early 1915, Casement was poorly received and was manhandled by the POWs, greeted by cheers for John Redmond and taunted by shouts of 'how much are the Germans paying you?'[52] Most of the Irish POWs were apparently put on a starvation diet in an attempt to force them to join the Brigade.[53]

The handful of men who joined the Irish Brigade were not regarded as ardent Republicans. British military intelligence officers suggested that men joined the Brigade to receive better treatment and even Casement had to admit that few men joined him out of any real sense of patriotism.[54] This perception of the members of the Brigade as misguided rather than treacherous may account for the lenient treatment afforded to its two members captured by the British authorities during the war. Sergeant Daniel Bailey, late of the Royal Irish Rifles, who accompanied Casement to Ireland in 1916 and was captured there was 're-instated on account of his previous good character in the Army, and not as some people believe, because he gave, or offered to give King's evidence against Casement'.[55] Private Joseph Dowling, captured in Galway in May 1918, having been landed from a U-boat to ascertain if another rising was possible, was tried by a General Court Martial held in the Guildhall, Westminster on 8 July 1918. He was sentenced to penal servitude for life rather than to be executed. In 1923 Dowling was still being detained in Wandsworth prison, when pressure from the Irish Free State government had already seen the release of those imprisoned following the Connaught Rangers mutiny of 1920. This strongly suggests that the Irish government did not view Dowling as a political prisoner.[56] The mercenary nature of the force is further demonstrated by the fact that one of its members, Timothy Quinless, acted as an informer to the British forces during the Anglo-Irish War and was murdered by the IRA following his attempt to capture Michael Collins.[57]

The experience of Casement's Irish Brigade demonstrates that the concept of a crisis of morale, or indeed, of discipline, in the 1914/15 period, at least in the Irish regiments, can be overstated. Nevertheless, this period did see serious problems in the morale of the BEF. Regular soldiers expected a short war and when the Great War settled into stalemate, serious weaknesses in the British army were revealed. The supply of replacement officers and other ranks on such a large scale had never been envisaged with the result that units were frequently understrength and contained some poorly trained men. Many of the essentials of trench warfare, such as grenades, trench mortars, machine guns and heavy artillery, which the Germans appeared to have in abundance, were conspicuous by their absence in the BEF.

Losses obviously affected different units at different times during the first fourteen months of the war and battalions showed different propensities to maintain their regular character. Second Lieutenant Hitchcock, joining the 2nd Leinster Regiment in May 1915, commented, 'My platoon paraded in the trench for rifle inspection. They were a fine body of men; the majority hailed from Tipperary, King's and Queen's Counties and Westmeath and were time serving soldiers ... There was a splendid *esprit de corps* throughout the Battalion.'[58] Other units were less fortunate, Captain Burgoyne of the 2nd Royal Irish Rifles commented in April 1915, 'an Irish Militia Regiment, and that is all we are now, for the class of man we have in it now is a class which would not be accepted for the regular Army'.[59] By May, the situation was improving; Burgoyne commented, 'since last February our drafts have been improving both in quality and training, and we've got rid of our wasters, and I had some 155 quite useful lads under me; a small company, but quite good; none better in Flanders outside the guards.'[60]

These observations suggest that, in some respects, the disciplinary record of regiments is not necessarily a good guide to their battle readiness. The courts martial record of the 2nd Leinster Regiment was much worse than that in the 2nd Royal Irish Rifles, despite (or perhaps because of) the fact that the Rifles had suffered higher losses and were made up to strength with what were, in many cases, poorly trained drafts.

The poor quality of replacements sent out to Irish units, even in the very early stages of the war, was frequently commented on. The Medical Officer of the 1st Connaught Rangers reported a number of serious problems in that unit. Some of the men were over fifty years of age and were thus too old for work in the trenches.[61] Others had no teeth and found it impossible to eat ration biscuits.[62] Worse still, from a medical point of view, Lieutenant Colonel Loveband of the 2nd Royal Dublin Fusiliers noted in October 1914 that,

> Several cases of crabs have occurred recently amongst the men of this Battalion. On investigation it was found that most of the cases were men of the last reinforcement. I suggest that a careful medical examination should be made of all drafts before they leave the overseas base and all suspected case[s] be kept back as owing to the insanitary life men are forced to lead when in trenches any disease of this nature spreads with great rapidity.[63]

The 1st Connaught Rangers may be an extreme example in regard to poor quality drafts, given their serious recruiting problems. However, in other units there were also problems of men being over age and poorly trained for front-line service. Burgoyne, commenting on his company of the 2nd Royal Irish Rifles in December 1914, noted, 'One of my beauties had the following conversation with Kearns (a second lieutenant), "Sure, Sir, I'm over 50, haven't I done over 30 years service Sir, and sure Sir I don't know how to fix the sights of this rifle, I who haven't seen a gun for 15 years!!!" And we found another man who didn't know how to work his rifle. Useful sort to send out to us!'[64]

Service with such men can have done little to raise the morale of other ranks in this period. But it must be remembered that some army reservists, who had been away from 'colour service' for up to seven years, found rejoining the army and especially serving under younger NCOs unsatisfactory. John Lucy, then a Lance Corporal in the 2nd Royal Irish Rifles, noted, 'Of my eight men four were reservists, older men who were not so easy to command as the serving regulars. They groused rather too much and offered gratuitous advice on soldiering.'[65] It also seems likely that men whose colour service was due to come to an end in late 1914 were not happy with being forced to stay on in the army for another year.[66]

The replacement of experienced officers was a serious
problem for some Irish units. Following heavy losses at their
landing at Gallipoli in May 1915, Lieutenant Guy Nightingale
was dismissive of many of the officers sent to rebuild the 1st
Royal Munster Fusiliers. He noted, 'We have now got 38 officers. Geddes is commanding + with 5 of us originals and 36
Territorials, Militia + Special Reserve people – we are a most
peculiar crowd. There are nearly as many officers as men now!
The new ones are very funny – extraordinarily helpless, fright-
fully keen + about as much idea of soldiering as the man in the
moon.'[67]

Rather less needs to be said regarding the inferiority of the
BEF equipment during this initial period of the war. Most
soldiers were painfully aware that devices, unknown in the pre-
war British army, such as hand grenades and trench mortars,
were plentiful in the German forces. Even worse than this, in
their effect on morale, were some of the improvised weapons
produced in the BEF during this period. On 17 December 1914
the 1st Connaught Rangers relieved the 1st Manchester
Regiment in the front line:

> A trench-mortar was taken over in these trenches and used with
> some success until December 19th., on which day it burst, killing
> Private Murray, the man working it. The first weapons of the type
> used in the British Army, the barrels being made of wooden
> battens frapped round with wire or metal hoops, had been
> constructed just three weeks previously, originating in the Indian
> Division. The enemy opposite were at this time using *minenwer-*
> *fers* against the Rangers' trenches, but with indifferent success.[68]

During this period, the BEF had adapted fairly successfully to
the conditions of trench warfare. Certainly its disciplinary
record showed a few black spots (most notably the 'Colonels'
Surrender' at St Quentin), nevertheless in what was, even in
August 1914, a hastily improvised force, which during much of
this period was not only under-equipped, but also received
many replacements of poor quality, this is hardly surprising. By
September 1915, it would appear that some of the worst cases of
indiscipline had been ironed out in the Irish regular units and
officers and men were slowly adjusting to the prospect of a long
war with high casualties.

Notes

1 See P. Simkins, *Kitchener's Army: The Raising of the New Armies, 1914–16* (Manchester University Press, 1988), pp. 217–21; and K. Simpson, 'The Officers', in I. F. W. Beckett and K. Simpson (eds.), *A Nation in Arms: A Social Study of the British Army in the First World War* (Manchester University Press, 1985), pp. 69–72.

2 See for example J. Brent Wilson, 'The Morale and Discipline of the British Expeditionary Force, 1914–18', unpublished MA thesis, University of New Brunswick, Canada, 1978, p. 67; and J. M. Bourne, *Britain and the Great War, 1914–18* (Edward Arnold, London, 1989), p. 223.

3 F. E. Whitton, *The History of the Prince of Wales' Leinster Regiment (Royal Canadians)*, vol. II (Gale and Polden Ltd, n.d. (1926?)), p. 15.

4 T. Johnstone, *Orange, Green and Khaki: The Story of the Irish Regiments in the Great War, 1914–18* (Gill and Macmillan, Dublin, 1992), p. 75. It also appears that in some Dublin firms the outbreak of war saw a repeat of the lock out, as men were forced by their employers to join the British army. See, P. Murray, 'The First World War and a Dublin Distillery Workforce: Recruiting and Redundancy at John Power & Son, 1915–1917', *Saothar*, 15, 1990, p. 50.

5 See, J. F. Lucy, *There's a Devil in the Drum* (Faber and Faber, London, 1938), pp. 13 and 43; and JAD, H. V. Gill, 'As seen by a Chaplain with the 2nd Battalion, Royal Irish Rifles', unpublished manuscript, p. 7; and N. Perry, 'Nationality in the Irish Infantry Regiments in the First World War', *War and Society*, XII, 1, 1994, p. 68.

6 I would like to thank Mr Nicholas Perry for providing me with these figures for deaths in the Irish units during 1914 and 1915. It should be noted that, while the court martial record has been calculated from the unit's arrival in France until 30 September 1915, the total number of deaths per unit was calculated from the unit's arrival in France until 31 December 1915.

7 Brent Wilson, 'The Morale and Discipline of the British Expeditionary Force', p. 57.

8 PRO, WO95/1482, war diary of 1st Royal Irish Fusiliers, entry for 18 March 1915.

9 F. C. Hitchcock, *'Stand To', A Diary of the Trenches, 1915–18* (Hurst and Blackett, London, 1937. Reprinted by Gliddon Books, London, 1988), p. 70.

10 C. Davison (ed.), *The Burgoyne Diaries* (Thomas Harmsworth Publishing, London, 1985), pp. 34 and 122–3.

11 *Ibid.*, p. 43.

12 PRO, WO71/432, transcript of Private Thomas Hope's court martial.

13 PRO, WO71/432, transcript of Lance Corporal Peter Sands's court martial, comments of Brigadier General P. R. Stephens, commanding 25th Infantry Brigade.

14 PRONI, D.1868/1, diaries of Father McCrory, PRONI, p. 34.

15 The North and South Irish Horse were both Special Reserve units, while the 1/14th London Regiment was a unit of the Territorial Force.

16 E. M. Spiers, 'Army Organisation and Society in the Nineteenth Century', in T. Bartlett and K. Jeffery (eds.), *A Military History of Ireland* (Cambridge University Press, 1996), p. 337.

17 PRO, PRO30/57/58, papers of Field Marshal Lord Kitchener, letter, Seely to Lord Kitchener, 21 January 1915.

18 NAM, 6508–5, A. T. Mathews, 'The Thin Khaki Line', pp. 16–17.

19 J. Greenhut, 'The Imperial Reserve: The Indian Corps on the Western Front, 1914–15', *The Journal of Imperial and Commonwealth History*, XII, 1, 1983, p. 57.

20 *Ibid.*, p. 58.

21 See PRO, WO95/3923, war diary of the Medical Officer, 1st Connaught Rangers, entries for 15 December 1914 and 20 June 1915.

22 See PRO, WO154/15 and 16, war diary of the Deputy Judge Advocate General, Indian Corps.

23 PRO, WO95/25, Adjutant General's war diary, General Routine Orders for 19 September 1914.

24 PRO, WO90/7, General Courts Martial Register (India), pp. 62–3.

25 J. Putkowski and J. Sykes, *Shot at Dawn: Executions in World War One by Authority of the British Army Act* (Leo Cooper, London, 1993), p. 292.

26 On this issue see PRO, WO32/5460, ' "Cruxifixion" as Field Punishment at the Front, Protest re.'.

27 See especially, P. T. Scott, 'Dishonoured': The 'Colonels' Surrender' at St. Quentin, The Retreat from Mons, August 1914 (Tom Donovan Publishing, London, 1994).

28 *Ibid.*, p. 54.

29 A. E. Mainwaring, *A Statement by A. E. Mainwaring* (Privately published, n.d.), cited, *ibid.*, p. 54; and G. T. M. Bridges, *Alarms and Excursions: Reminiscences of a Soldier* (Longmans, Green and Co., London, 1938), p. 87.

30 A. Osburn, *Unwilling Passenger* (Faber and Faber, London, 1932), p. 83.

31 *Ibid.*, p. 87.

32 *Ibid.*, p. 83.

33 S. McCance, *The History of the Royal Munster Fusiliers, vol. II, From 1861 to 1922 (Disbandment)* (Gale and Polden, Aldershot, 1927),

p. 119; and H. S. Jervis, *The 2nd Munsters in France* (Gale and Polden, Aldershot, 1922), p. 8.

34 Jervis, *The 2nd Munsters*, p. 12; Johnstone, *Orange, Green and Khaki*, pp. 27–34; and M. Staunton, 'The Royal Munster Fusiliers in the Great War' (MA thesis, University College Dublin, 1986), p. 26.

35 JAD, H. V. Gill, 'As seen by a Chaplain', p. 8.

36 H. F. N. Jourdain, *The Connaught Rangers* (Royal United Services Institution, London, 1924–28),vol. II, pp. 417–18.

37 PRONI, D.1868/1, diaries of Father McCrory, pp. 12–13. McCrory states that the action took place at Louducies.

38 Jourdain, *The Connaught Rangers*, vol. I, p. 450. The 2nd Connaught Rangers were only re-established after the war, when the 5th Battalion became the 2nd, the only New Army battalion to become part of the Regular forces.

39 IWM, 96/29/1, diary of Sergeant J. McIlwaine, entry for 30 September 1914.

40 Brent Wilson, 'The Morale and Discipline of the British Expeditionary Force', p. 67.

41 On this issue see M. Brown and S. Seaton, *Christmas Truce: The Western Front, December 1914* (Papermac, London, 1994).

42 IWM, 82/30/1, the papers of Brigadier General The Hon. J. F. Trefusis.

43 Royal Irish Fusiliers' Museum, Armagh, Captain Burrows' diary, entry for 13 January 1915.

44 Whitton, *The History of the Prince of Wales' Leinster Regiment*, pp. 77–8.

45 *Ibid.*, pp. 142–3.

46 Brown and Seaton, *Christmas Truce*, pp. 225–30.

47 The most comprehensive study of this unit is A. Roth, '"The German Soldier is not Tactful": Sir Roger Casement and the Irish Brigade in Germany during the First World War', *Irish Sword*, XIX, 78, 1995.

48 An original of this pamphlet is enclosed with notes by Colonel Maurice Moore on the court martial of Private Dowling in July 1918, in Irish Labour History Museum and Archives, Dublin, COS 46.

49 K. Jeffery, 'The Irish military tradition and the British Empire', in K. Jeffery (ed.), *'An Irish Empire?' Aspects of Ireland and the British Empire* (Manchester University Press, 1996), p. 114. Evidence given to MI5 by repatriated POWs put the size of the Brigade at between fifty and sixty-three men, see PRO, WO141/9, 'Formation of an "Irish Bde." among Prisoners of War in Germany'. Roth states that the maximum size of the Brigade was fifty-six men, A. Roth, '"The German soldier is not tactful"', pp. 311–12.

50 See PRO, WO141/9, memo of 1 July 1916 regarding Private M. O'Toole.
51 B. Inglis, *Roger Casement* (Hodder and Stoughton, London, 1973), pp. 287–8.
52 *Ibid.*, p. 289; and the evidence of Private Thomas Higgins, 2nd Royal Dublin Fusiliers and Private Andrew Duffy, RAMC in PRO, WO141/15, 'Sir R. Casement's visits to Limburg Camp'.
53 PRO, WO141/9, evidence of Private William Dooley, 2nd Royal Irish Regiment and Private John Cronin, 2nd Royal Munster Fusiliers.
54 B. E. W. Childs, *Episodes and Reflections, Being Some Records from the Life of Major General Sir Wyndham Childs* (Cassel and Co. Ltd., London, 1930), p. 113; PRO, WO141/9, letter, 5 April 1916, Major Price to Lieutenant Colonel V. G. W. Kell, MI5 G, War Office; and Jeffery, *'An Irish Empire?'*, p. 114.
55 Irish Labour History Museum and Archives, Dublin, COS46, Cathal O'Shannon Papers, notes by Colonel Maurice Moore.
56 All details of Dowling's case were taken from NLI, Ms.8456, Art O'Brien papers. This collection includes a transcript of his court martial and details on the campaign for Dowling's release.
57 L. Ó Broin, *Michael Collins* (Gill and Macmillan, Dublin, 1991), p. 54.
58 Hitchcock, *'Stand To'*, A *Diary of the Trenches*, pp. 25–6. The recruiting area of the Leinster Regiment was Counties Longford, Meath and Westmeath and King's and Queen's Counties.
59 Davison (ed.), *The Burgoyne Diaries*, p. 172.
60 *Ibid.*, p. 210.
61 PRO, WO95/3923, war diary of the Medical Officer, 1st Connaught Rangers, entries for 6 December 1914 and 26 July 1915. No such diary survives relating to any other Irish unit.
62 *Ibid.*, entries for 14 May 1915 and 1 June 1915.
63 PRO, WO95/1481, war diary of the 2nd Royal Dublin Fusiliers, Appendix I, to October 1914.
64 Davison (ed.), *The Burgoyne Diaries*, p. 39.
65 Lucy, *There's a Devil in the Drum*, p. 80.
66 S. Wilkes, 'A Touch of Memory', IWM, Misc.163, item 2508.
67 PRO, PRO30/71/3, letter, Guy Nightingale to his mother, 4 April 1915.
68 Jourdain, *The Connaught Rangers*, vol. I, pp. 451–2.

3

Raising the
Service battalions

The outbreak of the Great War saw in Ireland, as in the rest of
the United Kingdom, the rapid expansion of the army. In
Ireland, the 10th (Irish), 16th (Irish) and 36th (Ulster) Divisions
were raised and all spent a considerable amount of time training
in the United Kingdom. The 10th (Irish) Division first went overseas in July 1915, while the 49th Brigade of the 16th (Irish)
Division finally departed for France in February 1916. It is clear
that deficiencies in equipment, training and leadership affected
these units' performance at the front. Similarly, the political
affiliations of the 16th (Irish) and 36th (Ulster) Divisions were a
mixed blessing to the formations concerned, providing political
patrons and, in the case of the 36th (Ulster) Division, access to
Ulster Volunteer Force equipment but leading to problems in
recruitment and officer selection.

Expansion of the armed forces in Ireland was more straight-
forward than that in the rest of the United Kingdom. There was
none of the competition between New Army and Territorial
Force units, which led to such recriminations in Great Britain
and few Irish depots were overwhelmed with recruits to the
extent that many of their English counterparts were.[1]
Conversely, the expansion of the army in Ireland created a
number of problems for the military authorities which were
unparalleled in Great Britain. The 16th (Irish) and, to a greater
extent, 36th (Ulster) Divisions, were 'political' divisions. Both
had strong political patrons, the Irish Parliamentary Party and
the Ulster Unionists respectively; and this affected the formation

and training of these units in many ways. For example, there was great political pressure brought to bear to appoint certain officers involved in the pre-war paramilitary bodies to high ranks in the Irish New Army divisions, seen most clearly in the appointment of senior officers in the 36th (Ulster) Division. Certainly this lumbered both divisions with numbers of officers whose qualifications rested more on their political influence than their military competence.

These political pressures also extended to other issues, such as the exact names of units, the type of flags carried and badges worn and the type of regimental mascots used. While seemingly innocent enough in itself, this overdue interference of politicians in military minutiae had some serious side effects. It not only distracted officers from the more important task of preparing units for active service, but threatened the British regimental system, itself long prized in maintaining morale amongst British soldiers.

Difficulties arose as the War Office and Irish politicians did not agree on the exact roles of these political divisions. This was particularly the case for the Irish Parliamentary Party. Certainly John Redmond was very keen to see an 'Irish Brigade' formed from the Irish National Volunteers sent on overseas service but at the same time he wanted the British government to provide equipment and instructors for the Irish National Volunteers (INV) units left in Ireland. Redmond's plan was that, post-war, the 'Irish Brigade' and INV would provide the basis for an Irish army, capable of enforcing Home Rule on reluctant Ulster Unionists.[2]

In this chapter, the contribution of the pre-war paramilitary bodies to the creation of the Irish New Army divisions will be considered and the appointment, experience and training of officers will be discussed. This will be followed by a consideration of the composition of the other ranks of these divisions and how they differed from pre-war recruits and adapted to military discipline. The training, equipping and billeting of these units will be investigated and the political pressures on unit names and divisional symbols will then be examined. Consideration will be given to the disciplinary problems faced by these divisions while based in the United Kingdom and the efforts made by the military authorities and civilian bodies to improve morale.

Originally, Lord Kitchener had planned to treat recruitment in Ireland in exactly the same manner as that in the rest of the United Kingdom and on 21 August 1914 the 10th (Irish) Division was authorised. However, by 29 August 1914 he noted, '10th. Division (Irish) none of the battalions are doing well. If not improved next week this Division might be pushed over to K2 and raise a new Division from Ulster Volunteers – and from some of the Reg[iment]s. which show good results in 13th. Western Divi[ision].'[3] On 5 September, a detailed return showed that none of the battalions in the 10th (Irish) Division had reached their full establishment. The strongest battalion, the 6th Royal Irish Rifles had 905 men while the weakest battalion, the 6th Royal Irish Fusiliers, had just thirty-nine men.[4] This was at a time when most other divisions in the First New Army had recruited in excess of their establishment.[5]

These recruiting problems meant that the 10th (Irish) Division, despite its title, had to be completed with British recruits. Bryan Cooper, the Division's historian, suggested that 70 per cent of the other ranks in the Division were either from Ireland or of Irish descent.[6] Nicholas Perry's detailed work on casualty figures broadly agrees with this figure, noting that 66 per cent of fatalities in the Division in August and September 1915 were Irish.[7] At the battalion level, many officers and NCOs referred to the strange composition of their supposedly 'Irish' units. Sergeant J. McIlwaine was very surprised, when posted to the 5th Connaught Rangers in March 1915, to find that his platoon 'consisted largely of insubordinate Yorkshiremen'. Meanwhile, Terence Verschoyle, posted as a second lieutenant to the 5th Royal Inniskilling Fusiliers noted, 'the company was undoubtedly a "difficult" one. For, surprisingly, about one-third of its strength consisted of a draft of Londoners who had, as they thought, enlisted in the D.[uke of] C.[ornwall's] L.[ight] I.[nfantry], and almost a half came from Glasgow or Paisley.' Writing of his experiences as a second lieutenant in the same battalion, Ivone Kirkpatrick referred to 'my platoon of Glasgow Irishmen'. Similarly, F. E. Whitton noted that 600 men from Bristol were used to bring the 6th Leinster Regiment up to strength.[8]

Faced with recruiting difficulties in Ireland, Kitchener reconsidered his position regarding both an Ulster Division and an

'Irish Brigade'. On 3 September 1914, Sir Edward Carson opti-
mistically noted that a meeting with Kitchener, 'was a
wonderful success + now I am in great hopes we will get our
men in large numbers. The promise of making them into a division has been a great help – Tomorrow we commence recruiting
+ tonight I go down to address some of the troops.'[9]
Authorisation for the formation of the 36th (Ulster) Division was
finally given on 28 October 1914. Ulster Unionists drove a hard
bargain over the newly formed division, insisting that it had its
own distinctive badge, the title 'Ulster' in its name, local battalion titles and the appointment of officers sympathetic to the
Unionist cause, to senior positions in the Division. While it may
appear that Kitchener had acceded to Unionist demands, by
agreeing to form an Ulster Division, the point must be made that
the concessions granted to Ulster Unionists were similar to those
made to interest groups in Great Britain at the same time.
Indeed, concessions to the 36th (Ulster) Division appear minor,
given those granted to the 38th (Welsh) Division, which enjoyed
the patronage of David Lloyd George.[10]

As a result of a well-organised Ulster Unionist campaign,
which started almost immediately after the outbreak of the
Great War, the 36th (Ulster) Division has been seen as an
entirely Protestant and Unionist Division, formed solely from
the pre-war UVF. Writing in 1922, Cyril Falls, who served as a
captain in the Division, noted, 'The Ulster Division was not
created in a day. The roots from which it sprang went back into
the troubled period before the war. Its life was a continuance of
the life of an earlier legion, a legion of civilians banded together
to protect themselves from the consequences of legislation
which they believed would affect adversely their rights and
privileges as citizens of the United Kingdom.'[11] This view of the
link between the UVF and the 36th (Ulster) Division has been
echoed by modern historians.[12]

While there was, undoubtedly some continuity between the
UVF and the 36th (Ulster) Division, this constant reliance on
Fall's original account has tended to overemphasise this relationship.[13] While Falls is remembered as the Chichele Professor of
Military History at Oxford University, it is forgotten that in 1922
he was writing both with the patronage of Sir Edward Carson
and Sir James Craig[14] and at a time when Ulster Unionists felt

that their position in the newly formed Northern Ireland state was by no means secure. Thus his study emphasised the extent to which Ulster Unionists had rallied to the Empire in her hour of need, the clear implication being that the British government now owed them a debt of honour by maintaining the integrity of Northern Ireland. A more detailed, and impartial, consideration of the formation of the 36th (Ulster) Division suggests that the overlap between the UVF and this division varied considerably from battalion to battalion. This issue is of importance to the current study, as the extent to which the morale, discipline and, indeed, unit cohesion of the UVF transferred to the 36th (Ulster) Division, influenced this formation's own discipline and morale.

Extensive surviving papers enable a study to be carried out of the composition of the 14th Royal Irish Rifles. This battalion did have its origins in the Young Citizen Volunteers of Belfast and there were connecting factors with this UVF regiment; for example the distinctive grey, pre-war uniform was issued to all men in the new battalion, Lieutenant Colonel Robert Chichester always addressed his men as 'young citizens' and those who had been NCOs in the Young Citizen Volunteers became NCOs in the 14th Royal Irish Rifles.[15] However, the pre-war Young Citizen Volunteers had a stength of just 750 men[16] and of those who voluntarily enlisted in the 14th Royal Irish Rifles over 25 per cent were from England, Scotland and Wales and 17 per cent from Ireland excluding Belfast.[17] Thus, despite the unit title, a UVF regiment certainly did not seamlessly transform itself into a New Army battalion.

In Belfast, it would appear that most units of the 36th (Ulster) Division were filled relatively quickly with former UVF members. By 3 October 1914, the 8th, 9th, 10th and 15th Royal Irish Rifles, recruited from Belfast, had over 1,000 men each.[18] However, even in Belfast, it would be wrong to see UVF units entering the 36th (Ulster) Division en bloc. For example, in a political display on 4 September 1914, Sir Edward Carson and Sir James Craig reviewed 800 men of the North Belfast Regiment, UVF as they went to enlist.[19] At first sight this appears a high figure; however, it must be remembered that the North Belfast Regiment, UVF, in May 1914 had consisted of 6,001 men organised into seven battalions.[20] Seen in this context this political display appears far from impressive.

Outside Belfast overlap between the UVF and the 36th (Ulster) Division was even less distinct. By 3 October 1914 the Belfast-raised battalions of the Division had between 1,038 and 1,119 men. However, amongst rural battalions only the 13th Royal Irish Rifles had recruited well with 1,246 men. Other rural battalions had between 471 men (in the 11th Royal Inniskilling Fusiliers) and 940 men (in the 9th Royal Irish Fusiliers). Overall, the rural battalions had an average strength of just 768 men.[21]

In the case of the 13th Royal Irish Rifles, it appears that this unit obtained the vast majority of its men from UVF units in County Down. However, even within the county the response was variable. Bangor, in North Down contributed 97 men and the Ards Peninsula 85 men, yet the entire South Down UVF Regiment found just 102 men.[22] While this Battalion recruited up to strength very quickly, it effectively marked County Down's manpower ceiling. The 16th Royal Irish Rifles (2nd County Down), the divisional pioneer battalion, formed on 20 October 1914, had severe recruiting difficulties and did not reach its established strength until 24 June 1915.[23] Other rural battalions in the 36th (Ulster) Division faced more serious recruiting problems. In late October 1914, Lieutenant Colonel Ambrose Ricardo, 9th Royal Inniskilling Fusiliers, issued a handbill, which stated ominously, 'Come and join your comrades. If the Ballot Act is put into force you will not be able to choose your regiment.' Privately, he stated, 'We have done fairly well, but require 300 men to complete, if we do not get these at an early date there is a great risk of our being filled up from outside which would be a great slur on our country [sic].'[24] The 11th Royal Inniskilling Fusiliers relied on non-Irish recruits to fill its ranks. Indeed 'C' company was raised in Great Britain by the British League for the Support of Ulster and the Union.[25] Nicholas Perry's work suggests that almost half of the 11th Royal Inniskilling Fusiliers were non-Irish, although most battalions in the Division obtained over 90 per cent of their original establishment from Ireland.[26] Ultimately, the 36th (Ulster) Division, before it left for overseas service was to contain a number of men from Glasgow and Liverpool.[27] Therefore, there were, clearly, strong links between the UVF and the 36th (Ulster) Division, but these should not be over-stated. No UVF unit transferred en bloc into the British army and the overlap between the UVF and the 36th (Ulster) Division varied greatly from battalion to battalion. Not surprisingly, UVF recruitment into the 36th (Ulster) Division was weakest in rural areas, where many UVF members were the sole proprietors of small farms and in what were to become 'border' areas, where threatened sectarian tensions over the Home Rule issue were an incentive for men to stay at home.

While Kitchener saw the UVF as an efficient military force and was prepared to offer concessions to secure the service of UVF personnel in the British army his view of the INV was very different. Therefore, while the 16th (Irish) Division became known as the 'Irish Brigade' the overlap between the INV and the 16th (Irish) Division was considerably less than that between the UVF and the 36th (Ulster) Division. In many ways this was because John Redmond began bidding for higher stakes with a weaker hand. While Carson had insisted that Home Rule be suspended until Ulster exclusion could be considered at the end of the war, his actual demands in respect of the 36th (Ulster) Division were not extortionate and could easily be accommodated within the existing British army structure. By contrast Redmond, to demonstrate his support for the war, primarily wanted the INV to be recognised by the War Office as a military force, for home defence duties only and equipped at government expense.[28]

The INV were, even in comparison to the UVF, an inefficient military force in 1914, lacking trained officers, finance and equipment. Kitchener certainly was not inclined to, as he saw it, waste valuable officers and equipment on a force which, at best, would relieve Territorial Force units from garrison duties and, at worst, would provide Irish Nationalists with the ability to enforce Home Rule on their own terms. Despite receiving support from Asquith, Redmond's attempts to have the INV recognised had failed by mid-August 1914.[29] It was against this background that Redmond 'adopted' the 16th (Irish) Division. As Terence Denman notes, 'There was no indication at first that the division was intended to satisfy Redmond's demands for a specifically nationalist and Catholic formation. But on 12 October [Lieutenant General Sir Lawrence] Parsons was ordered to "clear" a brigade to receive recruits from the Redmondite Volunteers.'[30]

Despite this development, the links between the INV and the British army remained very loose. A proposal that the 8th Royal Munster Fusiliers should have the title 'Limerick Battalion' was agreed in principle by Parsons. However, insufficient numbers of Limerick INV enlisted to allow this proposal to go ahead.[31] Certainly numbers, and indeed bodies of the INV, joined the 16th (Irish) Division and it is noticeable that some units based their recruitment on politics rather than place of domicile. Thus, 100 men of the Enniskillen INV and 500 of the Belfast INV joined the 6th Connaught Rangers,[32] despite the fact that all of these recruits came from outside the Connaught Rangers' regimental recruiting area.

The political nature of the 16th (Irish) and 36th (Ulster) Divisions shaped their development in a number of ways: firstly, in terms of the officers and other ranks joining these units; secondly, in the actual structure of the divisions; thirdly, in relation to the emblems and mascots adopted by these divisions; and lastly, in the more practical issue of the equipment made available for these units.

In terms of officers, both the 16th (Irish) and 36th (Ulster) Divisions were at a disadvantage as most of the experienced officers in Ireland had already been posted to the 10th (Irish) Division, or to non-Irish units. Writing about officer appointments in the 10th (Irish) Division, Cooper noted that the senior service battalions usually secured their commanding officer, one captain and one subaltern from the regimental depot and three officers and ten to sixteen NCOs from the regular battalion which had been on home service when war broke out. In addition to this the Division secured the services of eight to ten District Inspectors of the Royal Irish Constabulary, who were commissioned as captains and the service of at least one Indian Army officer per battalion.[33] Considering the officers in the 6th Royal Dublin Fusiliers in August 1914, N. E. Drury noted that 12 of the officers had previous military experience; 6 in the Royal Dublin Fusiliers, 3 in the Indian Army, 2 in the Royal Irish Constabulary and 1 in the Rifle Brigade.[34]

This left very few experienced officers for the later Irish divisions. UVF influence certainly managed to secure some regular officers for the 36th (Ulster) Division, who otherwise would have gone to other units. Brigadier General T. E. Hickman noted, 'When Carson offered the Ulster Volunteers to Lord K.[itchener] and the latter ordered me to go over and raise the men, both K.[itchener], Sclater + Codrington distinctly promised Carson + myself that we should certainly have all the original Ulster Vol.[unteer] officers we asked for.'[35] Thus, the UVF requested the services of a number of officers who had reported for duty with other units on the outbreak of war. A number of these, for example, Lieutenant Colonel R. D. P. S. Chichester (Guards Reserve), Major S. W. Blacker (Royal Field Artillery) and Captain W. B. Spender (South Eastern Coastal Defences) were returned for duty with the 36th (Ulster) Division.[36] Meanwhile, F. P. Crozier, a captain in the Reserve of Officers, who on the outbreak of war was commanding a UVF battalion in West Belfast, following consultation with James Craig, simply ignored orders to report to the Royal Irish Fusiliers, preferring to stay with the UVF. He became a major and later a lieutenant colonel in the 9th Royal Irish Rifles.[37]

UVF influence also saw the appointment of Major General C. H. Powell, ex-Indian Army, and in 1914, the commander of the North Down Regiment, UVF as GOC of the 36th (Ulster) Division,[38] Colonel G. H. H. Couchman, late Somerset Light Infantry and UVF commander in Belfast, as Brigadier General commanding the 107th Infantry Brigade, Colonel G. W. Hacket Pain, late Worcestershire Regiment and UVF Chief of Staff, as Brigadier General commanding 108th Infantry Brigade and Colonel T. E. Hickman, MP, Inspector General of the UVF as Brigadier General commanding the 109th Infantry Brigade.[39] In addition, James Craig, MP, who had served as a captain in the Imperial Yeomanry during the Boer War, was appointed Assistant Adjutant and Quartermaster General of the 36th (Ulster) Division, with the rank of lieutenant colonel.[40] Former UVF officers therefore monopolised the high command of the 36th (Ulster) Division.

The usefulness of these officers, secured by UVF influence was variable. Brigadier General Couchman did not prove to be an effective commanding officer, and one of Major General Oliver Nugent's first acts on becoming GOC of the 36th (Ulster) Division was to remove Couchman from his command.[41] While Craig was able to secure some UVF equipment for the 36th (Ulster) Division, he was on sick leave from 5 July 1915 until he finally resigned his commission due to ill health on 10 March 1916.[42] By contrast Lieutenant Colonel S. W. Blacker turned the 9th Royal Irish Fusiliers into, arguably, the best battalion in the 36th (Ulster) Division, in terms of both discipline and combat effectiveness.[43]

Nevertheless, political influence could do nothing to remedy the shortage of experienced officers in either the 16th (Irish) or 36th (Ulster) Divisions. The 8th Royal Munster Fusiliers had two regular officers, while the 9th Royal Munster Fusiliers had only one regular officer.[44] The 9th Royal Irish Rifles had only two officers with previous regular experience: Lieutenant Colonel G. S. Ormerod, late Royal Munster Fusiliers, who had retired in 1904 and Major F. P. Crozier, a reformed alcoholic who had been forced to resign from both the 2nd Manchester Regiment in 1907 and the 3rd Loyal North Lancashire Regiment in 1909 for dishonouring cheques. Indeed, a confidential memorandum on Crozier noted, 'When commissioned in 1914 it was not discovered that this was the Captain Crozier who had had to resign his commission.'[45]

At the battalion level these officers were, again, a variable quantity. Crozier proved to be an efficient, if controversial, officer and ended the war as a brigadier general. Other veteran officers proved a severe embarrassment. During December 1914, Captain Charles St Aulwyn Wake reported for service with the 14th Royal Irish Rifles. Wake had lost his leg on active service and proved himself to be in no condition to train men. Following a route march,

> Capt. Wake gave the command 'Halt!', as the men had been 'Marking Time', Capt. Wake's next command was 'Fall out the Gentlemen.' For some unknown reason he then fell off his horse. He lay where he fell, apparently unhurt. He made no attempt to rise. He then gave the final command, 'Battalion Dis-miss', whereupon the parade did a Right Turn, saluted and then dispersed. Only then did Capt. Wake get up, and hand his mount over to the groom, who was waiting. Captain Wake remained only a short time with the 14th. Battalion.[46]

However, there is some evidence that other ranks in the New Armies were prepared to tolerate and work for officers who were not entirely competent in their duties. Rifleman

MacRoberts of the 14th Royal Irish Rifles noted that his company commander, Major Peter Kerr-Smiley, MP, 'was a cavalry officer, as most of us knew, and had little experience with infantry and was therefore bound to make mistakes, but we were to do the right thing, to support him loyally and he would do his best, so we would get along well together. He had a good voice and seemed to be very cool and collected.'[47]

Apart from regular officers, there were two other types of officers with some previous military experience available to the 16th (Irish) and 36th (Ulster) Divisions. Namely, former militia or special reserve officers and officers from pre-war paramilitary bodies. Retired militia officers appear to have been largely unsuccessful appointments. Major Sir Francis Vane, writing of his fellow officers in the 9th Royal Munster Fusiliers, noted,

> Several old officers of Irish Militia regiments had volunteered to come out, expecting jobs on the remounts etc. They were enthusiastically patriotic and admirable, but as captains of modern companies the work was much too great for their strength, and having left the Army for a score of years they did not know much about modern drill. When I was on parade they were constantly coming to me for advice – one asked me how many men there were in a modern company, another to give him a few useful words of command, etc. I did my best to help them at their request, but applied for them to be removed to more convenient employment. This was eventually done – but one at least died of the strain of it all.[48]

A number of officers whose only military experience was in pre-war paramilitary groups received commissions in the 16th (Irish) and 36th (Ulster) Divisions. In the 16th (Irish) Division, Lieutenant General Sir Lawrence Parsons refused to give commissions to such officers *en masse*. While Parsons gave four or five commissions in the Divisional Artillery to INV officers, he would only give commissions in infantry battalions to INV officers who brought a number of their men with them. Thus John Wray, an officer in the Enniskillen INV, received a commission in the 6th Connaught Rangers when he brought 200 of his men with him. Therefore, by November 1914, Colonel Maurice Moore, the Inspector General of the INV, was referring INV officers, desirous of a commission in the British army, to the

Tyneside Irish Brigade, where their claims would be dealt with
more sympathetically.[49]

In the 36th (Ulster) Division, many more openings were available for former paramilitary officers. While assessments of the
overlap between the UVF and 36th (Ulster) Division for other
ranks remain somewhat generalised, it is possible, following the
recent release of officers' personal records at the PRO to build
up a detailed picture of the officer corps of the division and its
continuity with the pre-war UVF. These officers' personal
records demonstrate that UVF membership was important, but
despite the claims of some contemporary Nationalist politicians
and recent historians, not paramount in officer selection for the
36th (Ulster) Division.[50]

The importance of UVF membership in officer appointments
varied considerably between units. In most of the rural units
(especially the 12th and 13th Royal Irish Rifles, 9th Royal Irish
Fusiliers and 11th Royal Inniskilling Fusiliers) UVF membership
played an important role in officer selection. For example, in the
9th Royal Irish Fusiliers of the fourteen surviving officers' files
it is clear that nine had served in the UVF. However, in the
Belfast-raised battalions, with the exception of the 14th Royal
Irish Rifles, few officers had UVF experience. In the 10th
Royal Irish Rifles of the eighteen surviving officers' files, it is
clear that only three had served in the UVF.[51] Those with UVF
experience were often commissioned into the army at a relatively high rank, although they had no proper military training.
For example, Lieutenant Colonel S. W. Blacker successfully
nominated George Robert Irwin to a captaincy solely on the
basis that he had been Adjutant of the 1st Armagh Regiment,
UVF and Lieutenant Colonel Pakenham successfully nominated
Adam Penrose Jenkins to a captaincy as he had commanded a
UVF battalion.[52] However, UVF officers were not automatically
nominated for higher rank; for example Major the Earl of
Leitrim nominated Charles Fausset Falls to a mere second lieu-
tenancy, despite the fact that Falls had commanded the 3rd
Fermanagh Regiment, UVF.[53] A more prominent example of the
claims of a UVF officer being ignored is in the case of William
Copeland Trimble. Trimble, a prominent Fermanagh Unionist
and editor of the influential local paper, *The Impartial Reporter*,
had raised the Enniskillen Horse of the UVF. However, he was

not given military rank in the service squadron of the 6th Inniskilling Dragoons, formed largely from this UVF unit, probably due to his advanced age and lack of any formal military experience.[54]

When the supply of regular, reserve, ex-special reserve, militia and former paramilitary officers had been exhausted, other methods had to be resorted to in order to obtain officers. Lieutenant General Sir Lawrence Parsons established a cadet company in the 7th Leinster Regiment. This was created in response to what Parsons saw as the poor quality of candidates presenting themselves for commissions. He noted, 'Many of the Candidates are quite socially impossible as Officers – men who write their applications in red or green ink on a blank bill-head of a village shop. These are the class most successfully weeded out by the enlisting ordeal [into the cadet company], as they think it beneath their dignity to enlist as "Common" Soldiers to be herded with "riff-raff".'[55] Parsons's cadet company was to prove a great asset to the 16th (Irish) Division: between November 1914 and December 1915, 161 cadets passed through it to become officers in the Division.[56] This company was particularly useful as in Ireland very few schools or colleges had established OTCs by 1914 and these institutions were attended, almost exclusively, by Protestants. Parsons's cadet company thus provided a manner in which Irish Catholics could receive an OTC type of training.

However, the cadet company in the 7th Leinster Regiment was not endorsed by a number of leading Nationalists. Colonel Maurice Moore, the Inspector General of the INV noted in November 1914,

> though the latter [Parsons] is very sympathetic and an old friend of mine, he may be inclined to take from us the only privilege we have, viz. – the appointment of officers. He says he has 200 applications and is going to lump them together into a company for drill and choose the best, that is I admit a very good plan from his point of view, but may mean the officering of the [Irish] Brigade by Unionists, whereas we want it as a training place for our officers to be ready after the war.[57]

Parsons's cadet company gained unpopularity amongst Nationalists as it developed. It was clear that Parsons did not see it as a training school for INV officers. His decision that some Irish Parliamentary Party MPs, most notably William Archer Redmond, would have to serve in the ranks before qualifying for commissions was tactless in the extreme.[58] There were, of course, sound military reasons why such men should go through some form of training before being commissioned. However, for the Irish Parliamentary Party this policy was damaging. As Nora Robertson, Parsons's daughter, noted of the cadet company, 'as a means of training officers it could not have been more satisfactory nor, for the majority, more popular. But as a political device for a distracted leader trying to entice M.P.s, J.P.s, touchy publicans, and financial supporters to send their sons to an extremely dangerous and not very popular war it was, to say the least of it, rebuffing.'[59]

Parsons's cadet company and whole policy on commissions was further discredited by three factors. Firstly, pitifully few Catholics received commissions in the 16th (Irish) Division. Scarcely one officer in five was a Catholic and of the officers above the rank of major, only one was not a Protestant.[60] Redmond highlighted the problems this created for the morale of men serving in the 16th (Irish) Division, stating that, 'The fact that every one of the three Brigadier Generals of the 16th Division is an Englishman, every Colonel in the Division, and, with one or two exceptions, every Major and Captain, Protestants, and that the smallest possible proportion of Officers of these Regiments are Catholics has been, and is, doing the greatest possible harm.'[61] Secondly, the cadet company was easily by-passed by a number of Englishmen who obtained temporary commissions. Some received direct commissions from the War Office, while a number of Englishmen, who had been privates in exclusive London Territorial Force units, were directly commissioned into the 16th (Irish) Division.[62] Finally, many Nationalists contrasted the difficulty they had in obtaining commissions in the 16th (Irish) Division, with the apparent ease with which Ulster Unionists received commissions in the 36th (Ulster) Division.[63]

In the 36th (Ulster) Division, no cadet company on Parsons's model was established and, indeed, it does appear that many men without any previous military experience found it relatively easy to obtain commissions in this unit. Nora Robertson argued that, 'practically all Ulstermen of officer standing had had some form of military training, even at school in the OTC. The Nationalist type had not.'[64] However, given the small number of OTC units existing in Ulster in 1914 (namely, those at Campbell College and The Queen's University of Belfast) this does appear to be overstating the case.

Figures calculated from surviving officers' records suggest that 20 per cent of those in the 36th (Ulster) Division received commissions on the basis of having attended a school or university OTC, 11 per cent had previously been officers in regular or reserve units and 24 per cent had previously served in the ranks.[65] Many men appear to have been commissioned into the 36th (Ulster) Division simply as they were prominent businessmen, or had some professional qualifications. The only training given to such men, except informally by senior officers in their own battalion, was at a special officers' course which took place at The Queen's University of Belfast. J. H. Stewart-Moore, commenting on the usefulness of this course stated, 'I do not think that we learnt much that was useful but the course provided an opportunity for one or two pleasant tea parties.'[66] At a more mundane level, Brigadier General Couchman nominated many young men as second lieutenants on the basis that they had attended a grammar school in Belfast. When even this failed to secure enough junior officers for the 107th Brigade he nominated a few young men, with no military experience or UVF links, from working-class areas of Belfast.[67]

Enthusiastic amateurs or military adventurers who obtained their commissions through political connections occasionally did not become efficient officers. Captain Lewis Walter McIntyre, who had obtained his commission in the 11th Royal Inniskilling Fusiliers of the 36th (Ulster) Division on the basis that he was personally known by Major the Earl of Leitrim and had served as a UVF company commander, was forced to resign his commission in May 1915 due to his excessive consumption of alcohol.[68] Probably the worst example of an officer removed for incompetence while Irish New Army units were training in the UK was that of Captain Richard Edward Toker of the 10th Royal Inniskilling Fusiliers. Toker had served as an officer in the Indian Army from August 1905 to March 1913. From April 1914 it appears that he may have had some connection with the UVF in the Londonderry area. Lieutenant Colonel Ross Smyth, the CO of the 10th Royal Inniskilling Fusiliers, recommended Toker for a captaincy and the position of Adjutant in his battalion. Toker ran up a large drinks bill in the regimental mess, issued a number of dishonoured cheques and left his wife and children without any financial support. The battalion CO was very concerned about the poor example set by Toker to younger officers and it was decided to let Toker resign his commission in September 1915 in consideration for his father, who was a general.[69]

The other ranks in the Irish New Army divisions appear to have come from less varied social backgrounds than their counterparts in Great Britain, few being skilled workers or middle class in origin. Pauline Codd, writing in relation to County Wexford, and Martin Staunton, regarding County Clare, suggest that over 80 per cent of recruits from these areas during the war were labourers. Even from industrial Belfast, many of the recruits were unskilled workers. For example, in June 1917 a roll of honour unveiled in Harland and Wolff shipyard's boiler shop listed 260 men from that workshop on active service. Of these, 36 were skilled workers, 42 apprentices and 182 unskilled workers. In the 10th Royal Inniskilling Fusiliers, it appears that 74 per cent of men serving in this unit between October 1914 and July 1916 were unskilled workers.[70] This contrast to the general British experience was important as it made the number of potential NCOs very small, especially in the 16th (Irish) and 36th (Ulster) Divisions, which had few veterans in the ranks. David Starret noted the situation at Donard Camp, where the 107th Brigade was quartered: '"Acting" sergeants came round half-a-dozen times a day to ask your name. I doubt if some of them could spell their own.'[71] Likewise, J. H. M. Staniforth, serving in the 6th Connaught Rangers, wrote, 'Well, our sergeant was a mild, helpless old thing with a "strong weakness" [for alcohol] himself, so he let us get out of hand altogether and we scattered over the town, drinking hard.'[72]

Middle-class recruits to the Irish New Army divisions found it difficult to adapt to army life. When J. H. M. Staniforth joined the 6th Connaught Rangers in October 1914 he described his fellow recruits as 'these, filthy, sodden, smelling, staggering, slobbering lepers who sang and cursed and quarrelled and snore by turns'.[73] By early February 1915 such problems were being rectified in the 14th Royal Irish Rifles, as Rifleman J. MacRoberts noted, 'we were beginning to recall the little conventions that constitute modern good manners and everyone who forgot himself at table now, was tossed in a blanket, after having been properly tried and condemned by a special judge with jury. We had quite a number of offenders each night.'[74]

In disciplinary terms, the backgrounds of some recruits posed potential problems. Former soldiers or militia men could cause difficulties for their new officers. A. M. Cooper, serving in the 8th Royal Inniskilling Fusiliers, remembered, 'There were militia-men among us, wearing South African war ribbons, who were amused at the large body of civilians who had become soldiers overnight. They were always ready to make fun of any arduous drill and training which they thought to be unnecessary – for them anyway.'[75] David Campbell, a theology student at Trinity College Dublin, who was commissioned into the 6th Royal Irish Rifles, recounted similar problems, 'My platoon looked a pretty tough lot. Most of them, as I learned later, were reservists and were accustomed to being called up annually for a month's training. Many of them were middle aged and beery looking, they were not easy to manage at first, they hated violent exercise and physical jerks or doubling round the barrack square were anathema to them. The regular exercise and ample food, however soon began to tell before very long, they began to face their work cheerfully enough, and to take pride in their smartness.'[76]

The formation and training of the Irish New Army units faced problems on a number of other levels, all of which influenced the morale of the Service battalions. Firstly, there were political issues surrounding the names of units and the badges, flags and mascots used. Secondly, there was the purely practical problem of trying to train men with insufficient numbers of trained officers and NCOs or equipment. Thirdly, there were problems associated with the slow recruitment of units. Lastly, there were difficulties with billeting the large numbers of new recruits.

As has already been discussed, the overlap between the INV and 16th (Irish) Division and the UVF and the 36th (Ulster) Division was far from absolute. However, these divisions' polit-

ical patrons wanted to influence how the divisions developed
and what symbols they used. Many of these political trappings
caused controversy and were potentially damaging to morale.
One of the earliest decisions to be made in these divisions was
the exact name of the units concerned. The title 'Ulster' for the
36th Division was reluctantly conceded by Kitchener, although
the title had never appeared in the British army before.[77]
Likewise the so-called, 'Dixie' badge (an oval, bronze disc,
showing the red hand of Ulster) was issued to the 36th (Ulster)
Division. The latter decision shocked a number of officers
serving in the Division. As F. P. Crozier related,

> A single instance will illustrate this pride of regiment. Someone –
> I know not who – devised a Divisional cap badge, comprising the
> Red Hand of Ulster, to be worn by the whole of the Ulster
> Division. The political suggestion was approved by the higher
> authorities, without our knowledge. The badges arrived, were
> issued, and of course worn, since an order is an order; but regi-
> mental tradition prevailed over political stupidity. Protests
> reached Divisional Headquarters in such large numbers, in the
> regulation manner, that within a week the Royal Irish Rifles
> badge was again in every cap. It is possible to play on regimental
> tradition to almost any extent, provided the way is known, but it
> cannot be cut across for apparently no good military reason.[78]

Redmond was keen that, to evoke the memory of the 'Wild
Geese', the 16th Division should be known as the 'Irish Brigade'
and given a distinctive badge and uniforms.[79] However, Parsons
was generally unsympathetic to the 'Irish Brigade' title and the
trappings which this entailed. In a letter to John Redmond in
December 1914 he noted, 'I have always been opposed to any
special Badge being stuck to the 16th. Div.[ision] ... The only
reason I can see is that the Ulster Div[isio]n. has a silly badge
replacing the time honoured badges of the Regiments they
belong to. I am not in favour of copying the Ulster Div[isio]n.'[80]
Finally, no less a personage than Field Marshal Lord Kitchener
decided that a shamrock would be the divisional badge.[81]

In terms of morale, the preservation of the regimental system
was probably the most important result of these discussions.
Given the fact that the 49th Infantry Brigade did not arrive in
France until February 1916, three months after the rest of the
16th (Irish) Division and the early date at which some Service

battalions in the Division were disbanded, it is questionable whether the 16th (Irish) Division ever attained a corporate identity like that enjoyed in the 36th (Ulster) Division.[82]

The 10th (Irish), 16th (Irish) and 36th (Ulster) Divisions all faced problems in their training, which were similar to those experienced by other New Army units in Britain.[83] Training in the 10th (Irish) Division was reasonably comprehensive, given the large number of regular or recently retired officers and NCOs available in this formation. Indeed, the 10th (Irish) Division was the only Irish division to complete the course laid down by the War Office.[84]

In the 16th (Irish) Division, training was less organised, and this has led to some debate. Terence Denman believes that Sir Lawrence Parsons was an effective training officer, stating, 'Parsons was energetic and methodical in his frequent inspections of his troops in a determined, and largely successful, attempt to prepare his division for the realities of trench warfare and to counter the debilitating effects of long months of training and waiting.'[85] By contrast, Tom Johnstone believes the training programme to have been insufficiently intensive, involving only eight to nine hours work per day; also noting that Parsons set no uniform standards which battalions were expected to meet and, as late as August 1915, Parsons had not even visited some of the units under his command.[86] Certainly, training in the 16th (Irish) Division could verge on the shambolic and war games in the 48th and 49th Brigades descended into farce, with units on supposedly the same side attacking each other and a company of the 7th Royal Inniskilling Fusiliers, specifically ordered not to take part in the war game, launching a bayonet charge.[87]

By June 1915, deficiencies in the 16th (Irish) Division's training were blindingly obvious. Lieutenant S. E. J. C. Lushington, serving in the 11th Hampshire Regiment, the divisional pioneer unit, noted, 'we just heard the very unwelcome news that we have been turned into the 4th. Reserve army which means which [sic] shan't go out for another six months, all because these rotten Irishmen are absolutely hopeless.'[88] At about this time, Major Sir Francis Vane commented that the 16th (Irish) Division had become 'a patchwork of men in different stages of instruction'.[89]

While Parsons must be held responsible for some of the defects in divisional training, Johnstone's criticisms are, to some extent, unjustified. The training of the 36th (Ulster) Division was not noticeably better. David Starret, on arriving at Donard Camp, as a member of the 107th Brigade in mid-September 1914 remembered, 'Things were topsy-turvy ... The first two-three days was Babel. My! it was a picnic. Others as well as myself did not know to what they belonged so roamed together in and about the camp.'[90] Indeed, the work schedule in late September was actually less intense than that in the 16th (Irish) Division, with only five and three-quarters hours work a day.[91] While the 36th (Ulster) Division did have access to UVF arms, equipment and uniforms,[92] under Major General Powell, the training of the Division appears to have consisted merely of marching. Certainly, when Major General Oliver Nugent took over command of the Division, he felt it to be unfit for front-line service.[93]

The experience of the 36th (Ulster) Division suggests that Parsons coped as well as could be expected in the circumstances with the training of the 16th (Irish) Division. Johnstone's criticism also ignores another key factor which retarded the training of and, as discussed later, possibly caused discontent in, the 16th (Irish) Division: the serious manpower problem faced in its formation. By March 1915 the 16th (Irish) Division did, indeed, present a 'patchwork appearance' in terms of unit strengths; the strongest battalion in the Division, the 6th Connaught Rangers contained 1,235 men, while the weakest, the 7th Royal Irish Rifles contained just 352 men.[94]

The varying unit strengths in this division at this date had a political dimension. Due to Redmond's influence, it had been decided to 'clear' one brigade of the 16th (Irish) Division in October 1914 to be filled up with men recruited from the INV. Parsons viewed this clearing scheme as 'all damned rot' but selected the 47th Infantry Brigade for this dubious honour, presumably as its units had the largest geographical catchment areas.[95] This clearing scheme was certainly beneficial to the 47th Brigade which by March 1915 had a total of 4,004 men, whereas by this date the 49th Brigade had a mere 2,197 men.[96]

While some of Parsons's battalions were thus politically favoured, others were not as fortunate. The Royal Inniskilling Fusiliers, Royal Irish Rifles and Royal Irish Fusiliers were all linked, in nationalist eyes, with the 36th (Ulster) Division, as their recruitment areas were all in the nine counties of Ulster.[97] The bizarre result of this was that Derry INV members from the Royal Inniskilling Fusiliers regimental area enlisted in large numbers in the 6th Royal Irish Regiment, and Belfast INV members from the Royal Irish Rifles regimental district enlisted in the 6th Connaught Rangers and 7th Leinster Regiment.[98] Parsons's attempt to equalise the numbers of men in his battalions ran into immediate difficulties. R. J. Tennant mistakenly believed that when Parsons transferred men from the 47th to the 49th Infantry Brigades, he was forcing INV members to serve with UVF personnel.[99] Parsons replied, noting, 'What would Lord K.[itchener] say if he saw my returns of strength showing some Battalions as 1,300 strong, others 400!'[100]

This situation became increasingly complicated for Parsons, when, in March 1915 the 7th Royal Irish Rifles received six officers and 225 other ranks from the Jersey Militia and the 6th Royal Irish Regiment, a complete company and machine gun section of the Guernsey Militia. The Jersey Militia personnel must have been welcome to a battalion which was all but failing. The Guernsey Militia, however, were a mixed blessing; not only had the Guernsey Militia company been posted to the strongest battalion in the Division by the War Office, but the fact that the Guernsey Militia had been disbanded in 1896 due to a mutiny suggested that this company would not provide a stabilising influence in the 16th (Irish) Division.[101]

Parsons was also under pressure from John Redmond, given the weakness of some units in the 16th (Irish) Division, to apply for the Tyneside Irish Brigade to join this formation.[102] Parsons managed to alienate much nationalist support by stating that Irishmen living in British industrial cities 'are slum-birds that we don't want. I want to see the clean, fine, strong, temperate, hurley-playing country fellows such as we used to get in the Munsters, Royal Irish, Connaught Rangers.'[103]

Another controversy over the manning of the 16th (Irish) Division came in June 1915 when the Division had to send 1,200 men to the 10th (Irish) Division to replace men who had been found medically unfit.[104] Redmond was incensed that these men were all drawn from the 49th Brigade, 'which was the one Brigade of the Division undermanned'.[105] This loss of manpower led to serious, albeit unfounded, concerns amongst

Nationalist politicians that this brigade, if not the entire 16th (Irish) Division, would be used as a draft-finding body.[106]

The political nature of the 36th (Ulster) Division also affected its recruiting policy. Some units in this division were perfectly happy to accept Catholic recruits; for example, the 14th Royal Irish Rifles had five officers and ninety-eight other ranks serving in it during this period who were Catholics.[107] However, the case of P. J. Kelly, a Catholic who had tried to enlist into a Royal Engineer unit highlighted the sectarian nature of some units in the 36th (Ulster) Division. The officer who interviewed Kelly apparently told him that to join the 36th (Ulster) Division he would have to change his religion. When this case appeared in the newspapers an unrepentant Richard Dawson Bates, Secretary of the Ulster Unionist Council, pointed out that Catholics were free to join other units and erroneously suggested that there were only fifteen Catholics in the Division, all sergeant instructors, sent by the War Office. This blatant piece of misinformation, with the implication that Catholics were not welcome in the 36th (Ulster) Division, can have done little to improve either the morale of Catholics serving in the Division or, indeed, recruitment for some of the rural battalions of the Division which had not reached their establishment. The War Office traced Kelly to Noble's Explosive Works in Ayrshire and persuaded him to enlist in another Royal Engineer unit.[108]

One final issue which caused discontent in New Army units were the poor accommodation arrangements. At Birr Barracks cramped and insanitary conditions led to an outbreak of 'spotted fever' which led to four deaths in the 11th Hampshire Regiment.[109] In autumn 1914 a severe storm levelled the 109th Brigade camp at Finner.[110] Similar conditions at Donard Camp led to a mutiny in early winter 1914, when tents began to collapse due to heavy rain. A number of men of the 9th Royal Irish Rifles left the camp, stating that they were returning home to Belfast. Colonel Wallace, the camp commandant, and Major F. P. Crozier rode after the men, and they all agreed to return when these officers promised them new billets. No disciplinary action was taken against these men.[111] Meanwhile, by July 1915, Captain O. L. Beater noted of the camp inhabited by the 9th Royal Dublin Fusiliers, near Buttevant, 'This camp is getting into a very unhealthy state and fairly stinks. The sooner they shift us the better.'[112]

The billeting of men in private houses during the Great War was a controversial issue throughout the United Kingdom.[113] However, in Ireland billeting attained sectarian overtones. In September 1914 when Clandeboye camp was flooded by heavy rain, the 11th Royal Irish Rifles were billeted in Lisburn. This led to accusations that an outrageously large number of men were billeted in Nationalist homes.[114] The billeting of men in public buildings caused other problems. When the 109th Brigade's tented accommodation was levelled by storms at Finner in autumn 1914, the 9th, 10th and 11th Royal Inniskilling Fusiliers simply had to re-erect their tents and stayed there throughout the winter. By contrast, following this disaster, the 14th Royal Irish Rifles moved to hotels in Ballyshannon, 'The Y.[oung] C.[itizen] V.[olunteers] [14th Royal Irish Rifles] were from the more affluent families of Belfast and there was a certain degree of antagonism between them and the men from the west of Ulster, many of whom were from very poor homes. It would take a long time before they were fully accepted by the rest of the Brigade.'[115]

A number of breaches of discipline occurred in the Irish New Army divisions during training. The worst of these were mutinies, of which at least nine took place during this period. Absenteeism was another serious problem, especially in the 10th (Irish) and 36th (Ulster) Divisions, when men were quartered near their homes. Drunkenness was a persistent problem and resulted in action from both the local and military authorities. However, it appears that none of these military crimes was of a political nature. In 1915 the Athgorvan company of the Irish Volunteers was spectacularly unsuccessful in attempting to purchase rifles from Irish soldiers training at the Curragh camp.[116]

As with other New Army divisions, the 16th (Irish) and 36th (Ulster) Divisions contended with a number of mutinies during their training, although none appear to have occured in the 10th (Irish) Division.[117] Uniquely, men in the 16th (Irish) Division were actually tried and found guilty of mutiny by courts martial.[118] On 17 June 1915, Lance Corporal J. Austin of the 8th Royal Irish Fusiliers was tried at Tipperary for mutiny by a

District Court Martial and sentenced to eighty-four days detention. Meanwhile, on 6 September 1915, seven privates of the 8th
Royal Inniskilling Fusiliers were tried for mutiny and drunkenness at Enniskillen, and were each sentenced to one year hard
labour. Unfortunately the case transcripts, or, indeed, any
contemporary accounts of these incidents do not survive.
Nevertheless, it is possible to posit, with some certainty, the
reasons why these mutinies occurred.

Both of these mutinies took place in the 49th Brigade, which
had the most serious recruiting problems in any Irish New
Army formation. The mutiny in the 8th Royal Irish Fusiliers
occurred in June 1915, the very time when the 49th Brigade had
to send 1,200 men to the 10th (Irish) Division.[119] The result of
this was not only to split up men who had joined the army on
the explicit understanding that they would serve together, but
to disperse the Brigade, as battalions were sent to Ulster to
recruit. The mutiny in the 8th Royal Inniskilling Fusiliers would
appear to have occurred for similar reasons, with the added
grievance that, by September 1915, it appeared that the 49th
Brigade was being converted into a draft-finding unit. Indeed, it
is possible that even by this date, men in the Brigade were aware
that they would not accompany the rest of the 16th (Irish)
Division overseas.[120]

A number of other incidents which can properly be described
as mutinies occurred in the 16th (Irish) and 36th (Ulster)
Divisions during their training. While no men were court-
martialled for their part in these incidents, at least a clearer
picture is available as to why they occurred. The unit most
dogged with mutinies during this time was the 6th Connaught
Rangers. It would appear that mutinies occurred in this battalion on 23 October 1914, another later in October 1914 and,
finally, one on 24 or 25 December 1914.[121] The most serious of
these was that occurring in late October, as the then Sergeant
Staniforth observed,

> We had a fearful mutiny last week. The prisoners in the guard-
> room and cells (50 men, all drunk) rose again ... and got
> possession of the place and smashed it to splinters, and then
> sallied out armed with bayonets upon the crowd outside. For
> about a quarter of an hour there was all hell let loose: bayonets
> going and bricks flying, until they could get the fire-hose

limbered up and turn on to them. That settled them, but there were six men lying unconscious, and many more bleeding from small wounds. Two subsequently died in hospital, one from a stick of a bayonet and one from a bang of a brick over the heart. We had a frightful kick-up over it next day; they brought the General over from Mallow to curse us.[122]

Despite these fatalities, Parsons decided not to institute court martial proceedings, as he noted in his diary, 'Motored to Fermoy on getting news of drunken row in [6th] Connaught Rangers. Made a speech to N.C.O.s of [6th] Connaught Rangers and [7th] Royal Irish Rifles and then to men and gave them pepper.'[123] It would appear from this comment that similar problems had occurred in the 7th Royal Irish Rifles. Staniforth believed that the first two mutinies were simply drunken brawls which got out of hand. The third mutiny in the 6th Connaught Rangers, occurred on either Christmas Eve or Christmas Day 1914 and appears to have been viewed simply as seasonal high spirits. On this occasion the men invaded the mess while the officers were having dinner and carried them outside.[124]

In the 36th (Ulster) Division, at least three mutinies took place during the Division's training. That in the 9th Royal Irish Rifles, over poor accommodation, has already been referred to. Another mutiny occurred following manoeuvres by the 109th Brigade in the Antrim hills in June 1915. In this incident, the men of the 14th Royal Irish Rifles refused to march back to Shane's Castle camp, insisting on a train being provided. The battalion's CO, Lieutenant Colonel Robert Chichester, diffused the situation by conceding to this demand and chartering a train. No man in the 14th Royal Irish Rifles received any official punishment for this action, but from then on the other battalions in the Brigade referred to them as 'Chocolate Soldiers'.[125]

Much more serious was the mass mutiny of the 36th (Ulster) Division in early September 1915. At this time a number of battalions of the Division mutinied as they believed, wrongly, that they were to be sent overseas immediately, without home leave first. Rifleman J. MacRoberts related how this situation was diffused in the 14th Royal Irish Rifles,

One evening a rumour reached us from the huts that no leave was going to be granted before going to the front, and that several of the battalions had – to use the only possible word – mutinied. That night we were paraded and addressed by Major B[ruce?], at that moment in a lamentable, intoxicated state.

If we did not get leave he said, we were not to mutiny, no matter what other battalions might do and what they might say about us. We had joined the army for King and Country and had undertaken to obey its rules and commands. This was the first war most of us had been in and probably it would be the last, thus it behaved [sic] us to abide by the rules like men. So let us play the game and to hell with the Pope. The proceedings were a scandal and a shame to the British Army, but the reckless, dare-all manner of the Major had a great influence with the troops.[126]

Perhaps not surprisingly, the main crimes committed by New Army units while based in the United Kingdom involved absence or drunkenness (although the latter crime was on a small scale when compared to figures for regular battalions in table 2.1). Of the 305 cases considered in a sample number of Irish Service battalions, as detailed in table 3.1, only twenty-five involved insubordination.[127] Consideration of the courts martial records of these battalions during training shows a far from uniform pattern. The 14th Royal Irish Rifles had only four courts martial during this period, as the Battalion's Adjutant, Captain Bentley, refused to refer absent without leave cases to courts martial.[128] The difference between the courts martial records of the 6th (115 cases) and 8th (seventeen cases) Royal Dublin Fusiliers may be explained, partly, by the different social classes represented,[129] and partly by the proximity in which the 6th Royal Dublin Fusiliers were stationed to Dublin. Hervey de Montmorency, serving as a captain in the 7th Royal Dublin Fusiliers, along with the 6th Battalion in 30th Brigade stated,

It is quite true that the Irishmen in my battalion have been recruited from the poorest, unskilled casual labourers of Dublin, the lowest strata of our society – and there has been undoubtedly a great deal of absence without leave, but absence without leave is a purely military offence, it is not immoral, besides the prevalence of this 'crime' is, in no small measure, due to the men being stationed within reach of Dublin i.e. within reach of temptation.[130]

It should be noted that even absent without leave cases were seen as potentially political crimes in the 36th (Ulster) Division,

Table 3.1. Offences for which men serving in sample Service battalions were tried, while training in the United Kingdom

Offence	8RInnsF	10RInnsF	9RIRifs	13RIRifs	14RIRifs	6CR	6RDF	8RDF
War Treason	0	0	0	0	0	0	0	0
DORA	0	0	0	0	0	0	0	0
Offence against an inhabitant	0	0	0	0	0	0	0	0
Mutiny	7	0	0	0	0	0	0	0
Cowardice	0	0	0	0	0	0	0	0
Desertion	1	0	12	0	1	1	2	6
Absence	2	1	8	1	0	0	65	1
Striking or violence	6	1	1	0	0	3	0	0
Insubordination	2	3	1	0	0	2	6	0
Disobedience	0	0	0	0	0	0	0	0
Quitting post	0	0	0	0	0	0	0	0
Drunkenness	1	1	2	0	0	2	2	0
Injuring property	0	0	0	0	0	0	0	0
Loss of property	0	0	0	0	0	0	1	0
Theft	0	1	1	1	0	2	1	0
Indecency	0	0	0	0	0	0	0	0
Resisting escort	0	0	0	0	0	0	0	0
Escaping confinement	0	0	1	0	0	0	0	0
Miscellaneous and multiple military offences	31	11	21	3	4	33	38	9
Miscellaneous civil offences	0	0	0	4	0	0	0	0
Self-inflicted wound	0	0	0	0	0	0	0	0
Fraudulent enlistment	0	0	0	0	0	0	0	0
Enlisting after discharge	0	0	0	0	0	1	0	0
Falser answer	0	0	0	0	0	0	0	1
Neglect	0	0	0	0	0	0	0	0
Fraud	0	0	0	0	0	0	0	0
Totals	50	18	47	9	5	44	115	17

as it appears that the War Office moved the Division to England in early July 1915, partly due to the fears that many men would desert to take part in Orange Order parades on 12 July if the formation remained in Ireland.[131]

It is also noticeable that there is no uniform disciplinary record amongst or between units in the 16th (Irish) or 36th (Ulster) Divisions. Thus the 10th Royal Inniskilling Fusiliers and 9th, 13th and 14th Royal Irish Rifles all have very different courts martial records, although all served in the 36th (Ulster) Division. Similarly, the 8th Royal Inniskilling Fusiliers, 6th Connaught Rangers and 8th Royal Dublin Fusiliers, all of the 16th (Irish)

Division, have very different records. Therefore, New Army battalions, while being raised, officered and trained in broadly similar ways, all developed the unique courts martial records seen in regular units in table 2.1. It is, however, noticeable that crime rates were generally lower in New Army than in regular units.

In terms of punishments, there are three points worthy of note, with reference to table 3.2. Firstly, Special Reserve battalions, generally, had more men sentenced to hard labour than Service battalions and more courts martial cases overall. Three Special Reserve battalions studied for this period – the 3rd Royal Irish Regiment, 3rd Royal Irish Rifles and 4th Royal Dublin Fusiliers – had 70, 60 and 34 courts martial cases, respectively. This is an indication of the tolerance with which the military authorities treated the 'temporary soldiers' of the New Armies. Secondly, four of the nine men tried in the 13th Royal Irish Rifles were found not guilty. This is explained by the fact that four soldiers charged with rape were all acquitted. Finally, the eight quashed or not confirmed cases, out of a total of eighteen in the 10th Royal Inniskilling Fusiliers is abnormally high. This reflects the number of men incorrectly tried by Field General Courts Martial while serving in the United Kingdom.[132]

Of course, while training in the United Kingdom, soldiers

Table 3.2. Sentences passed by courts martial, relating to sample Service battalions while training in the United Kingdom

Sentences	8RInnF	10RInnF	9RIRifs	13RIRifs	14RIRifs	6CR	6RDF	8RDF
Death	0	0	0	0	0	0	0	0
Penal Servitude	0	0	0	0	0	0	0	0
Hard Labour	21	1	2	0	2	5	20	1
Imprisonment	0	0	0	0	0	2	2	0
Detention	23	6	32	4	3	30	75	10
FP1	2	0	0	0	0	0	3	0
FP2	0	1	0	1	0	2	8	5
Discharged with ignominy/cashiered	0	0	0	0	0	0	0	0
Reduced or reprimanded	1	0	10	0	0	2	5	0
Stoppages, fines, etc.	1	0	1	0	0	0	1	0
Quashed/not confirmed	1	8	1	0	0	0	1	1
Suspended sentence	0	0	0	0	0	0	0	0
Not guilty, acquitted, etc.	1	2	1	4	0	3	0	0
Totals	50	18	47	9	5	44	115	17

were subject to civil law for various offences. On 28 October 1914, magistrates in Bangor, Co Down took pre-emptive action and agreed to a request by District Inspector Gerrity, Royal Irish Constabulary, that all public houses in Bangor should close at eight o'clock in the evening on Saturdays as the 108th Brigade, 36th (Ulster) Division was encamped at nearby Clandeboye.[133] Magistrates again became involved following a fight between two civilians and unidentified soldiers on 6 March 1915 at Conlig public house. This led to the two civilians concerned being fined five shillings each, with recognisances of five pounds, and the public house being closed to troops at all times.[134] No soldier at Clandeboye camp during this period was tried by the civil authorities for drunkenness, and this would appear to be as a result of intimidation of the police by the troops.[135] Certainly, at Finner camp, County Donegal, men of the 10th Royal Inniskilling Fusiliers clashed with Royal Irish Constabulary officers in April 1915, resulting in three men being tried by a court martial.

One military crime which had been a constant problem in the British army, namely the contraction of venereal disease, appears to have been practically absent from the Irish New Army divisions while they were training in Ireland. Apart from the Curragh camp, where prostitutes were a well-established local feature by 1914, few provincial towns in Ireland provided such dubious delights.[136] F. P. Crozier noted that men of the 9th Royal Irish Rifles only began to visit prostitutes when the battalion moved to Seaford in England.[137]

A number of the measures which had proved successful in maintaining morale in Irish units on the Western Front were adopted by the Irish Service battalions during their training. Sports were an important element of this process. The 16th Royal Irish Rifles established regimental rugby and cricket teams at an early date and played against a number of local teams.[138] On a larger scale, the 108th Brigade held a sports day in Bangor on 17 April 1915. This event was open to the public and the band of the 13th Royal Irish Rifles performed, while Riflemen Saunders and Montgomery and Lance Corporal Rule of the same Battalion entertained the crowd, dressed as clowns.[139]

Even at this early date, other measures had been taken to reinforce morale, some battalion comforts funds had been

formed,[140] and the YMCA had established canteens and huts at
the various military camps.[141] Individuals and organisations
also provided entertainment for the troops. For example, on
26 January 1915, the entire 14th Royal Irish Rifles was admitted,
free of charge, to a concert in Randalstown, where Percy French,
the famous Ulster singer, songwriter and artist was the star
performer.[142] Meanwhile, in Bangor, County Down, Trinity Hall
was made avaliable to men of the 108th Brigade for recreational
purposes.[143]

Military bands were also seen as an important method to
maintain morale. However, when Lord Kitchener sanctioned the
New Army divisions he made no official provision for these.
Nevertheless, private initiatives ensured that most Irish Service
battalions did secure a band of some description. By January
1915 the 14th Royal Irish Rifles had no less than three bands:
bugle, pipe and flute.[144] Following an approach by Major Sir
Francis Vane, Gordon Selfridge of the famous London department store provided instruments for the 9th Royal Munster
Fusiliers.[145] Finally, and most famously, John Redmond
presented a complete set of band instuments to each battalion in
the 16th (Irish) Division.[146]

Reaching a balanced assessment of the state of discipline in
the Irish New Army divisions during their training period in the
United Kingdom is not a simple task. While the 16th (Irish) and
36th (Ulster) Divisions both had a relatively large number of
mutinies, the court martial record of these units appears to have
compared very favourably with that of the 10th (Irish) Division.
Nevertheless, a few factors are clear: firstly, the Irish New Army
units during this period appear to have had a worse record than
any other New Army units in Britain; certainly the Irish units
appear to have had a decidedly disproportionate number of
mutinies.

Secondly, the political influence exerted, at least on the 16th
(Irish) and 36th (Ulster) Divisions, appears to have been mostly
malign. This saddled both divisions with some incompetent
officers from the pre-war paramilitary organisations, and
threatened many of the regular army's tried and trusted
methods of maintaining morale, most notably the regimental
system. Perhaps most damagingly, sectarian recruitment poli-
cies, fostered by the political nature of these divisions, meant

that both were painfully slow at recruiting to establishment; indeed the 49th Brigade was one of the last New Army formation to be sent overseas. This delay in sending Irish divisions to the front led to boredom and discontent, especially in battalions which had recruited up to their full strength by the end of 1914.

Thirdly, the localities in which the New Army units were billeted almost encouraged indiscipline. Men of the 10th (Irish) Division stationed in Dublin and of the 36th (Ulster) Division, located in the vicinity of Belfast, were based in areas which were very close to their own homes, often leading to desertion and absence without leave.

Fourthly, we should note that units which adopted many of the tried and tested regular army methods of maintaining morale appear to have maintained much better disciplinary records. For example, the courts martial record of the 13th Royal Irish Rifles, serving in the 108th Brigade, where a large number of sporting activities were organised, compares favourably with that of the 10th Royal Inniskilling Fusiliers and the 9th Royal Irish Rifles, where such activities did not take place to the same extent.

Finally, it should be stressed that, as in the regular army, each Service battalion had its own unique courts martial record. The 14th Royal Irish Rifles, for example, appears to have maintained an excellent record, not because it was a particularly good battalion in terms of either discipline or combat effectiveness, but because its Adjutant did not want to try men by courts martial! It appears that men in the Service battalions very quickly adopted the same patterns of military crime as their regular counterparts.

Notes

1 P. Simkins, *Kitchener's Army: The Raising of the New Armies, 1914–16* (Manchester University Press, 1988), pp. 41–6; and I. F. W. Beckett, *The Amateur Military Tradition, 1558–1945* (Manchester University Press, 1991), pp. 226–8.
2 T. P. Dooley, 'Politics, Bands and Marketing: Army Recruitment in Waterford City, 1914–15', *The Irish Sword*, XVIII, 72, 1991, p. 209.
3 PRO, WO162/20, Kitchener papers, memorandum on recruiting, 29 August 1914.

4 PRO, WO162/4, 'New Armies, Establishments and Strengths'.
5 T. Denman, 'The 10th (Irish) Division, 1914–15: A Study in Military and Political Interaction', *The Irish Sword*, XVII, 66, 1987, p. 18.
6 B. Cooper, *The Tenth (Irish) Division in Gallipoli* (Irish Academic Press, Dublin, 1993. First published by Jenkins, London, 1918), p. 24.
7 Nicholas Perry, 'Nationality in the Irish Infantry Regiments in the First World War', *War and Society*, XII, 1, 1994, p. 78.
8 IWM, 96/29/1, diary of Sergeant J. McIlwaine, entry for 20 March 1915; IWM, papers of Major Terence Verschoyle, p. 1; I. Kirkpatrick, *The Inner Circle: Memoirs of Ivone Kirkpatrick* (Macmillan, London, 1959), p. 4; and F. E. Whitton, *The History of the Prince of Wales' Leinster Regiment (Royal Canadians)*, vol. II (Gale and Polden, London, n.d. (1926?)), p. 97.
9 PRONI, D.1507/A/8/4, Carson papers, letter, Carson to Miss Ruby Frewen, 3 September 1914.
10 C. Hughes, 'The New Armies', in I. F. W. Beckett and K. Simpson (eds.), *A Nation in Arms: A Social Study of the British Army in the First World War* (Manchester University Press, 1985), p. 106; and C. Hughes, *Mametz: Lloyd George's 'Welsh Army' at the Battle of the Somme* (Gliddon Books, London, 1990), pp. 29–30.
11 C. Falls, *The History of the 36th (Ulster) Division* (Constable, London, 1996. First published by McCaw, Stevenson and Orr, Belfast, 1922), pp. 1–2.
12 T. Johnstone, *Orange, Green and Khaki: The Story of the Irish Regiments in the Great War, 1914–18* (Gill and Macmillan, Dublin, 1992), p. 216; and P. Orr, *The Road to the Somme: Men of the Ulster Division Tell Their Story* (Blackstaff Press, Belfast, 1987), p. 45.
13 For a more detailed consideration of this issue, see my 'The Ulster Volunteer Force and the Formation of the 36th (Ulster) Division', *Irish Historical Studies*, XXXII, 128, 2001.
14 Falls, *The History of the 36th (Ulster) Division*, p. XIII; and A. Jackson, 'Irish Unionism', in D. George Boyce and A. O'Day (eds.), *The Making of Modern Irish History, Revisionism and the Revisionist Controversy* (Routledge, London, 1996), p. 126.
15 Royal Ulster Rifles Museum, Anon, 'Service with the 14th Battalion, Royal Irish Rifles (Young Citizen Volunteers), 1914–18 War', pp. 23–42.
16 E. Mercer, 'For King, Country and a Shilling a Day: Recruitment in Belfast during the Great War, 1914–18', unpublished MA thesis, The Queen's University of Belfast, 1998, pp. 10–11.
17 Figures calculated from Royal Ulster Rifles Museum, Membership roll of the 14th Royal Irish Rifles, 1914–15.

18 *Belfast Evening Telegraph*, 3 October 1914, p. 6.

19 I. Colvin, *The Life of Lord Carson* (Victor Gallancz, London, 1936), vol. III, p. 34.

20 Royal Irish Constabulary returns for 31 1914 and 31 May 1914, in B. Mac Giolla Choille, *Intelligence Notes, 1913–16* (State Paper Office, Dublin, 1966), pp. 37 and 100.

21 These comments are based on figures given in the *Belfast Evening Telegraph*, 3 October 1914, p. 6.

22 Royal Ulster Rifles Museum, Anon., 'Historical Records of the 13th Service Battalion of the Royal Irish Rifles, part 3', pp. 1–4.

23 S. N. White, *The Terrors: 16th. (Pioneer) Battalion, Royal Irish Rifles, 1914–19* (The Somme Association, Belfast, 1996), p. 11.

24 Royal Inniskilling Fusiliers Museum, box 12, handbill and covering letter to Mr Robinson, ? October 1914.

25 W. J. Canning, *Ballyshannon, Belcoo, Bertincourt: The History of the 11th Battalion, The Royal Inniskilling Fusiliers (Donegal and Fermanagh Volunteers) in World War One* (privately published by W. J. Canning, Antrim, 1996), p. 15.

26 N. Perry, 'Maintaining Regimental Identity in the Great War: The Case of the Irish Infantry Regiments', *Stand To*, 52, 1998, pp. 6 and 11.

27 F. P. Crozier, *A Brass Hat in No-Man's Land* (Cedric Chivers, Bath, 1968. First published by Cape, London 1930), p. 33; IWM, 79/35/1, D. Starret, 'Batman', pp. 28–30; and Simkins, *Kitchener's Army*, p. 71.

28 C. Hannon, 'The Irish Volunteers and the Concepts of Military Service and Defence 1913–24', unpublished PhD thesis, University College Dublin, 1989, pp. 82–3 and 115–16.

29 *Ibid.*, p. 83.

30 T. Denman, *Ireland's Unknown Soldiers: The 16th (Irish) Division in the Great War, 1914–1918* (Irish Academic Press, Dublin, 1992), p. 38.

31 NLI, Ms.10,561/19–40, Maurice Moore papers, letter, Parsons to Colonel Maurice Moore, 29 October 1914.

32 NLI, Ms.21,278, correspondence and diary extracts of Lieutenant General Sir Lawrence Parsons, 1915–18, letter, Parsons to Tennant, 27 February 1915, and Denman, *Ireland's Unknown Soldiers*, pp. 49–50.

33 *Ibid.*, p. 23.

34 NAM, 7607–69–1, diaries of Captain N. E. Drury, p. 1.

35 PRO, WO339/39413, personal record of Major Peter K. Kerr Smiley, MP, letter, Hickman to General Robb, War Office, 20 February 1915.

36 PRONI, D.1498/7, Lieutenant General Sir George Richardson papers, 'Nominal Roll of Officers recently recalled to the colours, whose services are applied for, for the Ulster Division' (undated, but c. August 1914).

37 Crozier, *A Brass Hat in No-Man's Land*, pp. 18–19.

38 M. T. Foy, 'The Ulster Volunteer Force: Its Domestic Development and Political Importance in the Period 1913 to 1920', unpublished PhD thesis, The Queen's University of Belfast, 1986, p. 208.

39 PRONI, D.1498/7, Lieutenant General Sir George Richardson papers and PRONI, D.1507/A/10/10, Carson papers, 'Return of Officers on Reserve or Special Reserve – serving as Commanders and Staff officers with the Ulster Volunteer Force', undated but 1914.

40 PRO, WO339/3792, Lieutenant Colonel James Craig's personal file.

41 PRONI, D.3835/E/2/5/20A, Farren Connell papers, letter, Nugent to his wife, 26 October 1915.

42 PRO, WO339/3792, James Craig's personal file, especially letter, resigning his commission, Craig to Secretary, War Office, 10 March 1916.

43 Orr, *The Road to the Somme*, p. 131.

44 M. Staunton, 'The Royal Munster Fusiliers in the Great War, 1914–19', unpublished MA, University College Dublin, 1986, p. 214.

45 Crozier, *A Brass Hat in No-Man's Land*, pp. 32–4; IWM, 79/35/1, D. Starrett, 'Batman', p. 14; and PRO, WO374/16997, personal file of Brigadier General F. P. Crozier, memorandum from APS to Adjutant General, 24 April 1930.

46 Royal Ulster Rifles Museum, Anon, 'Service with the 14th Battalion Royal Irish Rifles', p. 54.

47 LC, diary of Rifleman J. MacRoberts, 14th Royal Irish Rifles, p. 14.

48 F. Vane, *Agin the Governments* (Samson Low and Marston, London, 1928), p. 248.

49 NLI, Ms.10,561/19–40, Maurice Moore papers, letters, Parsons to Colonel Maurice Moore, 27 October 1914 and 29 October 1914, Denman, *Ireland's Unknown Soldiers*, pp. 43–4; and NLI, Ms.10,561/19–40, Maurice Moore papers, letter, Moore to Captain Fitzgerald, 26 November 1914.

50 See, for example, S. Gwynn, *John Redmond's Last Years* (Edward Arnold, London, 1919), p. 173; and D. Fitzpatrick, *The Two Irelands, 1912–39* (OPUS, Oxford, 1998), p. 52.

51 A more detailed discussion of officer appointments in the 36th (Ulster) Division is included in my 'The Ulster Volunteer Force and the Formation of the 36th (Ulster) Division'.

52 PRO, WO339/14269, personal file of Captain George Robert Irwin and PRO, WO339/14333, Major Adam Penrose Jenkins.

53 PRO, WO339/21314, personal file of Major Charles Fausset Falls.

54 PRONI, D.1507/A/11/3, Carson papers, letter, W. Copeland Trimble to Carson, 15 January 1915.

55 NLI, Ms.21,278, Parsons papers, letter, Parsons to Secretary, War Office, 29 November 1914.

56 NLI, Ms.21,278, Parsons papers, list of officers.

57 NLI, Ms.10,561/1–18, Moore papers, letter, Moore to Joseph Devlin, MP, 7 November 1914.

58 Denman, *Ireland's Unknown Soldiers*, p. 48. W. A. Redmond was eventually commissioned into the Irish Guards, who proved less discriminating than Parsons in their officer appointments.

59 N. Robertson, *Crowned Harp: Memories of the Last Years of the Crown in Ireland* (Allen Figgis, Dublin, 1960), p. 126.

60 Return in NLI, Ms.15,259, Redmond papers, cited Fitzpatrick, *The Two Irelands, 1912–39*, p. 53; and Denman, *Ireland's Unknown Soldiers*, p. 45.

61 NLI, Ms.15,261(7), Redmond papers, memorandum by John Redmond relating to an interview with Lord Kitchener at the War Office, 29 September 1915.

62 Denman, *Ireland's Unknown Soldiers*, p. 46; Vane, *Agin the Governments*, p. 248; and Staunton, 'The Royal Munster Fusiliers in the Great War', p. 215.

63 Gwynn, *John Redmond's Last Years*, p. 173.

64 Robertson, *Crowned Harp*, p. 125.

65 Figures calculated from officers' personal files in the WO339 and WO374 series at the PRO.

66 IWM, J. H. Stewart-Moore, 'Random Recollections', p. 6.

67 See, for example, PRO, WO339/14295, personal file of Lieutenant D. B. Walkington and PRO, WO339/4100418, personal file of Captain R. McLaurin.

68 PRO, WO339/21306, personal file of Captain L. W. McIntyre, letter, Lieutenant Colonel W. F. Hessey to Headquarters, 109th Infantry Brigade, 29 April 1915.

69 PRO, WO339/21333, personal file of Captain R. E. Toker, memorandum dated 29 September 1915.

70 Simkins, *Kitchener's Army*, p. 71; P. Codd, 'Recruiting and Responses to the War in Wexford', in D. Fitzpatrick (ed.), *Ireland and the First World War* (Lilliput Press and Trinity History Workshop, Dublin, 1988), p. 15; M. Staunton, 'Kilrush, Co. Clare and the Royal Munster Fusiliers: The Experience of an Irish Town in the First World War', *The Irish Sword*, XVI, 65, 1986, p. 269; *Belfast*

Newsletter, 22 June 1917, cited in Mercer, 'For King, Country and a Shilling a Day', p. 14; and IWM, Roll Book for No 3 Platoon, No 9 Section, 'A' Company, 10th Royal Inniskilling Fusiliers, compiled by Sergeant R. Campbell.

71 IWM, D. Starrett, 'Batman', p. 5.
72 IWM, 67/41/1, J. H. M. Staniforth, 'Kitchener's Soldier, 1914–18', p. 3.
73 *Ibid.*, p. 4.
74 LC, diary of Rifleman J. MacRoberts, 14th Royal Irish Rifles, p. 7.
75 M. Cooper (ed.), *We Who Knew: The Journal of an Infantry Subaltern during the Great War* (The Book Guild, Lewes, 1994), p. 16.
76 LC, diaries of Second Lieutenant David Campbell, p. 2.
77 H. Montgomery-Hyde, *Carson* (Constable, London, 1987), p. 378.
78 Crozier, *A Brass Hat in No Man's Land*, p. 45.
79 Hannon, 'The Irish Volunteers and the Concepts of Military Service and Defence, 1913–1924', pp. 115–16.
80 NLI, Ms.15,519, Redmond papers, letter, Parsons to Redmond, 12 December 1914.
81 NLI, Ms.15,519, Redmond papers, letter, Parsons to Redmond, 27 June 1915.
82 On the divisional loyalty in the 36th (Ulster) Division, see, PRONI, D.1295/2/1A–9, Wilfrid Spender, 'History of the U.V.F. and the 36th Division', p. 32. Spender was the GSO2 of the 36th (Ulster) Division during this period.
83 J. M. Bourne, *Britain and the Great War, 1914–1918* (Edward Arnold, London, 1989), p. 160; and J. M. Winter, *The Great War and the British People* (Macmillan, London, 1985), p. 31.
84 Johnstone, *Orange, Green and Khaki*, p. 94.
85 Denman, *Ireland's Unknown Soldiers*, p. 56.
86 Johnstone, *Orange, Green and Khaki*, pp. 193 and 197.
87 G. A. Cooper Walker, *The Book of the 7th Service Battalion, the Royal Inniskilling Fusiliers: from Tipperary to Ypres* (Brindley and Son Printers, Dublin, 1920), p. 5; and IWM, 86/65/1, Captain O. L. Beater diaries, entry for 14 July 1915.
88 IWM, 96/37/1, Miss D. Daubeny papers, letter, Lushington to D. Daubeny, 3 June 1915.
89 Vane, *Agin the Governments*, p. 250.
90 IWM, 79/35/1, D. Starrett, 'Batman', p. 5.
91 *County Down Spectator and Ulster Standard*, 25 September 1914, p. 5.
92 P. Buckland, *James Craig* (Gill and Macmillan, Dublin, 1980), p. 36; and St J. Ervine, *Craigavon: Ulsterman* (George Allen & Unwin, London, 1949), p. 298; Falls, *The History of the 36th (Ulster) Division*, p. 6; and Cooper Walker, *The Book of the 7th Service Battalion, the Royal Inniskilling Fusiliers*, p. 3.

93 Falls, *The History of the 36th (Ulster) Division*, pp. 13–14; and PRONI, D.3835/E/2/5/12A, Farren Connell papers, letter, Nugent to his wife, 16 October 1915.

94 Denman, *Ireland's Unknown Soldiers*, p. 50.

95 NLI, Ms.21,524, Parsons papers, Parsons's diary entries for 12 October 1914, 17 October 1914, 23 October 1914 and 30 October 1914.

96 Denman, *Ireland's Unknown Soldiers*, p. 50.

97 Gwynn, *John Redmond's Last Years*, pp. 194–5; and Mercer, 'For King, Country and a Shilling a Day', p. 12. Parsons complained that 'the unfortunate Tipperary Brigade has been regarded as an Orange Brigade, even by people who ought to have known better', NLI, Ms.15,261(3), Redmond papers, letter, Parsons to Redmond, 6 May 1915.

98 Gywnn, *John Redmond's Last Years*, p. 177.

99 NLI, Ms.21,278, Parsons papers, letter, Tennant to Parsons, 26 February 1915.

100 NLI, Ms.21,278, Parsons papers, letter, Parsons to Tennant, 27 February 1915.

101 C. Falls, *The History of the First Seven Battalions, The Royal Irish Rifles (now the Royal Ulster Rifles) in the Great War* (Gale and Polden, Aldershot, 1925), vol. II, p. 20; S. Geoghegan, *The Campaigns and History of the Royal Irish Regiment, vol. II: From 1900 to 1922* (William Blackwood, Edinburgh and London, 1927), p. 111; E. Parks, *The Royal Guernsey Militia: A Short History and List of Officers* (La Société Guernesiaise, St Peter Port, Guernsey, 1992), pp. 20–2; and E. Parks, 'Guernsey's Contribution to the 16th (Irish) Division', *The Irish Sword*, XVIII, 73, 1992.

102 D. Gwynn, *The Life of John Redmond* (George G. Harrap & Co. Ltd., London, 1932), pp. 403–4. On the formation and career of the Tyneside Irish Brigade see F. Forde, 'The Tyneside Irish Brigade', *The Irish Sword*, XVI, 1984.

103 Gwynn, *The Life of John Redmond*, p. 400. This quote is apparently taken from a letter sent by Parsons to Mr Crilly, the Secretary of the United Irish League of Great Britain.

104 Denman, *Ireland's Unknown Soldiers*, p. 55.

105 NLI, Ms.15,225, Redmond papers, letter, Redmond to General H. C. Sclater, War Office, 9 August 1915.

106 NLI, Ms.15,225, Redmond papers, letter, Redmond to Sclater, 27 July 1915.

107 Details from Royal Ulster Rifles Museum, Membership roll for 14th Royal Irish Rifles, 1914–15.

108 *Irish News and Belfast Morning News*, 12 April 1915, p. 6. and 16 April 1915, p. 4; and *Belfast Newsletter*, 14 April 1915, p. 12.

109 E. M. Spiers, *The Late Victorian Army*, 1868–1902 (Manchester University Press, 1992), p. 216 and J. M. Brereton, *The British Soldier: A Social History from 1661 to the Present Day* (The Bodley Head, London, 1986), p. 10; A. R. Skelly, *The Victorian Army at Home: The Recruitment and Terms and Conditions of the British Regular, 1859–1899* (Croom Helm, London, 1977), pp. 38–9; and IWM, 96/37/1, Daubeny papers, letter, Lieutenant S. E. J. C. Lushington to Miss D. Daubeny, 18 February 1915.

110 G. Mitchell, *'Three Cheers for the Derrys!': A History of the 10th Royal Inniskilling Fusiliers in the 1914–18 War* (Yes! Publications, Derry, 1991), p. 24.

111 IWM, 79/35/1, D. Starrett, 'Batman', p. 13.

112 I.W.M., 86/65/1, Captain O. L. Beater diaries, entry for 31 July 1915.

113 P. Simkins, 'Soldiers and Civilians: Billeting in Britain and France', in I. F. W. Beckett and K. Simpson (eds.), *A Nation in Arms*, pp. 166–87.

114 PRONI, D.1295/2, Wilfrid Spender papers, cited, Orr, *The Road to the Somme*, p. 55.

115 Mitchell, *'Three Cheers for the Derrys!'*, p. 24.

116 C. Costello, *A Most Delightful Station: The British Army on the Curragh of Kildare, Ireland, 1855–1922* (The Collins Press, Cork, 1996), p. 290.

117 Simkins, *Kitchener's Army*, pp. 239–44.

118 PRO, WO86/65, p. 77 and WO86/66, p. 111.

119 Denman, *Ireland's Unknown Soldiers*, p. 55.

120 While the 47th and 48th Brigades went to France in November 1915, the 49th Brigade did not embark until February 1916, Johnstone, *Orange, Green and Khaki*, p. 198.

121 IWM, 67/41/1, J. H. M. Staniforth, letters to his parents, 24 October 1914, 1 November 1914 and 25 December 1914, cited in J. H. M. Staniforth, 'Kitchener's Soldier', pp. 14–15, 23 and 35–6.

122 IWM, 67/41/1, letter, Staniforth to his parents, 1 November 1914, cited in 'Kitchener's Soldier, 1914–18', p. 23.

123 NLI, Ms.21,524, Parsons papers, entry of 2 November 1914 in Parsons's diary. It is worth noting that a mutiny in the 1st Royal Inniskilling Fusiliers in 1887 appears to have been similarly dismissed as a 'drunken row'. See G. Dominy, 'More than just a "Drunken Brawl"? The Mystery of the Mutiny of the Inniskilling Fusiliers at Fort Napier, 1887', *Southern African–Irish Studies*, I, 1991.

124 IWM, 67/41/1, letter, Staniforth to his parents, 25 December 1914, cited, 'Kitchener's Soldier, 1914–18'.

125 Mitchell, 'Three Cheers for the Derrys!', p. 29; and Orr, The Road to the Somme, p. 64.
126 LC, diary of Rifleman J. MacRoberts, 14th Royal Irish Rifles, pp. 63–4.
127 The battalions considered were 8th and 10th Royal Inniskilling Fusiliers, 9th, 13th and 14th Royal Irish Rifles, 6th Connaught Rangers and 6th and 8th Royal Dublin Fusiliers.
128 Royal Ulster Rifles Museum, Anon, 'Service with the 14th Battalion, Royal Irish Rifles (Young Citizen Volunteers), 1914–18 War', p. 61.
129 I would like to thank Mr Tom Burke of the Royal Dublin Fusiliers Association for showing me his work in progress, which suggests that men killed while serving in the 6th Royal Dublin Fusiliers were born overwhelmingly in largely working-class areas of Dublin; those of the 8th Battalion came, in many cases, from lower-middle-class backgrounds.
130 NLI, Ms.15,261(2), Redmond papers, letter, de Montmorency to John Redmond, 24 January 1915.
131 IWM, J. H. Stewart-Moore, 'Random Recollections', p. 10; and Orr, The Road to the Somme, p. 78.
132 See PRO, WO81/144, Judge Advocate General's office books, letter, Judge Advocate General to the GOC, 36th Division, 22 April 1915, p. 504.
133 County Down Spectator and Ulster Standard, 30 October 1914, p. 5.
134 Ibid., 26 March 1915, p. 8.
135 Ibid., 14 May 1915, p. 5.
136 Costello, A Most Delightful Station, p. 171.
137 Crozier, A Brass Hat in No-Man's Land, pp. 49–50.
138 White, The Terrors, p. 15.
139 County Down Spectator and Ulster Standard, 23 April 1915, p. 5.
140 Royal Inniskilling Fusiliers Museum, Colonel F. J. M. Mc Crory, 'The History of the 36th (Ulster) Division: The 10th Royal Inniskilling Fusiliers (The Derrys)', p. 5.
141 Letter (undated, but c. July 1915), Powell to Black, cited, W. E. Dornan, 1850–1950, One Hundred Eventful Years: An Outline History of the City of Belfast Y.M.C.A. (Nicholson and Bass, Belfast, 1950), p. 44.
142 LC, J. MacRoberts papers, p. 5.
143 County Down Spectator and Ulster Standard, 27 November 1914, p. 5.
144 LC, J. MacRoberts papers, p. 2.
145 Vane, Agin the Governments, pp. 253–4.
146 NLI, Ms., 15,225, Redmond papers, letter, Redmond to General H. C. Sclater, 8 July 1915.

4

Adjusting and adapting

The period from July 1915 to September 1916 saw the peak of Irish involvement on the Western Front, with the arrival of the 16th (Irish) and 36th (Ulster) Divisions in that theatre and also saw a significant contribution of Irish troops, both regulars and members of the 10th (Irish) Division, to the British forces in the Eastern Mediterranean. This period saw a number of disciplinary problems occurring in Irish units. Some regular units, which had reformed on a number of occasions, witnessed indiscipline from members of the unit who felt insulted at being left as a cadre when their comrades went into action. The 16th (Irish) and 36th (Ulster) Divisions, as examined in the previous chapter, suffered from a number of inherent defects in discipline which became increasingly obvious in France. A number of officers and NCOs proved completely unsuitable for front-line service and insufficient training contributed to poor trench discipline. Finally, the High Command feared that the Easter Rising of April 1916 would lead to serious breaches of discipline in some Irish units.

This chapter will begin with a consideration of disciplinary problems in Irish regular battalions serving on the Western Front during this period. Secondly, the discipline and morale of the 10th (Irish) Division at Gallipoli and Salonika will be evaluated. Thirdly, the experiences of the 16th (Irish) and 36th (Ulster) Divisions in adapting to active service will be considered, especially in terms of their courts martial records. Fourthly, the experiences of the 10th (Irish) Division at Gallipoli and Salonika, the 16th (Irish) Division at Hulluch and Ginchy and the 36th (Ulster) Division at Thiepval will be assessed with reference to discipline. Fifthly, the impact of the Easter Rising on Irish units serving on the Western Front will be assessed. Finally, consideration will be given to the development of measures, official and unofficial, designed at maintaining morale.

The disciplinary record of the regular Irish units serving on the Western Front between October 1915 and September 1916 was very varied. While the 2nd Royal Munster Fusiliers had a mere thirty-seven courts martial, the 2nd Royal Inniskilling Fusiliers had a staggering 117 cases. The overall average number of cases for Irish regular infantry battalions was fifty-eight. A number of units with large numbers of courts martial in August 1914 to September 1915 had improved considerably in the October 1915 to September 1916 period. For example, the 2nd Royal Dublin Fusiliers with 150 cases in the former period, shrank to just 95 in the latter, while the number of courts martial held on men serving in the 2nd Royal Irish Rifles fell from 119 cases to just 67. However, this picture is by no means uniform. The 2nd Royal Inniskilling Fusiliers had ninety-four men tried by courts martial between August 1914 and September 1915, but 117 from October 1915 to September 1916. Nevertheless, overall, the disciplinary record of the Irish regular units was improving over these periods. If we compare the 15 Irish units which served continuously on the Western Front from 1914 to September 1916, the number of men tried by courts martial had fallen in 10 units, remained the same in 2 and risen in 3.

As noted in chapter 2, it is very difficult to account for many of these variations. In terms of casualties the 1st Royal Inniskilling Fusiliers had a much higher number than the 2nd Royal Inniskilling Fusiliers but a better disciplinary record, whereas the 2nd Royal Dublin Fusiliers had a worse courts martial record than the 1st Royal Dublin Fusiliers and a higher casualty rate.[1] Nevertheless, a few trends are clear. It is noticeable that units which moved to other formations had improved disciplinary records while serving in their new formation. This is perhaps most noticeable in the case of the 2nd Leinster Regiment. This unit had 145 men tried by courts martial in the August 1914 to September 1915 period, but this fell to sixty-four during October 1915 to September 1916. This dramatic reduction would appear to be a result of this battalion's movement to the 73rd Brigade, 24th Division in October 1915. Similar reductions occurred in the 2nd Royal Irish Rifles which joined the 74th Brigade, 25th Division, also in October 1915 and the 2nd Royal Irish Regiment, which was transferred to the 4th Division in May 1916.

The impact which these moves had on discipline is somewhat surprising, given that they were breaking up formations which had served together since the start of the war. Certainly the transfer from the 6th to the 24th Division was regarded as 'sad news' by officers in the 2nd Leinster Regiment.[2] By contrast, men in the 2nd Royal Irish Rifles seem to have been very enthusiastic about their transfer. As Father Henry Gill noted, 'It is now certain that we are to be put into 25th. Division, one of K[itchener]'s. All are delighted at the prospect of getting away from Hooge and Salient ... We shall be the only regular Brigade in the Division and will I suppose, be its back-bone.'[3] Gill further noted that Major General Haldane, GOC 3rd Division, told the men that they were being sent to the 25th Division as they were his most senior brigade.[4] This tactful speech made it clear that the 2nd Royal Irish Rifles were, in no way, being passed to another formation as a form of punishment. John Lucy, commenting on how the 2nd Royal Irish Rifles acted as instructors, wrote,

> We were a bad lot to bring into that peaceful scene. Incredibly [sic] we listened to stories of flat-capped enemy troops who showed themselves at dawn and wished the British 'Good Morning'. Now we knew why the Regulars were broken up, and we automatically did what was expected. There was no choice anyway. The morning greeters were shockingly killed off ... The New Army battalions got used to the more warlike atmosphere we brought with us, and shortly took it very much for granted ... These battalions got over their awe of us when they discovered they could do some things as well or better than we could, and they were far keener in the main than we were, because they had a tradition to build up, whereas we had become used to ours, and did not exert ourselves in any outstanding way simply to maintain it.[5]

Lucy mentioned that this experience with Service battalions gave men of the 2nd Royal Irish Rifles a great respect for the

Kitchener units.[6] His account also suggests that the regulars of his battalion enjoyed their role of instructors. Therefore, they presumably did not want to see their battalion lose its prestige by having a worse court martial record than its New Army comrades. While the exchange of regular and New Army units, following the failures of the 21st and 24th Divisions at Loos,[7] may have improved the disciplinary record of the 2nd Royal Irish Rifles and 2nd Leinster Regiment, it has been judged, generally, as a failure. As Clive Hughes comments, 'The regulars were intended to "stiffen" the new formations, and, while there might have been some success in Lucy's case, generally it had little effect in the long term.'[8]

A number of other Irish units saw a change in their brigading, or duties, which it is worth examining with reference to discipline. The 1st Royal Inniskilling Fusiliers, 1st Royal Munster Fusiliers and 1st Royal Dublin Fusiliers, all in the 29th Division, arrived in France in March 1916, having served at Gallipoli. These battalions appear to have adapted well to service in France, indeed, in June 1916, Major General H. B. Delisle, GOC 29th Division, stated that, 'The discipline in the 1st. Batt.[alion] R.[oyal] Inn[i]s.[killing] F.[usiliers] is excellent.'[9]

Other battalions faced less popular assignments. Following heavy losses at Loos in September 1915, the 2nd Royal Munster Fusiliers became pioneers to 1st Division. As one officer noted,

From the end of November until early February 1916 over 2 months of a bitter winter, we spent our lives in the most demoralising assignment it is possible to imagine. Every night at dusk we marched up the line from Mazingarbe under intermittent shellfire to the trenches ... From then until an hour before dawn we worked solidly in the most appalling conditions, rebuilding trenches ... Dawn would find us back in Mazingarbe, a revolting and unrecognisable collection of sewer navvies caked from head to foot, mud in our hair, our ears, our eyes, and gritting between our teeth. To crown it all, we had casualties nearly every night and we were not even recognised as fighting men. The most heartbreaking part of the whole affair was that we had to spend the day trying to clean ourselves up and dry our clothing knowing all the time that we must start all over again that evening ... Throughout January drafts of young Irishmen arrived and put new blood into the regiment. When at last, in February, the news came through that the battalion was to rejoin the Third

> Brigade, morale went sky-high overnight. Pioneer work had
> slowly been eating out the souls of the old soldiers.[10]

This period of pioneer work, therefore, appears to have sapped
morale and led to a small, if significant rise in the numbers of
courts martial in the Battalion. It is, perhaps, no coincidence that
it was during this period that Private J. Graham was executed
for desertion and obtaining money with false pretences,
although, unfortunately no officer commenting on this case
gave any indication of how the High Command viewed discipline in the 2nd Royal Munster Fusiliers.[11]

Another issue with regard to discipline is that units with
good courts martial records were often sent to other theatres.
Thus the 1st Royal Irish Regiment, 2nd Royal Irish Fusiliers, 1st
Connaught Rangers and 1st Leinster Regiment were all sent to
Salonika. This would appear to suggest that units which main-
tained good disciplinary records while serving on the Western
Front were transferred to less arduous theatres as a reward,
although no direct evidence of such a policy has come to light.

The impact of officers being tried by courts martial is also
worthy of consideration. This was particularly evident in the 2nd
Royal Munster Fusiliers where the CO, Major and Temporary
Lieutenant Colonel T. T. Stubbs, was cashiered for drunkenness
on 25 March 1916. Six weeks later, Lieutenant S. S. Byrne, of the
same unit, was cashiered for cowardice and offences under
Section 40 of the Army Act. This failure of leadership, especially
in Stubbs' case, does not appear to have adversely affected discipline in the 2nd Royal Munster Fusiliers, which had one of the
best disciplinary records of any Irish unit during this period. This
would suggest that officers serving in regular units who were
clearly failing in their duties were quickly removed, before their
actions led to similar problems amongst the rank and file.

The 2nd Royal Munster Fusiliers faced another disciplinary
problem during this period over the establishment of a cadre
system, which, paradoxically, demonstrated high morale in this
unit. On 14 July 1916 the warrant officers of the battalion caused
'serious unrest':

> They had a grievance, and demanded an interview with the
> Commanding Officer. On inquiry by the latter, he elicited the
> information that the warrant officers considered *they were being*

very unfairly treated in being kept out of the battle, and wanted to know what they had done to deserve such a fate. Headed by Regimental Sergeant Major Ring ... they requested, almost demanded, that they should be allowed to take their usual places in action. Finally Colonel Lyons permitted two of the company sergeant-majors to fight with their companies, the remainder being left behind. The toss of a coin decided which these should be, and one of the losers to this day asserts that his rival used a double-headed penny.[12]

The 2nd Royal Munster Fusiliers had introduced the cadre system of keeping a reserve of NCOs on which to rebuild the battalion after a major action, in August 1914. This preservation of experienced NCOs, which was not introduced into the BEF as a whole until July 1916,[13] along with the constant refusal of Regimental Sergeant Major John Ring to accept promotion, may well explain how this battalion maintained such a good court martial record in the face of demoralising pioneer work and the court martial of its CO.

Discipline in the regular Irish units was under pressure from two other measures during this period, namely the partial collapse of the army's drafting system and the transfer of experienced officers, NCOs and, even other ranks, in Irish cavalry regiments to other units. Traditionally, regular units of the British army had relied on their depots and post-1908 Special Reserve battalions to send them drafts in the event of war.[14] However, given the high losses experienced by regular Irish units and the downturn in Irish recruitment, evident long before the Easter Rising, this system was beginning to break down.[15] This, of course, was not endemic to Irish units; as early as February 1916 it was decided to draft men of the 1/9th Argyll and Sutherland Highlanders and 1/4th Cameron Highlanders to their 1st and 2nd Battalions and to amalgamate the 1/4th and 1/5th Black Watch.[16] The collapse of the drafting system is demonstrated by the number of drafts from various Irish Special Reserve units, sent to the 2nd Royal Dublin Fusiliers, during a two-week period in July 1916. This battalion received 54 men from the Royal Dublin Fusiliers, 52 from the Royal Munster Fusiliers, 63 from the Royal Irish Regiment, 18 from the Leinster Regiment, 9 from the Royal Irish Fusiliers, 4 from the Royal Irish Rifles, 4 from the Royal Inniskilling Fusiliers and 2 from the Connaught Rangers.[17]

What frustrated officers in Irish regular units was the apparent insensitivity with which the War Office appeared to deal with their recruiting problems. As Hitchcock noted in July 1916,

> Owing to the heavy demands for reinforcements from the Somme area, there seemed to be no discrimination with regard to men being sent to their own units. Two hundred men of the Connaught Rangers were sent up the line to join the Munsters, who had suffered severely in the attack on Mametz Wood. A Leinster draft of over fifty was sent to the Black Watch! Posting men of one Irish regiment to another was reasonable, but sending Leinsters to join any regiment but an Irish one gave cause for much legitimate grousing.[18]

This indiscriminate drafting policy therefore appears to have been deeply resented by officers in the units concerned and, presumably, was also unpopular amongst members of new drafts, who had enlisted into a specific regiment and expected to serve in one of its battalions overseas. However, having acknowledged this, there is no indication that this policy led to any serious disciplinary problems in Irish regular units. Indeed, it may have led to greater discipline amongst members of a new draft, in the hope that this would lead to their acceptance by the battalion concerned.

The stalemate of trench warfare meant that, increasingly, cavalry units on the Western Front became redundant. This situation meant that they were seen as an excellent source of trained officers, NCOs and other ranks for infantry units and, indeed, many ambitious officers, seeking faster promotion, applied for transfer to front-line infantry units. On 28 November 1915, alone, the 6th Inniskilling Dragoons lost three of their squadron sergeant majors, who were promoted and transferred to other units; none of these men had less than sixteen and a half years service.[19] In May 1916 it would appear that a draft of one lieutenant and seventy-five other ranks of the 8th Hussars was sent to the 36th (Ulster) Division.[20] While, in August 1915 the 1st Royal Munster Fusiliers received a number of men compulsorily transferred from lancer regiments.[21]

With regard to officers, the 5th Lancers alone lost two experienced officers in this period. In September 1916 Lieutenant Sharpe transferred to the 2nd Leinster Regiment,[22] while in July

1916 Captain A. G. McClintock was promoted and became the CO of the 9th King's Own Yorkshire Light Infantry.[23] By October 1916 there were serious concerns that this process had gone too far and the GOC, Cavalry Corps stated that, in future, no officers or NCOs were allowed to transfer from cavalry to infantry or Royal Flying Corps units.[24]

Finally, with respect to regular units, the point must be made that, purely from a practical point of view, the number of men tried by courts martial in regular units would naturally fall as the war progressed. In August 1914 units of the original BEF embarked for active service with a relatively large number of men in their ranks who had already committed military crimes, and when they committed another, these men would automatically be tried by courts martial. By contrast, in October 1915, many of these men were dead, their places taken by wartime recruits, who would be tried by their CO for their first and, perhaps, even second or third military crime, as long as this was of a minor nature, before being referred to trial by court martial. This partially explains why, in the face of high losses, especially of officers and NCOs, the disciplinary record of regular Irish units based on courts martial records generally improved in the July 1915 to September 1916 period.

As noted in chapter 3, the 10th (Irish) Division was fortunate in having access to large numbers of recently retired officers and NCOs, which was not the case for the other two Irish New Army divisions. This, combined with the 10th (Irish) Division going into action immediately upon arriving at Gallipoli, without the acclimatisation period which the other Irish divisions had on the Western Front, meant that no changes were made to officer appointments before the division landed at Gallipoli.

The 10th Division is one that has received little attention from historians. The two books specifically concerned with it significantly end with the evacuation from Gallipoli.[25] At Gallipoli itself, the Division seems to have performed very well and certainly the disciplinary record of the three battalions studied, the 5th Royal Irish Fusiliers, 5th Connaught Rangers and 6th Royal Dublin Fusiliers appears to be very good with 8, 1 and 3 courts martial respectively during August and September 1915.

Following heavy losses at Gallipoli the 10th (Irish) Division was transferred to Salonika in early October 1915. While the

Division did see some action against Bulgarian troops, the
general impression one forms is that morale fell at Salonika due
to boredom, endemic malaria, frostbite and poor food
supplies.[26] Major Terence Verschoyle of the 5th Royal
Inniskilling Fusiliers remembered the summer of 1916, 'I think
everybody got pretty fed up. We were just sat there being
chewed alive by mosquitoes all night … We were fortunate by
then we had got back quite a number of our original officers
who had been wounded in Gallipoli and rejoined us. So we were
fortunate in not being filled up entirely with strangers. I think
that helped a lot.'[27] Lieutenant Colonel H. F. N. Jourdain went
so far as to state, 'The conditions on the Western front were as
nothing compared to the discomforts on the highlands of Serbia
and Bulgaria.'[28]

The disciplinary records of Irish Service battalions at Salonika
from October 1915 to August 1917 were, as with their counterparts on the Western Front, very variable. Over this period the
5th Royal Irish Fusiliers had 52 courts martial cases, the 5th
Connaught Rangers, 126 and the 6th Royal Dublin Fusiliers 72.
Overall these figures appear to compare badly with figures for
the Western Front, again supporting the impression of poor
morale. There is no clear pattern to these offences, although the
large number of cases occurring in the 5th Connaught Rangers
may be due to Lieutenant Colonel H. F. N. Jourdain's desire to
prevent men selling their equipment to local Greeks.[29]

Rebuilding battalions of the 10th (Irish) Division after their
heavy losses at Gallipoli, appears to have caused some problems
in terms of morale.[30] Lieutenant Colonel H. F. N. Jourdain was
very eager to obtain officers from reserve battalions of the regiment for the 5th Connaught Rangers, rather than officers from
the Royal Dublin Fusiliers who he had been sent, noting, 'The
reason that I make this urgent request is that it is above all
things necessary to get officers who have known the men with
whom they have to deal, which is extremely necessary in an
Irish Regiment.'[31] Captain David Campbell noted different
problems with the 6th Royal Irish Rifles, returning to the
Regiment in May 1916 having been wounded at Gallipoli,

> I was given command of A Company (my original Co[mpan]y)
> immediately I rejoined, and promoted to the rank of Captain. The

Company, however did not give me all that enthusiastic a welcome. The officer I superseded 2nd L[ieutenan]t. Lucas, had been in command for some 8 months and had built it from scratch with drafts which arrived from time to time from home and elsewhere. The drafts were young conscripts of various nationalities who had received perhaps a couple of months training. He was proud of them and it was obvious they were devoted to him.[32]

The disciplinary problems faced by Irish New Army units serving on the Western Front were, in the main, very different from those faced by the regular units and the 10th (Irish) Division during this period. Indeed, between October 1915 and September 1916 the major disciplinary issues faced by Service battalions were how they would adapt to active service and behave in major actions. The transition of the New Army divisions from training in the United Kingdom to active service was, by no means, an easy one and this is particularly apparent in the case of the 36th (Ulster) Division. This Division experienced a number of changes when arriving in France, most importantly the replacement of Major General Powell with Major General Oliver Nugent. No official reason was given for Powell's replacement, but it seems likely that this was due to his age and seniority and, possibly, due to the poor training provided to the 36th (Ulster) Division.[33] Unlike his predecessor, Nugent had experience of commanding troops in the Great War itself, having commanded 42nd Brigade, 14th (Light) Division, itself a New Army formation.[34] Also, unlike Powell, Nugent, despite his involvement in the UVF pre-war (as commanding officer of the Cavan Regiment), was to resist Ulster Unionist interference in the 36th (Ulster) Division. Thus, in his first address to the Division, following a field day, far from praising his new formation, he made it clear that he felt that it was poorly trained and unfit for front-line service. Most officers who heard this speech appear to have remembered it all too well. Second Lieutenant Guy O. L. Young of the 11th Royal Inniskilling Fusiliers recalled,

At the pow wow after the 'ceasefire' he [Nugent] told us quietly + firmly what he thought of us as a Division. His remarks in brief may be summed up as follows we had a good name as a division but he did not know how we got it. Every rudimentary mistake that could be made had been made by officers that day. They showed total ignorance of modern conditions + lamentable ignorance. He did not know what sort of training we had had in Ireland, but it was very poor. Such were the remarks General Nugent made to his new officers at his first 'pow wow'. They left an impression on the minds of many who heard them that will never die out, but they had their effect on all ranks.[35]

However, Nugent's lecture was not simply a critical diatribe, it included some considered and informed comments on modern military discipline,

> Discipline is the cement which binds every body of men into a homogeneous whole and without which any body of soldiers has little to distinguish it from an ordinary mob.
>
> Training, good behaviour, intelligence, education and physical fitness are all essential qualities in an army but without discipline what use are they in the field?
>
> It is the spirit of discipline which enables you and the men you have to lead to face losses, to go steadily to your front and to comfort difficulties and dangers which would probably [have] frightened you into a lunatic asylum 8 months ago ... All men are not equally brave or equally [steady?] under discipline, some have less control than others over their emotions. Those are the men who in a big fight begin to look behind them, who become seized with panic and try to get away to the rear.
>
> The bad example of one man is contagious and may affect a number in his vicinity.
>
> Every officer and N.C.O. has a great responsibility at such times. A rot must always be stopped before it spreads. You would be justified in using every means even to the most decisive to prevent an individual whose nerve has gone from being a cause of infection to others.
>
> You would be not only justified in any step you took to deal with such cases but I shall expect it of you ... Successful leading is largely a matter of the confidence of the men in the officers and N.C.O.s they know and trust, but men will not trust where they do not respect. They do respect the man who is strict and just. The easy going officer or N.C.O. who lets things pass which it is his duty to notice, may be popular in quarters, but he does not earn respect, and the men do not give him the obedience which a leader in battle must exact and get or pay the penalty in failure.
>
> It is to the regimental officers and N.C.O.s that all higher commanders look for maintenance of discipline. If you fail in that, you fail in all besides ... Avoid criticising your superiors.[36]

Nugent therefore made it clear to his officers, by example, that he felt that the officers and NCOs in his division should not court popularity. Instead, he believed in firm discipline, to be maintained if necessary by shooting retreating men. His final comment, regarding criticism of superiors, demonstrates his understanding of the new 'citizen soldiers' and propounded his view that problems in the Division should not take on a political dimension or appear in the press.

Nugent's criticisms of the 36th (Ulster) Division were sincerely felt. Writing to his wife on 16 October 1915, he stated, 'I had a field day today ... which was quite interesting and after which I delivered a long criticism. There were too many mistakes and shortcomings I am sorry to say in a Division supposed to be ready for war.'[37] Nugent acted quickly to remedy problems in the Division. On 10 October, he decided to replace Brigadier General Couchman as GOC 107th Brigade, noting, 'I have had to write to one of my Brigadiers and tell him he won't do, so beastly, but quite unavoidable. I might have delayed it, but what good and a good man is badly wanted at once.'[38] On 12 October he decided to remove his GSO1 as, 'Meynell is I am afraid a useless Staff Officer, always making heavy weather of everything and no more intelligent than a clerk. I have to think of every thing in his branch and he gets on my nerves. I am afraid I shall have to get him removed.'[39]

Nugent also moved quickly to replace other officers whom he judged to be incompetent. On 12 October 1915, Nugent stated, 'I have to recommend the removal of another C.O. today', as a result of which on 30 December 1915 Colonel H. T. Lyle was replaced by Lieutenant Colonel R. T. Pelly as CO of the 8th Royal Irish Rifles.[40] Lyle became the CO of the 17th Royal Irish Rifles, a General Reserve battalion based in Ireland. Similarly, on 2 December 1915 Lieutenant Colonel F. L. Gordon replaced Lieutenant Colonel G. H. Ford-Hutchinson as CO of the 15th Royal Irish Rifles.[41] As Ford-Hutchinson did not hold any further command in the British army, this would appear to be a clear case of dismissal for incompetence.[42] The surviving officers' personnel records for the 36th (Ulster) Division also show that at least four other officers, Captain E. R. Kennedy of the 8th Royal Irish Rifles, Lieutenant W. C. Drean also of the 8th Royal Irish Rifles, Captain J. C. Boynton of the 11th Royal Inniskilling

Fusiliers and Honorary Lieutenant and Quartermaster Frederick Hodgson of the 9th Royal Inniskilling Fusiliers were either sent home to train reserve units, or forced to resign due to incompetence shortly after Nugent took command of the Division.[43] It is, however, worth noting that these officers were relieved of their duties due to adverse reports by their battalion COs, not action initiated by Nugent. Thus, writing on 15 January 1916, Lieutenant Colonel R. T. Pelly of the 8th Royal Irish Rifles stated, 'I beg to recommend that Captain E. R. Kennedy of The Battalion under my Command be given employment either at home or at the Base. He is of too nervous a nature to stand the strain of Trench Life and in the event of active operations would in my opinion be a source of danger in his capacity as a Company Commander. I do not consider him to be fitted to command a Company in the Field, but he is capable of doing good work in an office.'[44] Similarly, Lieutenant Colonel Ambrose Ricardo stated,

> I consider Lieut[enant] + Q.M. F. HODGSON is not efficient to perform his duties as Quartermaster in the field.
> He is a good office man, but is unable to cope with his outdoor work successfully ... when he is called upon to cope with any stress of work he is apt to take too much liquor, thus rendering himself further incompetent [sic] ... He has done some good work for the past year + has kept his books + stores well + under a strict officer would be capable of good work at home, where I recommend he should be sent.[45]

However, Nugent found that one of his brigades needed more drastic changes. While he had observed the 108th and 109th Brigades during the field day on 16 October 1915, the 107th (often known as the 'Belfast') Brigade was serving in the trenches, on attachment to 4th Division. Reports on its performance were unfavourable and, as table 4.1 demonstrates, it had the worst disciplinary record in the 36th (Ulster) Division. Writing to his wife, following the 107th Brigade's return from the trenches, Nugent wrote,

> I am not too happy about the Ulster Division for it cannot be denied that some of them have very little discipline. The Belfast [107th] Brigade is awful. They have absolutely no discipline and their officers are awful. I am very much disturbed about them.

Table 4.1. The number of men tried by courts martial while serving in the 36th (Ulster) Division, 1 October 1915 to 30 September 1916

Units	Oct.	Nov.	Dec.	Jan.	Feb.	Mar.	Apr.	May	June	July	Aug.	Sept.	Total
107th Brigade													
8/Royal Irish Rifles	2	6	3	3	0	1	0	1	2	0	2	1	21
9/Royal Irish Rifles	6	3	3	4	3	1	5	2	1	0	2	1	31
10/Royal Irish Rifles	3	1	8	4	4	1	4	6	1	2	2	2	38
15/Royal Irish Rifles	2	3	5	3	6	2	1	0	3	0	6	1	32
108th Brigade													
11/Royal Irish Rifles	1	6	1	0	0	2	2	1	1	0	0	3	17
12/Royal Irish Rifles	2	0	0	1	0	3	0	0	1	1	1	0	9
13/Royal Irish Rifles	1	3	1	0	1	1	0	0	1	0	0	0	8
9/Royal Irish Fusiliers	0	1	0	1	0	0	0	3	0	0	2	0	7
109th Brigade													
9/Royal Inniskilling Fusiliers	2	0	5	3	1	4	2	1	0	1	0	4	23
10/Royal Inniskilling Fusiliers	0	4	3	1	1	1	6	4	1	1	2	2	26
11/Royal Inniskilling Fusiliers	0	3	4	5	4	0	4	2	1	1	2	1	27
14/Royal Irish Rifles	0	1	1	0	0	0	1	0	0	0	1	4	8
Divisional Pioneers													
16/Royal Irish Rifles	1	0	1	1	0	0	0	0	2	0	1	1	7

I don't think they are fit for service and I should be very sorry to have to trust these. Don't breathe one word of this to a living soul please. It is all due to putting a weak man [i.e. Brigadier General Couchman] in command of the Brigade to start with and giving commissions to men of the wrong class.[46]

Nugent had no hesitation in telling officers of the 107th Brigade exactly what he thought of their units. In November 1915 Nugent 'strafed' Major F. P. Crozier of the 9th Royal Irish Rifles, castigating him for bringing 'such a mob' to France.[47] As Crozier recollected, a number of senior NCOs in the 9th Royal Irish Rifles became 'dead drunk'[48] and,

It so happened that other unfortunate 'accidents', such as minor looting, take place in other battalions of the brigade at about the same time, with the result that Major-General Oliver Nugent, the newly appointed Divisional Commander, begins to think one of his brigades is an undisciplined mob! … General Nugent, taking the bull by the horns, assembles all the officers of our brigade in

a village schoolroom where he delivers a strafe, not wholly
deserved but very good for us, which I shall always treasure in
my mind as the complete example of what can be said by the
powerful to the powerless in the shortest space of time possible,
consistent with the regulations of words and space for breathing,
in the most offensive, sarcastic and uncompromising manner
possible ... At last the sentence is pronounced! 'Banishment – to
the 4th. Division!'[49]

The High Command offered a solution to Nugent's disciplinary problems, by breaking up the 36th (Ulster) Division.
Initially, Nugent was not enthusiastic about this; on 23 October
1915 he wrote,

> The Ulster Division is being broken up I am sorry to say. That is
> to say we are to lose 1 Brigade of Ulster men and get another
> Brigade in its place of regulars. This is to happen to all the New
> Divisions I understand. I am very sorry and I am afraid it will
> cause a great feeling of disappointment and will I fear have a bad
> effect on recruiting in Ulster. I hope it may only be for a while and
> that later on the 3 Ulster Brigades will be all under one roof again.
> It is in many ways a good idea no doubt as the new battalions will
> have a better opportunity of picking up useful knowledge when
> they have regular battalions along side of them.[50]

Nugent, faced by this situation, did what any sensible GOC
would do and jettisoned his problem formation, the 107th
Brigade, on to 4th Division, receiving the 12th Brigade in return.
Initially, it would appear that this transfer was to be permanent.[51] Nugent made it quite clear to officers of the 107th
Brigade that they were to regard this transfer as a punishment.
The incorporation of the 12th Brigade into the 36th (Ulster)
Division meant that the 11th Royal Inniskilling Fusiliers and
14th Royal Irish Rifles from the 109th Brigade were attached to
12th Brigade, while the 2nd Essex Regiment was attached to
109th Brigade and the 2nd Lancashire Fusiliers to 108th
Brigade.[52] The impact of these changes on discipline in the 108th
and 109th Brigades, as demonstrated in table 4.1, is debatable.
For example, in the case of the 11th Royal Irish Rifles, the
number of men tried by courts martial fell sharply during this
period of attachment (from November 1915 to January 1916).
However, in the case of the 11th Royal Inniskilling Fusiliers the
number of courts martial held increased.

Certainly this period of attachment did little to tackle more fundamental problems in the 108th and 109th Brigades. In October 1915, Lieutenant A. C. Herdman noted of Brigadier General G. W. Hacket Pain, GOC, 108th Brigade, 'Here we are with our Brigadier who must know he would be absolutely useless when it comes to anything especially trenches, as you know he could not walk 2 y[ar]ds along ours + here he is kidding himself + everyone else that he is fit + some day we shall have another + until then we run along wasting time + the nation's money.'[53] Herdman further felt that, by retaining his battalion in reserve, the military authorities were actually promoting indiscipline, noting, 'Everyone complaining of inaction, its affecting the Batt[alio]n in different ways, the chief way is for the S[er]g[ean]t[s] to get drunk + really I feel a certain amount of sympathy for some of them. A poor billet, leaky + drafty on a bad day + poor light naturally they go to the cafes + the blasted proprietors, in spite of regulations, sell them "Rum" which knocks them out.'[54]

In the 14th Royal Irish Rifles, other problems were not remedied by the attachment to 12th Brigade. When in the trenches between 8 and 13 November 1915, Rifleman J. MacRoberts noted,

> Once again we were under the control of our officers who were nearly all ignorant, conservative and bullying, to an intolerable degree.
> Captain S[lacke?] [55] was intoxicated for most of the time we were in the trenches ... Our Lieutenant was scarcely more visible during our stay in the trenches. He never came round to see how we fared for food, he never visited our dug-out and our rifles actually were never inspected once. But when in quarters, where we had every opportunity of taking care of our equipment, our lives were verily plagued with rifle, kit and billet inspections.[56]

Also during this period of attachment, Captain Hyndman tried to have forty men of the 14th Royal Irish Rifles court-martialled for losing their iron rations in the trenches. Following this the men felt that 'Captain Hyndman was unstable.'[57] This period of attachment did see one major benefit for the 14th Royal Irish Rifles. It occurred when the Brigadier General of the 107th Brigade discovered that the Battalion had under-drawn bread to the value of £600.[58] This discovery meant that the men's diet was improved greatly when full rations were again provided.

A number of the problems in the 14th Royal Irish Rifles
appear to have been the result of illness amongst veteran officers
and NCOs. Lieutenant Colonel R. P. D. S. Chichester, suffered
from persistent lung trouble and was away from the Battalion
during much of the October 1915 to September 1916 period.
Major H. R. Bliss of the Royal Irish Regiment became acting CO
for a three-month period while Major Llewellyn, who again was
posted from the 9th Royal Inniskilling Fusiliers, next took over
temporary command. Major Peter Kerr-Smiley, one of the few
officers with previous regular military experience, serving in the
unit, was invalided to England with a stomach infection. During
the same period, Regimental Sergeant Major Elphick and
Sergeant Irvine were sent to England with lumbago while the
health of Company Sergeant Major Griffith also broke down in
the trenches.[59]

Attachment to the 4th Division, equally, appears to have done
little to improve discipline in the 107th Brigade. Indeed, following this period of attachment, the Brigade had its first executions
in February 1916 when the death penalty was imposed on
Rifleman J. Crozier of the 9th Royal Irish Rifles and Riflemen J.
F. McCracken and J. Templeton of the 15th Royal Irish Rifles.
The fall in the number of courts martial in these battalions, and
indeed the entire 107th Brigade, after February 1916 (see table
4.1) suggests that it was these executions, rather than attachment
to the 4th Division, which reduced the cases of indiscipline in
this formation. It is worth emphasising, in the light of the allegations made by those supporting the campaign to pardon all of
those executed serving in the British army during the Great War,
that Nugent endorsed these executions as a last resort. As the
107th Brigade had incompetent officers replaced, most notably
Brigadier General Couchman, and had been attached to the 4th
Division in an attempt to introduce firm discipline into the
brigade, Nugent was left in the unenviable position of either
recommending these executions in the hope that they would
solve disciplinary problems in this formation, or reporting this
brigade as unfit for front-line service.

In the case of Rifleman James Crozier, while Brigadier
General Whithycombe noted that 'The discipline of the 9th.
R.[oyal] I.[rish] Rif[le]s. is good for a service Battalion', Major
General Nugent felt that the execution should proceed as 'There

have been previous cases of desertion in the 107th. Brigade.'[60] With reference to the cases of Riflemen McCracken and Templeton, both Brigadier General Whithycombe and Major General Nugent felt that the death penalty should be enforced to prevent further desertions from the 15th Royal Irish Rifles, Whithycombe noting that 'The discipline of the 15th. Batt.[alion] R.[oyal] I.[rish] Rif[le]s is fair for a Service Battalion.'[61]

The effect of the transfer of the 107th Brigade to the 4th Division on morale is difficult to assess. Falls comments, 'Any advantages they may have had were found insufficient to counterbalance the dislike of the break-up of their old formations felt by battalions of both Divisions.'[62] However, Crozier stated that men of the 107th Brigade wanted to stay with the 4th Division and petitioned the High Command, asking not to be returned to the 36th (Ulster) Division.[63]

F. P. Crozier noted that during the period with 4th Division, the 9th Royal Irish Rifles suffered from a number of problems, mainly as a result of the poor quality of officers in the unit. While in the trenches Captain Gaffikin turned to alcoholism and, one evening, attempted to lead two platoons into no man's land in a suicidal attempt to recover two men captured by a German patrol. Crozier prevented this attack, but refused to report Gaffikin. Instead, he simply requested that Gaffikin gave up alcohol while serving with the Battalion. Crozier also covered up for a young second lieutenant who contracted venereal disease, allowing him ten days leave to have this privately treated in Amiens.[64]

Crozier's decision in Gaffikin's case was to prove a sensible one. Gaffikin, by then a major, died bravely on 1 July 1916, leading his men into action.[65] However, in the case of the second lieutenant, who Crozier refers to as Rochdale, but who was actually Second Lieutenant A. J. Annandale, Crozier's oversight was to have serious consequences. On 1 February 1916, Annandale was tried by a General Court Martial for offences under Section 40 of the Army Act, for 'Conduct to the prejudice of good order and Military Discipline, in that he, in the fire trenches, when his Commanding Officer was discussing certain Military work with him, left the dug-out in which the discussion was taking place without permission and did not return.'[66] While the sentence of the court martial was that he be dismissed from the army, there was a recommendation to mercy on health grounds and it was not confirmed by the military authorities. Annandale had, by all accounts, run from the front-line trenches, in full view of his men, while under fire from trench mortars. Crozier stated that he refused to accept Annandale back into his battalion; however, it is unclear if this was, indeed, the case. Annandale was placed on sick leave from 2 March until 29 August 1916, when he was forced to relinquish his commission. A medical board concluded that not only had he developed serious eye problems, but that he was suffering from shell shock.[67]

Annandale's apparent free pardon, days after Rifleman Crozier had been sentenced to death for a similar offence, was an unpopular decision in his battalion. As Starrett noted, 'If the officer did not know what he was doing, did the man? We did not think so, and Bell actually chanced his three stripes, and was placed under arrest himself by taking the handcuffs off the chap.'[68]

Two other officers in the 9th Royal Irish Rifles proved themselves unfit to command front-line infantry. Lieutenant Colonel Ormerod was evacuated with pneumonia; not surprisingly the health of this veteran, nearing sixty years of age, broke down in the trenches.[69] In less meritorious circumstances, an elderly subaltern who Crozier refers to as Felucan became an alcoholic after his 'nerves went' and Crozier sent him home.[70]

However, not all disciplinary problems in the 9th Royal Irish Rifles were on the part of officers. Captain W. A. Montgomery noted that drunkenness was a serious problem in the Battalion, 'Over the drink troubles I have taken the drastic step of not paying the company ... I understand they were stunned with horror. They are now blacklisting all the doubtful boys with a view to taking care of them when within a mile of drink.'[71] Perhaps the most shocking aspect of this indiscipline in the 9th Royal Irish Rifles is that it was one of the better disciplined units in the 107th Brigade, as table 4.1 demonstrates.

Evaluating how well the 16th (Irish) Division adapted to service on the Western Front is much more difficult than in the case of the 36th (Ulster) Division, largely due to the absence of primary source material.[72] As in the case of the 36th (Ulster) Division, active service saw a new GOC for the 16th (Irish)

Division, in the form of Major General W. B. Hickie. The replacement of Lieutenant General Sir Lawrence Parsons was not a particularly popular move in the Division. For example, Captain William Redmond, MP, writing to Parsons, stated, 'I regret the fact that you are leaving us. This regret is universal in the Division which you have seen grow under your care.'[73] This is in sharp contrast to the 36th (Ulster) Division, where no-one appears to have felt any remorse at the removal of Major General Powell.

However, Hickie – one of that rare breed, a senior, Irish, Catholic officer – was a popular replacement. As Father J. Wrafter, chaplain to the 8th Royal Munster Fusiliers, noted, 'The General of the Division – Parsons – was changed yesterday. It was a great disappointment to everyone. He was very much liked + had raised the Division ... The new General is William Hickie, so we can't complain.'[74] Hickie was a much more diplomatic and tactful man than Nugent. Indeed, his political awareness is shown by the fact that he became one of the first senators in the Irish Free State,[75] and when taking over the 16th (Irish) Division, unlike Nugent, he spoke of the pride which his new command gave him.[76] Hickie was particularly tactful in that what he initially commanded was not actually an entire division; while the 47th and 48th Brigades arrived in France on 18 December 1915, the 49th Brigade did not reach the Western Front until February 1916.[77] As a result, it would probably be true to say that no-one expected a great performance from the 16th (Irish) Division, an incomplete formation, which had only been sent to France under pressure from the IPP.[78]

Certainly there were serious problems in the 16th (Irish) Division. The courts martial records of some units of the 16th (Irish) Division, for example the 6th Connaught Rangers with fifty-seven cases, compared very badly to battalions of the 36th (Ulster) Division. However, as demonstrated in table 4.2, unlike in the case of the 107th Brigade, 36th (Ulster) Division, no one brigade could be singled out as having a worse disciplinary record than the others.

Furthermore, the whole ethos in training the 16th (Irish) Division was very different to that in the 36th (Ulster) Division. While units of the 36th (Ulster) Division had been sent into the front line soon after their arrival in France, and then the 107th

Table 4.2.   The number of men tried by courts martial while serving in the 16th (Irish) Division, 1 December 1915 to 30 September 1916

Units	Dec.	Jan.	Feb.	Mar.	Apr.	May	June	July	Aug.	Sept.	Total
47th Brigade											
6/Royal Irish Regiment	0	1	2	1	1	2	4	2	0	1	14
6/Connaught Rangers	0	6	5	7	11	4	3	12	7	2	57
7/Leinster Regiment	0	3	1	2	1	0	1	3	2	0	13
8/Royal Munster Fusiliers	0	2	5	6	6	0	4	1	3	1	28
48th Brigade											
7/Royal Irish Rifles	0	3	0	2	3	3	3	2	5	2	23
9/Royal Munster Fusiliers	0	11	9	4	1	1	–	–	–	–	26
8/Royal Dublin Fusiliers	0	2	3	5	0	1	7	4	2	0	24
9/Royal Dublin Fusiliers	0	10	5	5	1	8	7	6	4	4	50
49th Brigade											
7/Royal Inniskilling Fusiliers	–	–	0	3	3	3	4	1	5	1	20
8/Royal Inniskilling Fusiliers	–	–	0	7	2	13	2	1	3	2	30
7/Royal Irish Fusiliers	–	–	0	1	1	5	9	4	4	0	24
8/Royal Irish Fusiliers	–	–	0	17	12	6	12	8	15	3	73
Divisional Pioneers											
11/Hampshire Regiment	0	0	0	0	0	0	0	0	0	0	0

Note: The 49th Brigade did not arrive in France until February 1916 and the 9th Royal Munster Fusiliers were disbanded in May 1916.

Brigade had been exchanged with the 12th Brigade, the system of training in the 16th (Irish) Division was to be very different. Whether this was a policy devised by Hickie or the Higher Command is unclear, but certainly Hickie was a firm advocate of this alternative system. As Staniforth noted,

> We saw General Hickey [sic] the day before yesterday, and he blamed other Divisions very much for sending their men up into the firing-line right away before they got used to new conditions and Boche habits. He intends to keep us in French billets for a month, to acclimatise us, far away from the war zone. Then a month somewhere behind the lines, taking up officers and men gradually bit by bit for a day or so each, for instructional purposes. Then a month with the whole Division in the trenches, not to take part in attacks, you understand, but to accustom the men to trench life and all that sort of thing.[79]

Nevertheless, some of Hickie's methods were identical to Nugent's, for example in the replacement of officers who were regarded as inefficient. Shortly after their arrival on the Western Front the GOCs of the 47th and 48th Brigades were replaced. In January 1916 Lieutenant Colonel G. E. Pereira took command of the 47th Brigade and Lieutenant Colonel F. W. Ramsay the 48th Brigade.[80] Clearly it was felt that the former GOCs of these brigades were not suitable for front-line commands. As Lieutenant General Sir Henry Wilson stated to Parsons, 'Hickie has thought it right to replace Br.[igadier] Gen[era]l.[s] Miles + Buchanan (47th + 48th B[riga]des) by younger officers who have had long + varied experience of this war. I have endorsed Hickie's action ... the command of all units in close contact with the Boch [sic] must be in the hands of young experienced officers.'[81] The removal of Brigadier Generals Miles and Buchanan was, apparently, popular in the 16th (Irish) Division. As Father J. Wrafter, Chaplain of the 8th Royal Munster Fusiliers, noted, 'Everyone likes Hickie + he is making things fine. He sacked two brigadier-generals since he came out. It was hard lines on them being sent home before they were a month out, but everyone said he was right.'[82] When the 49th Brigade arrived in France in February 1916, it likewise received a new GOC, Brigadier General P. Leverson-Gower.[83]

A number of battalion COs were also replaced shortly after the 16th (Irish) Division landed in France. The first CO to be replaced was Lieutenant Colonel D. L. Hartley of the 7th Royal Irish Rifles who on 5 February 1916 was superseded by Lieutenant Colonel S. G. Francis.[84] On 9 March 1916, Hartley became a Section Commandant in the Royal Defence Corps,[85] suggesting that he was not regarded as fit to command troops on active service. Lieutenant Colonel F. Williams was succeeded by Temporary Lieutenant Colonel E. Monteagle-Browne as CO of the 9th Royal Munster Fusiliers on 12 February 1916.[86] Williams had first been commissioned into the 104th Bengal Fusiliers in 1879; it therefore does not seem surprising that he was retired in 1916.[87] The last CO to be replaced in February 1916 was Lieutenant Colonel M. J. Hughes, who was succeeded by Lieutenant Colonel H. N. Young. Hughes was, apparently, compulsorily retired.[88]

In March 1916 two further battalions in the 16th (Irish) Division received new COs. Lieutenant Colonel S. T. Watson took over command of the 8th Royal Irish Fusiliers,[89] his predecessor, Colonel J. S. Brown, becoming CO of the 86th Training Reserve Battalion.[90] Likewise, on 14 March 1916, Lieutenant Colonel F. S. Thackery took over command of the 9th Royal Dublin Fusiliers.[91] He succeeded Lieutenant Colonel W. E. G. Connolly who became CO of the 2nd Garrison Battalion, Royal Irish Fusiliers in April 1916.[92] Finally, on 18 March 1916, Lieutenant Colonel H. J. Downing was relieved of his command, the 8th Royal Inniskilling Fusiliers, Major J. M. Wadmore becoming acting CO. On 19 June 1916, Downing took command of the 10th Reserve Battalion, East Lancashire Regiment.[93]

Therefore Hickie made sweeping changes amongst the senior officers in the 16th (Irish) Division, replacing all three brigadier generals and six battalion commanders. Of course, not all of these officers were completely incompetent, as testified by the fact that many were later posted to command reserve units. It is possible that most of these officers were removed from their commands as, like Lieutenant Colonel Ormerod of the 9th Royal Irish Rifles, their health had collapsed while on active service. Indeed, many officers who had proved perfectly satisfactory as COs of New Army units while in training, were simply regarded as too old for active service, especially when, in early 1916, there were a number of officers experienced in trench warfare available to command these units.

However, it is significant that Lieutenant General Sir Lawrence Parsons had never wanted Lieutenant Colonel H. J. Downing to serve as a CO in his division,[94] while Captain O. L. Beater was certain that Lieutenant Colonel W. E. G. Connolly had been removed for incompetence.[95] His suspicions are borne out by the recent release of Connolly's personal file. In January 1916, Major General W. B. Hickie stated to HQ, IV Corps,

> I have to report that I consider Temp.[orary] L[ieutenan]t. Col.[onel] W. E. G. Connolly (retired Major Royal Marines) unfitted for the command of a Battalion, and I beg that he may be relieved at once, from the command of the 9th. Royal Dublin Fusiliers ... I can recommend an officer, now serving with the Division, for the appointment.
>
> As this Battalion is very shortly for a tour of duty in the trenches I beg that I may be empowered to send L[ieutenan]T. Col.[onel] Connolly Home [sic.] pending the receipt of authority

for his relief ... He is not educated up to the requirements of modern War ... The Battalion is not well trained or as efficient as it should be. I cannot recommend L[ieutenan]t. Col.[onel] Connolly for employment for training purposes. I do not recommend that his services be dispensed with, as there may be work in his late branch of the Service in which he might be useful.[96]

Hickie's reservations, with regard to this officer, were well founded. Incredibly re-employed after Hickie's report, Connolly was relieved of his command of the 2nd Garrison Battalion, Royal Irish Fusiliers, in May 1917, after carrying out a poorly planned and costly trench raid at Salonika. As Lieutenant General G. F. Milne stated, 'the state of discipline in his [Connolly's] Battalion was bad and the raid, largely due to vague orders and to want of organisation, entirely failed, ending in a most discreditable retreat, I am sending him home.'[97] Nevertheless, the pruning of senior officers in the 16th (Irish) and 36th (Ulster) Divisions, while drastic, was not an atypical experience for New Army units embarking on active service. For example, two brigadier generals in the 38th (Welsh) Division were replaced by younger officers before this formation embarked for overseas service.[98]

As in the case of the 36th (Ulster) Division, units of the 16th (Irish) Division did not behave particularly well in their first tour of duty in the trenches. As J. H. M. Staniforth, then a Second Lieutenant in the 7th Leinster Regiment, noted in January 1916, 'We have got rather a bad name in the English Division to which we were attached in the trenches, because the men would not keep under cover in the daytime, and we had to put the sergeant-major with a rifle loaded with candle-grease bullets to keep them in the trenches.'[99] Likewise, Brigadier General Frederick Shaw, the then acting GOC of the 48th Brigade, informed Parsons of the 'Breaking up of discipline' in the 7th Royal Irish Rifles and 9th Royal Dublin Fusiliers while in the trenches.[100]

However, in general, the trench discipline in the 16th (Irish) Division was seen as good, as Lieutenant Colonel William Rennie, a senior staff officer in the 16th (Irish) Division, commented,

The 48th. [Brigade] have finished their attachment in the trenches it was of a pretty practical nature as it entailed about seventy

casualties including seven junior officers ... the 48th. [Brigade] as
far as one could learn did well except in such matters as looking
after their trench stores + similar side issues ... He [Major
General Hickie] was very pleased with the 8th. Munsters today
marching to forward billets + I think that battalion are going to
end by doing very well indeed. Williamson's rough + ready
methods seem really to have got a grip of this tough lot of
Limericks which he collected.[101]

Similarly, Lieutenant Colonel Fitzroy Curzon, CO of the 6th
Royal Irish Regiment, noted that the 47th Brigade had received
'a good report of our men's behaviour in the trenches', and that,
as a result, none of the battalion COs in the Brigade were to be
replaced.[102]

The actual performance of the 16th (Irish) and 36th (Ulster)
Divisions in action during the October 1915 to September 1916
period demonstrated no serious disciplinary problems and,
indeed, these actions have been well covered elsewhere.[103] At
Hulluch on 27 April, the 16th (Irish) Division suffered heavy
casualties from a gas attack and a number of contemporaries
alleged that these losses were a result of poor gas discipline in
the Division.[104] However, objective research has suggested that
high casualties at Hulluch were mainly due to defective gas
masks, the 'sack helmet' then in use being useless in concentrated gas clouds.[105]

The 36th (Ulster) Division, despite its many disciplinary
problems, performed very well on 1 July 1916. It would appear
that the success of the attack was largely due to inspired tactical
planning. Major General Nugent ordered his men into no man's
land ten to fifteen minutes before zero hour, which meant that,
unlike other divisions, they were able to attack the German
trenches immediately after the barrage lifted.[106] The artillery
support given to the 36th (Ulster) Division was also superior to
that afforded to most British formations. Tim Travers notes that
at a time when many artillery barrages were based on guess-
work officers of the 36th (Ulster) Divisional Artillery were
carrying out much more accurate, predicted shooting off a
1:10,000 map.[107]

This success should not disguise the fact that there were some
serious acts of indiscipline in the 36th (Ulster) Division. Colonel
H. C. Bernard of the 10th Royal Irish Rifles and Lieutenant

Colonel F. P. Crozier of the 9th Royal Irish Rifles disobeyed orders that senior officers were not to take part in the attack, believing that if their battalions met serious opposition they should be present to provide leadership.[108] Bernard was killed in action and Crozier faced no disciplinary action. The attack also witnessed some cases of straggling, especially after most of the officers had been killed and German counter-attacks were taking place.[109] Following the battle, a number of men in the 36th (Ulster) Division appear to have succumbed to drunkenness. Private Ellison Whitley of the 1/7th West Yorkshire Regiment was sent to relieve the 36th (Ulster) Division and remembered, 'The Ulster [sic] Rifles who were still alive were all roaring drunk.'[110]

Following this battle the 36th (Ulster) Division appears to have experienced low morale. Even Cyril Falls, the divisional historian, acknowledged this, although by 12 July he felt that 'confidence was returning' to the Division.[111] Rifleman John Doran of the 14th Royal Irish Rifles confessed to his mother, 'I don't feel in very good form after what we have went through so this note will be very short but I will write a longer one when I get my mind settled a little it was our first big fight and I am not feeling at all like myself.'[112] Likewise, Lieutenant Maxwell of the 16th Royal Irish Rifles wrote on 10 July,

> Now we are resting, but the experiences of the first week in July, 1916, will long remain as unpleasant memories that we long to curtain and blot out for ever. But even time can not erase these incidents – they are carved deep on our memories, haunting us in our waking moments like ghastly spectres, reminding us unceasingly of what the horrors of war really are, and reviewing again our sorrow for the loss of gallant comrades.[113]

In the 16th (Irish) Division's attack on Ginchy, on 9 September 1916 both morale and discipline appear to have been maintained, which is rather surprising, given that the battalions had been used 'piecemeal' in support of other units and were seriously under strength before the attack.[114] Major Rowland Feilding recalled that his battalion, the 6th Connaught Rangers, consisted of just 200 men, ninety-one of them from a recent draft and, as he commented, 'Those that were not raw recruits from the new drafts were worn out and exhausted by their recent fighting, and much more fitted for a rest camp than an attack.'[115]

Despite this the discipline of the 16th (Irish) Division held up well. Major General W. B. Hickie noted, 'The Division leaves the Somme with a very high reputation for discipline and good behaviour as well as for fighting.'[116] Meanwhile, the CO of the 9th Royal Dublin Fusiliers commented,

> When you come to think that we had bad weather + that our Brigade were five days in so-called trenches before we made the attack [on Ginchy] with never a hot meal and not much water their performance was wonderful ... after all our trials + loss when the remnants of my Battalion had accomplished a tiring dirty march of eleven miles the men sailed into the billets splendidly dressed and singing 'Brian Boru'. The next morning we paid the men + that afternoon every man had all his brass work shining + boots cleaned.[117]

These battles, with their attendant losses had, of course, serious repercussions for New Army units in terms of drafts. As early as September 1915, Lieutenant Colonel James Craig, MP had stated, 'the only fear in my mind is the break up of the Ulster [Division], in the event of casualties being heavy. The Reserve Battalions are not filling up as they should and consequently some of your batt[alion]s. when wasted away may be replaced by "strangers", or, worse again, yours [sic] Batt[alio]ns. may be given away to fill other Armies!'[118] Officers in the 16th (Irish) Division were also expressing concern about reinforcements. In September 1916, Lieutenant Colonel Bellingham of the 8th Royal Dublin Fusiliers wrote, 'Tomorrow we come out + it will be only a poor little shadow of a Division. There is every hope of our being filled up with English [drafts] as the other sort simply don't exist.'[119]

The impact of drafting non-Irish soldiers into Irish New Army units during this stage of the war is unclear. W. E. Collins, drafted into the 9th Royal Irish Rifles from the 25th London Regiment, remembered receiving a warm welcome in his new unit, continuing, 'The [9th.] R.[oyal] I[rish] R.[ifles] when I joined them had come back from the Somme 16 strong out of 600 men and so they were only too pleased to get all the reinforcements they could.'[120] However, some Service battalions had built up a firm *esprit de corps* and in these units 'strangers' were not well received.[121]

One major event of this period, the Easter Rising, is important to assess with relevance to its impact on Irish soldiers serving in the British army. A number of historians commenting on this issue have concluded that the Rising had no detrimental impact on Irish troops.[122] The courts martial held in Irish regiments serving on the Western Front between October 1915 and September 1916 would appear to confirm this analysis. However, three issues should be emphasised relating to the reaction of Irish soldiers to the Rising. Firstly, some soldiers did have some sympathy for the rebels. John Lucy, then a sergeant in the 2nd Royal Irish Rifles, noted, 'My fellow soldiers had no great sympathy with the rebels, but they got fed up when they heard of the executions of the leaders. I experienced a cold fury, because I would see the whole British Empire damned sooner than hear of an Irishman being killed in his own country by any intruding stranger.'[123]

Secondly, a number of men who had Republican sympathies served without any disciplinary problems in the British army until they were demobilised at the end of the war. For example, Second Lieutenant Emmet d'Alton won the Military Cross serving with the 9th Royal Dublin Fusiliers at Ginchy, but post-war became a leading figure in the Dublin IRA.[124]

Thirdly, the response of Irish battalions on the Western Front to the Rising varied enormously. The trench journal of the 14th Royal Irish Rifles, writing from a firmly Unionist perspective, carried a strongly worded editorial stating,

> Speaking for ourselves, we'd rather have seen a little less mercy to some of the rebels. If a man out here plays any old tricks he is given short shrift – shot at daybreak. Remember this man may have fought long and sturdily for his Empire – but still he'd be shot. Then what kind of death do those insurgent dogs deserve – those swine who seize upon the fact that the soldiery is away, fighting and dying to save Sinn Feiner worthless skins – to rifle and riot and murder a whole host of innocent people. Ugh! Doesn't it make your blood boil lads?[125]

Those serving in Service battalions with a more nationalist ethos, equally felt little sympathy for the rebels. Lieutenant

T. M. Kettle, a former IPP, MP, then serving in the 9th Royal Dublin Fusiliers, wrote, 'The Sinn Fein nightmare upset me a little, but then if you tickle the ear of an elephant with a pop-gun, and he walks on you that is a natural concatenation of events. We took the side of justice, we did the right thing, we helped to bring North and South together.'[126]

In other units, especially regular ones, there appears to have been little interest in the Rising. Father Henry Gill noted that in the 2nd Royal Irish Rifles, 'On the whole the event created very little comment.'[127] Meanwhile, Private A. R. Brennan, serving in the 2nd Royal Irish Regiment remembered, 'Although we were all mildly interested, nobody took the thing very seriously.'[128]

Finally, some battalions made a point of demonstrating their opposition to the Rising to opposing German troops. The 8th Royal Munster Fusiliers captured a placard erected by the Germans which read, 'Irishmen! Heavy uproar in Ireland, english [sic] guns are firing at your wives and children! 1st. May 1916.'[129] Lieutenant Colonel S. McCance stated that the 8th Royal Munster Fusiliers organised a raid to capture this placard and also 'straffed the huns.'[130] However, both Martin Staunton and Terence Dooley believe that a patrol simply found these in an abandoned dugout.[131] In whatever fashion this placard was acquired, it is significant that it was presented to the King by Lieutenant Colonel Williamson of the 8th Royal Munster Fusiliers.[132]

The response of the 7th Leinster Regiment was rather different,

> The Germans put up three large placards this morning. One said, 'IRISHMAN: [sic] GREAT UPROAR IN IRELAND ENGLISH GUNS ARE FIRING ON YOUR WIFES [sic] AND CHILDREN.' Another said, 'KUT CAPTURED 13,000 ENGLISH PRISONERS!' The third and largest said, 'IRISHMAN! [sic] IN IRELAND REVOLUTION ENGLISH GUNS FIRING ON YOUR WIFES [sic] AND CHILDREN ENGLISH DREADNOUGHT SUNK. ENGLISH MILITARY BILL REFUSED. SIR ROGER CASEMENT PERSECUTED. THROW YOUR ARMS AWAY. WE WILL GIVE YOU A HEARTY WELCOME.' Aren't they impudent devils? We played Rule Britannia and lots of Irish airs on a melodeon in the front trench to show them we weren't exactly downhearted. It was a company commander who played, and he stuck to it for an

hour, although they push all sorts of stuff at him. We also stuck up a notice which annoyed them so much that they threw rifle grenades at it. 'PLEASE TELL YOUR DESERTERS TO COME OVER SINGLY NEXT TIME, AS THE LAST SIX WERE TAKEN FOR A PATROL AND UNFORTUNATELY FIRED UPON', which was a fact.[133]

The 9th Royal Munster Fusiliers hung an effigy of Sir Roger Casement in no man's land.[134]

Finally, in assessing discipline in Irish units during this period, something should be said regarding comparisons between the various Irish battalions and the relationship of discipline in Irish units to that in the British army as a whole. The first point to make, relating to comparisons between Irish units, is that the number of men tried by courts martial was generally lower in Service than regular battalions. Secondly, the number of men tried in the 36th (Ulster) Division was lower than in the 16th (Irish) Division. Thirdly, it should be noted that the transition from training in the United Kingdom to active service affected Service battalions differently. For example, the crime rate in the 6th Connaught Rangers rose on active service, while that of the 9th Royal Irish Rifles fell.

A comparative study of eleven non-Irish infantry battalions suggests that courts martial records were higher than average in Irish battalions.[135] The overall average number of courts martial in these non-Irish battalions for the period covered by this chapter is only fourteen cases. However, again there is a great variation between units. The 1/14th London Regiment had just one court martial, while the 1st Border Regiment had thirty-nine. A number of Irish regular units, for example the 2nd Irish Guards and 2nd Royal Irish Regiment, compare favourably with their non-Irish counterparts, while the crime rate in the 14th Royal Welsh Fusiliers, with fifteen cases, is higher than that of five battalions in the 36th (Ulster) Division. In broader terms, it is interesting to note that the Anson Battalion of the 63rd (Royal Naval) Division, although raised as a wartime expedient and outside the British regimental structure, had a commendable record with only two courts martial cases during this period.

Another point worthy of note is the great variation between non-Irish as well as Irish units serving in the same formation. The 1st King's Own Scottish Borderers, 2nd South Wales

Borderers, 1st Border Regiment and 1st Royal Inniskilling Fusiliers comprised the 87th Brigade, 29th Division, yet each battalion had its own distinctive courts martial profile. Finally, the examples of the North Irish Horse, South Irish Horse (Special Reserve units) and 1/14th London (Scottish) Regiment and 6th Gordon Highlanders (Territorial Force units) suggest that the discipline of units which pre-war had been reserve formations only was very good.

An examination of courts martial records over this period demonstrates some interesting issues. A number of Service battalions (for example, the 9th Royal Irish Rifles, 6th Connaught Rangers, 14th Royal Welsh Fusiliers and 26th Northumberland Fusiliers) have patterns of offences which are very similar to those of regular units, with drunkenness remaining a persistent problem in regular and Service battalions. Desertion appears to have been a more serious problem in the Irish units; however, when comparing courts martial records, what is striking are the similarities between the types of military crime committed by Irish and non-Irish units.

In April and May 1916, some senior officers had expressed concerns about the loyalty of Irish units. Private A. R. Brennan noted that the 2nd Royal Irish Regiment was kept in reserve for two weeks, in case there was a reaction to events in Dublin.[136] Meanwhile the 1st Royal Munster Fusiliers was withdrawn from the front line due to similar concerns,[137] and the CO of the 1st Irish Guards was called to the War Office to discuss the implications of the Rising on his men.[138] These fears do not appear to have resulted in a harsher sentencing policy for men serving in Irish units, tried by court martial.

The disciplinary record of Irish units on the Western Front during October 1915 to September 1916 demonstrates a great deal of variation. Broadly speaking, Irish regular battalions had come to terms with their earlier disciplinary problems, the number of men tried by courts martial decreasing drastically in this period. It is interesting to note that as losses in units increased, discipline actually appears to have improved.

The arrival of Irish New Army units in France demonstrated many of the failings in training and officering these units, inherent in the rapid expansion of the British army in 1914. Major General Oliver Nugent, in particular, felt initially that the 36th

(Ulster) Division was unfit for service. The replacement of inefficient officers and the executions of three men in the 107th Brigade appear to have led to improved discipline in many battalions in his division. While, as argued above, much of the 36th (Ulster) Division's success on 1 July 1916 relied on tactical planning, remarkably few breaches of discipline occurred in a raw formation attacking for the first time. Equally, the 16th (Irish) Division's attack at Ginchy demonstrated that Service battalions could remain as effective combat units, even after suffering heavy losses.

Comparisons between Irish and non-Irish units suggest that the number of men tried by courts martial in Irish units was, generally, higher than that in their counterparts from Great Britain. However, it is worth stressing that each British, as well as Irish, or for that matter, Australian, unit, appears to have had its own unique courts martial profile.

The reaction of Irish units to the Easter Rising varied greatly. Nevertheless, an assessment of courts martial trials for this period simply confirms what historians have long believed: namely, that no acts of indiscipline occurred in the Irish regiments as a result of the Rising. Finally, as discussed in chapter 1, it is apparent that the military authorities, by this stage of the war, were supporting a wide range of morale-boosting activities, including divisional sports, concert troupes and cinemas, which collectively appear to have fulfilled their tasks well.

Notes

1 I am grateful to Mr Nicholas Perry for providing me with details on casualty figures.

2 F. C. Hitchcock, *'Stand To', A Diary of the Trenches, 1915–1918* (Hurst and Blackett, London, 1937. Reprinted by Gliddon Books, London, 1988), p. 106.

3 JAD, H. V. Gill, 'As seen by a Chaplain with the 2nd Battalion, Royal Irish Rifles', p. 59.

4 *Ibid.*, pp. 59–60.

5 J. F. Lucy, *There's a Devil in the Drum* (Faber and Faber, London, 1938), pp. 339–41.

6 *Ibid.*, p. 343.

7 C. Hughes, 'The New Armies', in I. F. W. Beckett and K. Simpson

(eds.), *A Nation in Arms: A Social Study of the British Army in the First World War* (Manchester University Press, 1985), p. 113.

8 *Ibid.*, p. 113.

9 Comment included in PRO, WO71/484, the transcript of the court martial of Private James Cassidy.

10 P. R. Reid, *Winged Diplomat* (Chatto & Windus, London, 1962), pp. 55–6, cited in M. Staunton, 'The Royal Munster Fusiliers in the Great War, 1914–18', unpublished MA thesis, University College Dublin, 1986, pp. 34–5.

11 PRO, WO71/438, transcript of the court martial of Private J. Graham.

12 S. McCance, *The History of the Royal Munster Fusiliers, vol. II, From 1861 to 1922 (Disbandment)* (Gale and Polden, Aldershot, 1927), p. 137. Italics as per original.

13 Liddell Hart Centre of Military Archives, King's College, London, Jeffries Papers, letter from Brigadier General William Francies Jeffries to Historical Section, CID, 29 March 1930.

14 E. M. Spiers, *Haldane: An Army Reformer* (Edinburgh University Press, 1980), p. 89.

15 P. Callan, 'Voluntary Recruiting for the British Army in Ireland during the First World War', unpublished PhD thesis, University College Dublin, 1984, pp. 85–6; and D. Fitzpatrick, 'The Logic of Collective Sacrifice: Ireland and the British Army, 1914–1918', *Historical Journal*, XXXVIII, 4, 1995, pp. 1018–21.

16 PRO, WO95/26, Adjutant General's war diary, entry for 14 February 1916.

17 PRO, WO95/2301, war diary of the 2nd Royal Dublin Fusiliers, entry for 21 July 1916; and H. C. Wylly, *Neill's 'Blue Caps'*, The History of the First Battalion, Royal Dublin Fusiliers, *vol. III, 1914–22* (Gale and Polden, Aldershot, 1925), pp. 71–2.

18 Hitchcock, *'Stand To', A Diary of the Trenches*, p. 130.

19 PRO, WO95/1176, war diary of the 6th Inniskilling Dragoons, entry for 28 November 1915.

20 PRO, WO95/1185, war diary of the 8th Hussars, entry for 27 May 1916.

21 M. G. Staunton, 'Soldiers Died in the Great War, 1914–19 as Historical Source Material', *Stand To!*, 27, 1989, p. 7.

22 Hitchcock, *'Stand To', A Diary of the Trenches*, p. 176.

23 J. R. Harvey, *History of the 5th (Royal Irish) Regiment of Dragoons from 1689 to 1799, afterwards the 5th Royal Irish Lancers, from 1858 to 1921* (Gale and Polden, Aldershot, 1923), p. 327.

24 *Ibid.*, p. 337.

25 B. Cooper, *The Tenth (Irish) Division in Gallipoli* (Irish Academic Press, Dublin, 1933. First published by Herbert Jenkins, London,

1918); and H. Hanna, *The Pals at Suvla Bay: Being the Record of 'D' Company of the 7th Royal Dublin Fusiliers* (Ponsonby, Dublin, 1916).

26 IWMSA, 8185/4, interview with Major Terence Verschoyle, 5th Royal Inniskilling Fusiliers; LC, Lieutenant David Campbell, 6th Royal Irish Rifles, 'Memoirs', pp. 33–4; LC, manuscript by Private G. T. Newell, 7th Royal Dublin Fusiliers.

27 IWMSA, 8185/4, interview with Major Terence Verschoyle, 5th Royal Inniskilling Fusiliers.

28 H. F. N. Jourdain, *Ranging Memories* (Oxford University Press, 1934), p. 190.

29 PRO, WO79/49, papers re. 5th Connaught Rangers, letter from Jourdain to HQ 29th Brigade, 26 October 1915.

30 Cooper, *The Tenth (Irish) Division in Gallipoli*, pp. 128–9.

31 PRO, WO79/49, papers re. 5th Connaught Rangers, letter, Jourdain to HQ, 29th Brigade, 23 September 1915.

32 LC, Lieutenant David Campbell, 6th Royal Irish Rifles, 'Memoirs', pp. 32–3.

33 Charles Herbert Powell was born in 1857, first commissioned in 1876 and promoted to Major General in 1907, War Office, *Monthly Army List for April 1914* (HMSO, London, 1914), column 23.

34 There is a brief biographical sketch of Sir Oliver Nugent in the Department of the Environment for Northern Ireland, *Annual Report 1992–93 of the Public Record Office of Northern Ireland* (PRONI, Belfast, 1994), pp. 53–6.

35 PRONI, D.3045/6/11, the diary of Second Lieutenant Guy Owen Lawrence Young, 11th Royal Inniskilling Fusiliers, pp. 18–19. A similar account is provided in The Royal Inniskilling Fusiliers Museum, Box 70, F. J. M. McCrory, 'The History of the 36th (Ulster) Division, The 10th Royal Inniskilling Fusiliers (The Derrys)', p. 4.

36 PRONI, MIC/571/11, Farren Connell papers, lecture by Major General Oliver Nugent to the 36th (Ulster) Division, October 1915.

37 PRONI, D.3835/E/2/5/12A, Farren Connell papers, letter, Nugent to his wife, 16 October 1915.

38 PRONI, D.3835/E/2/5/8, Farren Connell papers, letter, Nugent to his wife, 10 October 1915.

39 PRONI, D.3835/E/2/5/10, Farren Connell papers, letter, Nugent to his wife, 12 October 1915. Lieutenant Colonel G. Meynell had been serving as an Assistant Adjutant and Quartermaster General since 31 August 1915, War Office, *Army List for November 1915* (HMSO, London, 1915), column 38b. On 4 November 1915 Meynell returned to regimental duty as CO of the 6th King's Own Yorkshire Light Infantry, War Office, *Army List for July 1916* (HMSO, London, 1916), column 1362 a.

40 War Office, *Army List for July 1916*, column 1495a.

41 PRONI, D.3835/E/2/5/10, Farren Connell papers, letter, Nugent to his wife, 12 October 1915 and War Office, *Army List for July 1916*, column 1496f.

42 The *Army Lists* for January, July and December 1916 make no mention of Ford-Hutchinson being on the active or reserve lists, which suggests that he had been compulsorily retired.

43 PRO, WO339/14322, personal record of Captain E. R. Kennedy; PRO, WO339/14321, personal record of Lieutenant W. C. Drean; PRO, WO339/21313, personal record of Captain J. C. Boynton; and PRO, WO339/45912, personal record of Honorary Lieutenant and Quartermaster Frederick Hodgson.

44 PRO, WO339/14322, personal record of Captain E. R. Kennedy, letter, Pelly to Staff Captain, 107th Brigade, 15 January 1916.

45 PRO, WO339/45912, personal record of Honorary Lieutenant and Quartermaster Frederick Hodgson, letter, Ricardo to HQ, 109th Brigade, 20 October 1915.

46 PRONI, D.3835/E/2/5/20A, Farren Connell papers, letter, Nugent to his wife, 26 October 1915.

47 IWM, 79/35/1, D. Starrett, unpublished manuscript entitled 'Batman', p. 39, IWM, 79/35/1.

48 In October and November 1915, the 9th Royal Irish Rifles had nine NCOs and one rifleman found guilty of drunkenness.

49 F. P. Crozier, *A Brass Hat in No-Man's Land* (Cedric Chivers Ltd., 1968), pp. 61–2.

50 PRONI, D.3835/E/2/5/17, Farren Connell papers, letter, Nugent to his wife, 23 October 1915.

51 C. Falls, *The History of the 36th (Ulster) Division* (Constable, London, 1996. First published by McCaw, Stevenson and Orr, Belfast, 1922), p. 24.

52 PRONI, D.3045/6/11, diary of Second Lieutenant G. O. L. Young, pp. 46–7.

53 PRONI, T.2510/1, letter, Lieutenant A. C. Herdman to his mother, 31 October 1915. Hacket Pain remained the GOC of the 108th Brigade until 4 December 1916, Falls, *The History of the 36th (Ulster) Division*, p. 308.

54 PRONI, T.2510/1, letter, Lieutenant A. C. Herdman to his mother, 11 November 1915.

55 The only captain in the 14th Royal Irish Rifles at this time whose surname began with S. was Captain C. O. Slacke, a temporary officer, War Office, *Army List for January 1915*, column 1496d.

56 LC, diary of Rifleman J. MacRoberts, p. 92.

57 The Royal Ulster Rifles Museum, Anon., 'Service with the 14th

Battalion, Royal Irish Rifles (Young Citizen Volunteers), 1914–18 War', p. 110.

58 LC, diary of Rifleman J. MacRoberts, pp. 94–5.

59 All details from *The Incinerator* (troop journal of the 14th Royal Irish Rifles), May 1916, pp. 9–26.

60 Comments included in PRO, WO71/450, transcript of the court martial of Rifleman James Crozier.

61 Comment included in PRO, WO71/453 transcript of the court martial of Rifleman J. F. McCracken and PRO, WO71/454 transcript of the court martial of Rifleman J. Templeton.

62 Falls, *History of the 36th (Ulster) Division*, p. 25.

63 Crozier, *A Brass Hat in No-Man's Land*, p. 62.

64 *Ibid.*, pp. 64–70.

65 Falls, *History of the 36th (Ulster) Division*, p. 59.

66 PRO, WO339/14160, personal file of Second Lieutenant Arthur J. Annandale, Report on Annandale's General Court Martial.

67 Details on the Annandale case are based on Crozier, *A Brass Hat in No-Man's Land*, pp. 80–1; IWM, 79/35/1, D. Starrett, 'Batman', p. 56; and PRO, WO339/14160, personal file of Second Lieutenant Arthur J. Annandale.

68 IWM, 79/35/1, D. Starrett, 'Batman', p. 57.

69 Crozier, *A Brass Hat in No-Man's Land*, p. 74. On 1 September 1916 Ormerod was appointed CO of the 82nd Training Reserve Battalion, War Office, *Army List for December 1916*, column 1582k.

70 Crozier, *A Brass Hat in No-Man's Land*, p. 79. There was no officer named Felucan serving in the 9th Royal Irish Rifles; it is likely that Crozier was referring to Second Lieutenant E. W. P. Feneran, War Office, *Army List for January 1916*, column 1495b.

71 PRONI, D.2794/1/1/4, letter from Captain W. A. Montgomery to his parents, 13 December 1915.

72 In particular, the papers of Major General W. B. Hickie for this period do not survive.

73 NLI, Ms. 21,278, Parsons's papers, letter, Redmond to Parsons, 28 November 1915.

74 JAD, letter, Father Wrafter to his Father Provincial, 26 November 1915.

75 T. Johnstone, *Orange, Green and Khaki: The Story of the Irish Regiments in the Great War, 1914–18* (Gill and Macmillan, Dublin, 1992), pp. 427–8.

76 T. P. Dooley, *Irishmen or English Soldiers? The Times and World of a Southern Catholic Irish Man (1876–1916) Enlisting in the British Army during the First World War* (Liverpool University Press, 1995), p. 195.

77 Johnstone, *Orange, Green and Khaki*, p. 198; T. Denman, *Ireland's Unknown Soldiers: The 16th (Irish) Division in the Great War, 1914–18* (Irish Academic Press, Dublin, 1992), p. 62.

78 NLI, Ms.15,225, Redmond papers, letter, J. Redmond to General H. C. Sclater, 27 July 1915; NLI, Ms.15,165 (5), Redmond papers, letters H. H. Asquith to J. Redmond, 1 December 1915 and 11 December 1915 and T. Denman, *Ireland's Unknown Soldiers*, pp. 55–6.

79 IWM, 67/41/1, letter, Staniforth to his parents, 12 December 1915, cited in J. H. M. Staniforth, 'Kitchener's Soldier', p. 93.

80 PRO, WO95/1957, Assistant Adjutant and Quartermaster General's (16th (Irish) Division) war diaries, entries for 17 and 18 January 1916; Johnstone, *Orange, Green and Khaki*, p. 203; and Denman, *Ireland's Unknown Soldiers*, p. 62.

81 NLI, Ms.21,278, Parsons papers, letter, Wilson to Parsons, 14 January 1916.

82 JAD, letter, Wrafter to his Father Provincial, 21 January 1916.

83 Johnstone, *Orange, Green and Khaki*, p. 203.

84 War Office, *Army List for July 1916*, column 1495.

85 War Office, *Army List for December 1916*, column 1621.

86 *Ibid.*, column 1544a.

87 Dooley, *Irishmen or English Soldiers?*, p. 195. There is no mention of Williams on the active or reserve list of officers after his removal as CO of the 9th Royal Munster Fusiliers, see War Office, *Army List for July 1916* and *Army List for December 1916*.

88 War Office, *Army List for July 1916* and *Army List for December 1916*.

89 War Office, *Army List for July 1916*, column 1508a.

90 War Office, *Army List for December 1916*, column 1583a.

91 War Office, *Army List for July 1916*, column 1552a.

92 War Office, *Army List for December 1916*, column 1504e.

93 War Office, *Army List for July 1916*, columns 1159a and 1188.

94 Denman, *Ireland's Unknown Soldiers*, p. 45.

95 IWM, 86/65/1, Captain O. L. Beater's diaries, entry for 8 November 1916.

96 PRO, WO339/7608, personal file of Lieutenant Colonel W. E. G. Connolly, letter, Hickie to HQ, IV Corps, 25 January 1916.

97 Letter, Milne to Secretary, War Office, 30 May 1917, in *Ibid*. The personal records of other COs replaced when the 16th (Irish) and 36th (Ulster) Divisions arrived in France were not avaliable in the PRO, WO339 series.

98 C. Hughes, *Mametz: Lloyd George's 'Welsh Army' at the Battle of the Somme* (Gliddon Books, London), 1990, p. 38.

99 IWM, 67/41/1, letter, Staniforth to his parents, 30 January 1916, cited in J. H. M. Staniforth, 'Kitchener's Soldier'.

100 NLI, Ms. 21,524, Parsons papers, entry for 10 February 1916 in Parsons' diary.

101 NLI, Ms. 21,278, Parsons papers, letter, Rennie to Parsons, 15 January 1916.

102 NLI, Ms. 21, 278, Parsons papers, letter, Fitzroy Curzon to Parsons, 8 February 1916.

103 See especially, Denman, *Ireland's Unknown Soldiers*, pp. 59–103; Falls, *The History of the 36th (Ulster) Division*, pp. 22–75; Johnstone, *Orange, Green and Khaki*, pp. 224–56; P. Orr, *The Road to the Somme: Men of the Ulster Division Tell Their Story* (Blackstaff Press, Belfast, 1987), pp. 85–203; and M. Staunton, 'Ginchy: Nationalist Ireland's Forgotten Battle of the Somme', *An Cosantoir*, XLVII 1986, pp. 24–6.

104 See the comments of A. Solly Flood, 25 July 1929, C. Grant, 30 April 1929 and J. K. D. Cunyngham, 20 May 1929, PRO, CAB 45/2898, p. 70.

105 Denman, *Ireland's Unknown Soldiers*, pp. 70–1; and M. Staunton, 'The Royal Munster Fusiliers in the Great War, 1914–18', p. 228.

106 Falls, *The History of the 36th (Ulster) Division*, pp. 51–2; and Orr, *The Road to the Somme*, p. 165.

107 T. Travers, *The Killing Ground: The British Army, the Western Front and the Emergence of Modern Warfare, 1900–1918* (Allen and Unwin, London, 1987), pp. 162–3.

108 Crozier, *A Brass Hat in No-Man's Land*, pp. 97–8.

109 *Ibid.*, p. 110; and Orr, *The Road to the Somme*, pp. 181–3.

110 Whittley's and Eastburn's accounts are cited in P. Morris, 'Leeds and the Amateur Military Tradition: The Leeds Rifles and their Antecedents, 1859–1918', unpublished PhD thesis, University of Leeds, 1983, p. 586.

111 Falls, *The History of the 36th (Ulster) Division*, p. 63.

112 IWM, Misc.89, item 1306, letter, Doran to his mother, 3 July 1916.

113 Letter, cited in S. N. White, *The Terrors: 16th (Pioneer) Battalion, Royal Irish Rifles* (The Somme Association, Belfast, 1996), p. 101.

114 Denman, *Ireland's Unknown Soldiers*, p. 83.

115 R. Feilding, *War Letters to a Wife: France and Flanders, 1915–19* (The Medici Society, London, 1929), pp. 111–13 and 117.

116 NLI, Ms.21,278, Parsons papers, letter, Hickie to Parsons, 17 September 1916.

117 NLI, Ms.21,278, Parsons papers, letter Lieutenant Colonel E. Bellingham to Parsons, 20 September 1916.

118 PRONI, D.1295/3/11, Spender papers, letter, James Craig, MP to Major Wilfrid Spender, GSO2, 36th (Ulster) Division, 24 September 1915.

119 NLI, Ms.21,278, Parsons papers, letter, Bellingham to Parsons, 9 September 1916.
120 IWMSA, 14142/1, interview with W. E. Collins.
121 IWM, 67/41/1, letter, Staniforth to his parents, 28 August 1916, cited in J. H. M. Staniforth, 'Kitchener's Soldier'; and Mitchell, *'Three Cheers for the Derrys!'*, p. 126.
122 G. Dallas and D. Gill, *The Unknown Army: Mutinies in the British Army in World War I* (Verso, London, 1985), p. 58; Denman, *Ireland's Unknown Soldiers*, p. 144; K. Jeffery, 'The Irish Military Tradition and the British Empire', in K. Jeffery (ed.), *'An Irish Empire'? Aspects of Ireland and the British Empire* (Manchester University Press, 1996), p. 106; P. Karsten, 'Irish Soldiers in the British Army, 1792–1922: Suborned or Subordinate?', *The Journal of Social History*, XVII, 1983, pp. 41–2; J. Leonard, 'The Reactions of Irish Officers in the British Army to the Easter Rising of 1916', in H. Cecil and P. H. Liddle (eds.), *Facing Armageddon: The First World War Experienced* (Leo Cooper, London, 1996), p. 265.
123 Lucy, *There's a Devil in the Drum* pp. 351–2.
124 M. Dungan, *Irish Voices from the Great War* (Irish Academic Press, Dublin, 1995), p. 138; and C. Dalton, *With the Dublin Brigade, 1917–1921* (Peter Davies, London, 1929), p. 127.
125 *The Incinerator*, June 1916, p. 19.
126 PRONI, D.3809/67/2, McLaughlin papers, letter, T. M. Kettle to Sir Henry McLaughlin, 7 August 1916.
127 JAD, H. V. Gill, 'As seen by a Chaplain', p. 80.
128 IWM, P.262, diary of Private A. R. Brennan, p. 7.
129 Cited, T. P. Dooley, 'The Royal Munster Fusiliers', p. 38.
130 McCance, *History of the Royal Munster Fusiliers, vol. II*, p. 197.
131 Dooley, 'The Royal Munster Fusiliers', p. 38; and Staunton, 'The Royal Munster Fusiliers in the Great War', p. 230.
132 Staunton, 'The Royal Munster Fusiliers in the Great War', p. 230.
133 IWM, 67/41/1, letter, Staniforth to his parents, 1 May 1916, in J. H. M. Staniforth, 'Kitchener's Soldier', pp. 157–8.
134 Leonard, 'The Reactions of Irish Officers in the British Army to the Easter Rising', p. 263; and Staunton, 'The Royal Munster Fusiliers in the Great War', p. 231.
135 The court martial records of eleven non-Irish battalions were used in this comparison. The battalions involved were: 1st Gloucestershire Regiment, 1/14th London Regiment, 1st King's Own Scottish Borderers, 2nd South Wales Borderers, 1st Border Regiment, 6th Cameron Highlanders, 26th Northumberland Fusiliers, 14th Royal Welsh Fusiliers, 6th Gordon Highlanders, Anson Battalion, Royal Naval Division and 1st Australian Imperial Force.

136 IWM, P.262, diary of A. R. Brennan, p. 7.
137 Letter from John Murphy, September 1965, cited in Dallas and Gill, *The Unknown Army*, p. 59.
138 Denman, *Ireland's Unknown Soldiers*, p. 143.

5

Amalgamations, reductions and conscription

The period October 1916 to February 1918 is a crucial one for understanding the development of discipline and morale in the Irish units of the BEF. The aftermath of the Battle of the Somme left both the 16th (Irish) and 36th (Ulster) Divisions seriously understrength, at the very time that voluntary recruiting in Ireland had all but ceased. This resulted in the disbandment and amalgamation of many Irish units, a process which meant that by February 1918, both the 16th (Irish) and 36th (Ulster) Divisions were mainly composed of Irish regular battalions. Conscription did not apply to Ireland; however, a number of Irish battalions did receive drafts of English conscripts and, in assessing discipline and morale, it is important to assess the impact of this change of personnel. Also, Irish units stationed in Ireland were moved to Great Britain in late 1917, suggesting that the military authorities were suspicious of Sinn Fein infiltration into Irish regiments.

In broader terms 1917 was a crisis year for many European armies. The Italian army collapsed at Caporetto, the Russian army dissolved in the revolution, the French experienced serious mutinies, the Austro-Hungarian army faced growing ethnic tensions and, recent research suggests the German army faced serious disciplinary problems. Out of this picture of a general crisis of morale, only the BEF emerged immune from collapse.

By October 1916 it was abundantly clear to both senior officers and leading politicians that Irish recruiting was at a standstill.[1] In late September 1916 the Adjutant General, Sir Nevil Macready, stated that the Irish infantry units were 17,194 men below strength. He offered five solutions to this problem, namely, the introduction of conscription in Ireland, amalgamating the 16th (Irish) and 36th (Ulster) Divisions, reinforcing Irish units with English conscripts, allowing the divisions to waste away, or transferring Irish units from non-Irish to Irish formations.[2] The Army Council opted for the second of these options, the amalgamation of the 16th (Irish) and 36th (Ulster) Divisions.[3]

The Army Council realised the political sensitivity of such a move and felt that the final decision, regarding the fate of the Irish divisions should be made by the War Cabinet.[4] David Lloyd George wrote, quite bluntly, to John Redmond, 'The state of the two Irish Divisions in France – the 16th. and 36th. – has been giving a good deal of anxiety lately. The 16th. Division in particular is now little stronger than one Brigade, and the Ulster Division is hardly up to two-thirds of its war establishment ... I propose to amalgamate the two Divisions into one.'[5]

Both Carson and Redmond were eager to retain their own 'private armies' on the Western Front, even when their political prestige had fallen to depths where they could no longer provide recruits for them. This meant that this decision was politically unacceptable. After some discussion, Redmond came to the conclusion that the amalgamation was unnecessary as,

> if a Dublin Brigade could be established, we would have little difficulty in obtaining the necessary recruits to keep it up to its strength ... My idea is, that the two Dublin battalions, I think the 7th. and the 8th. [actually the 8th and 9th], that are in the 16th. Division already should have associated with them the 10th. Dublins, which was sent to the Naval Division, and also the 2nd. Dublins. In this way, a Dublin Brigade could be created. I am sure that this creation would arouse a great deal of interest and satisfaction in Dublin City.[6]

Meanwhile, Carson favoured amalgamation, but proposed that the 36th (Ulster) Division should merge with the 51st (Highland) Division, rather than the 16th (Irish) Division.[7] Significantly, Major General Oliver Nugent, himself an Ulster Unionist, felt that, 'If however the question of amalgamation becomes imperative, I hope the 16th. and 36th. will be amalgamated so that there may be at least one Irish Division. I am sure that this will be the view of Officers and men of both Divisions and I have written to Carson to tell him so.'[8]

Of course, the Army Council's decision had not been an inspired one. The amalgamation of the 16th (Irish) and 36th (Ulster) Divisions would have simply created a formation which, after another two to three months service, would again have proved unviable. Political interference did nothing to provide a solution. The rather bizarre compromise reached was that men recruited in Ireland would be sent to Irish regular battalions, while English drafts would be used to maintain Irish Service battalions.[9] This, in itself, threatened both the regimental system and the national identity of Irish units, both of which Nicholas Perry believes were important in maintaining Irish troop morale in 1917 and 1918.[10]

The political compromises over the reinforcement of the Irish units also caused some difficulties for the Adjutant General's office. Army Council Order 1246 of 1916 meant that any man conscripted in Great Britain who was of 'Irish nationality' was, if he expressed the desire to join an Irish regiment, to be sent to the depot of the regiment he requested.[11] This imprecise phraseology meant that the system was open to abuse. Redmond took up the case of a Private, J. Barret, conscripted into the 3rd East Lancashire Regiment, who stated that his request to join an Irish unit had been ignored. After making enquiries, the Adjutant General stated, 'Steps have been taken to transfer him to an Irish unit. It looks to me like one of those cases in which a man does not take advantage of the privileges at his disposal and gives us all a great deal of trouble through his own carelessness and neglect. If this turns out to be the case, I hope you will vent your displeasure on him.'[12] Conceivably, almost every man conscripted in Great Britain with a vaguely Irish-sounding name, or Irish relations, could have requested a transfer to an Irish unit under this regulation. This would seriously have disrupted the dispatch of replacements to France.

The impact of absorbing English drafts and conscripts, on discipline and morale in the Irish regiments, appears to have varied considerably. In October 1917, the 1st Royal Inniskilling Fusiliers rather incredulously received a large draft from the

Army Pay Corps, who had only been afforded rudimentary training, 'but they were not as bad as all that, for they looked pretty good physically and, when, after Paschendale [sic.], we were able to knock them into shape, they became really good fighting men.'[13] Indeed, this draft was found to be much more intelligent and thus quicker to learn than the average soldier and, significantly, it was discovered that these men had all voluntarily enlisted in 1914.[14]

Conscripts generally appear to have received a less enthusiastic welcome. Like most British officers, those in Irish battalions mainly viewed conscripts with suspicion.[15] For example, Sir Barclay Nihill, emphasising the volunteer nature of his old battalion, stated, 'My Division was the 16th, Irish and my regiment the 1st. Battalion The Royal Munster Fusiliers, recruited largely from the counties of Cork and Kerry. We were a professional unit of the pre-war regular army ... although by March 1918 most of the officers and men were in for the duration of the war only. Except for a handful of Tyneside Irish who joined us early in 1918, there was not a conscript among us.'[16]

Conscripts, or even suspected conscripts received poor treatment when joining Irish units. A draft of English conscripts to the 14th Royal Irish Rifles appears to have been dubbed the 'Gawd blimy brigade'.[17] Edward Bowyer-Green, drafted into the 15th Royal Irish Rifles from the 25th London Regiment, received an even less effusive welcome. As he noted, 'We were the pariahs you see, although we were helping their battalion we weren't one of them, they made out we were conscripts but we weren't, we were volunteers, territorials.'[18] Some officers felt that the policy of drafting Englishmen to Irish battalions had all but destroyed the regimental system.[19]

Nevertheless, some Irish officers did have a more positive view of English drafts. Lieutenant Colonel G. A. M. Buckley of the 7th Leinster Regiment was even complimentary about conscripts, 'I got a draft of 109 from the Shropshire L.[ight] Inf.[antry] during the show. [Third Battle of Ypres]. They were conscripts – mere boys of 19 – never seen a shot fired. I hated taking them straight into a fiery furnace like we've been through but I had no alternative. They behaved splendidly our fellows were very pleased with them but after the way of new drafts they were unfortunate and suffered heavily.'[20] The ever pragmatic Major General Oliver Nugent stated in September 1916, 'We can't get Irishmen so we must have others and personally I don't care tuppence who they are as long as they make us up.'[21] Nugent must have been reflecting the views of many officers, that it was better to hold a trench with a company nearing full establishment, than with one which, if more ethnically pure, was not an effective fighting unit.

Ironically, the use of English drafts to maintain Irish battalions proved to be unviable. By February 1917 the Army Council believed that the strength of the BEF could not be maintained at its current level.[22] In this situation amalgamations and the disbandment of some Irish battalions to provide drafts for others became increasingly necessary. Indeed, as early as May 1916 the 9th Royal Munster Fusiliers had been disbanded and its men sent to the other three battalions of the regiments serving on the Western Front.[23] While the issue of the reduction of Irish battalions in the October 1916 to February 1918 period has already been well researched by Nicholas Perry,[24] it is vital to examine these reductions with regard to discipline and morale.

Of course Irish Service battalions were not the only elements of the BEF to face amalgamation in this period. January 1918 saw the introduction of the nine-battalion infantry division, which cut the infantry strength of all British divisions by almost one quarter.[25] However, in the BEF as a whole, these disbandments were carried out in a logical fashion. As Ian Beckett notes, 'in 1916 and in 1918 second line territorials in particular took the brunt of the reductions consequent upon the reorganisation of the expeditionary force.'[26] At the regimental level this meant that for example, when the 1/8th West Yorkshire Regiment, the most junior territorial battalion of the Regiment serving on the Western Front, was disbanded in early 1918, most of its personnel were drafted to the 1/6th Battalion of the Regiment. Likewise, when the 2/7th West Yorkshire Regiment was disbanded in June 1918, men serving in it were given the option of transferring to the 1/7th Battalion.[27]

By contrast, many of the disbandments and amalgamations of Irish Service battalions appear totally illogical. In the Royal Irish Rifles, for example, the most senior Service battalion in France, the 7th, was disbanded in November 1917, while the most junior battalion of the Regiment on active service, the 16th survived

until the end of the war. There are similar anomalies in other
Irish regiments, for example, the 10th Royal Dublin Fusiliers,
disbanded in February 1918, outlived the 8th and 9th Royal
Dublin Fusiliers, amalgamated in November 1917. Of course,
some very localised political and regional concerns influenced
the choice of units to be disbanded. Major General Oliver
Nugent, explaining the rationale for reductions in the 36th
(Ulster) Division in February 1918, stated,

> The Division now consists of 5 Regular North Irish battalions and
> of 5 battalions of the original Division.
>
> As General Officer Commanding the Division, I had the most
> unpleasant duty of selecting 2 battalions of Inniskilling Fusiliers
> and 4 battalions of Royal Irish Rifles for disbandment.
>
> I decided that the battalions to remain in the Division should be
> those which were composed of the men who first came forward
> to form the Ulster Division.
>
> I therefore selected the senior of the three battalions of
> Inniskilling Fusiliers to remain.
>
> In the case of the Royal Irish Rifles, I selected the senior battal-
> ion to remain. This was the 15th. Battalion, a Belfast Battalion,
> originally raised as the 7th. Battalion.
>
> The next senior of the original battalions of the Ulster Division
> would have been the 10th. Royal Irish Rifles.
>
> This was also a Belfast Battalion and I decided that it would be
> unfair to the Counties of Down and Antrim that they should have
> no representation amongst the original units of the Division. I
> therefore selected the 12th. Royal Irish Rifles as the other battal-
> ion to remain.
>
> The remaining third battalion of Royal Irish Rifles is the 16th.
> Royal Irish Rifles, the Pioneer Battalion, which was not affected
> by the reorganisation of the Division.[28]

This explanation to James Johnston, the Lord Mayor of Belfast
does shed some light on the decisions taken on disbanding
specific units. However, Nugent, doubtlessly aware that this
letter would be publicly circulated,[29] did not reveal all of the
considerations behind his decision. While he had informed
Belfast's leading citizen that he regretted that the 14th Royal
Irish Rifles, a Belfast raised unit, which Johnston had been eager
to save, had been disbanded,[30] the truth was rather different. In
December 1917, Nugent, writing confidentially to the Adjutant
General, stated,

The 14th. Royal Irish Rifles now in the 109th. Brigade, to be broken up and used to make up casualties in the Royal Irish Rifles battalions in the Division.

This battalion should in my opinion be broken up in any case.

About a year ago, I reported them as totally wanting in military spirit and asked for a C.O. and a large draft of Englishmen to try and create a fighting spirit in them. You gave me both, and while Cheape was in command they certainly improved, but since he left they have been tried and found wanting. It is significant that their present C.O. told me two days ago that most of the English draft sent to them a year ago have become casualties.

The Brigadier says he cannot trust them and I know that he is right.

They are poor stuff, either as workers or fighters and have been a constant source of anxiety during the past three weeks.[31]

Nugent's comments in this letter suggest that, in addition to local interests, disciplinary records and combat effectiveness also determined a battalion's fate. Nicholas Perry, mentioning the circumstances behind the disbandment of the 14th Royal Irish Rifles, noted that its number of English drafts was not disproportionate to that in other battalions in the 36th (Ulster) Division and that Nugent had written this letter in a fit of temper.[32] The disciplinary record of the 14th Royal Irish Rifles appears to be a very good one, and this, to some extent, bears out Perry's views.

However, there is strong evidence to suggest that both discipline and combat effectiveness were considerably worse than courts martial statistics suggest. At Langemarck in August 1917 the 14th Royal Irish Rifles appear to have retreated precipitately when facing German machine-gun fire.[33] This battalion had suffered from a number of problems, particularly inefficient officers, during the December 1915 to September 1916 period and there is little to suggest that there was any marked improvement during most of late 1916 and 1917. Indeed, J. MacRoberts noted that, following the Battle of the Somme, tensions between officers and other ranks increased in the battalion, as veterans did not enjoy being commanded 'by those new officers whose experience of warfare had been obtained at Newcastle in Ireland.'[34]

On the broader question of disbandments in the 36th (Ulster)

Division, it would appear to be no coincidence that the 8/9th and 10th Royal Irish Rifles, which were both disbanded in February 1918, had the worst courts martial records of the Service battalions then serving in 107th Brigade. It is also interesting to note that the amalgamations policy, adopted in late 1917, provided very mixed disciplinary results. The number of courts martial in the 8/9th Battalion, Royal Irish Rifles soared from the amalgamation of August 1917 until November 1917 while, by contrast, the 11/13th Royal Irish Rifles had no courts martial cases from the amalgamation until disbandment. It is also worth noting that the incorporation of 300 men, compulsorily 'transferred from the North Irish Horse to the 9th Royal Irish Fusiliers in September 1917,[35] appears to have actually improved that battalion's already exemplary disciplinary record.

In terms of the 16th (Irish) Division, we can be less sure about the reasons for the disbandments of some units. Indeed, some of the measures taken to reinforce this division appear bizarre. For example, when the decision was taken to utilise the South Irish Horse as infantrymen, instead of being incorporated into existing units, they were formed into the 7th (South Irish Horse) Royal Irish Regiment. This unit survived until the end of the war, while the more senior 6th Royal Irish Regiment was disbanded in February 1918.

Unlike the case of the 36th (Ulster) Division, disbandments in the 16th (Irish) Division appear to have taken little account of local sensibilities. Of the four provinces of Ireland, only two were represented by service battalions in the 16th (Irish) Division by the end of February 1918. It is perhaps a comment on the perceived decline of the IPP that this state of affairs had been reached and that, despite John Redmond's proposal to form a Dublin Brigade, no Royal Dublin Fusiliers Service battalion serving in the 16th (Irish) Division survived beyond February 1918. The latter is even more surprising, given that Dublin was one of the very few areas in Ireland which had provided anything resembling a satisfactory number of recruits.

In terms of discipline it would appear that the 7th Royal Irish Rifles and the 9th Royal Dublin Fusiliers were both disbanded due, at least partly, to disciplinary problems. In March 1917 Major General W. B. Hickie noted that the 7th Royal Irish Rifles had been unable to retaliate effectively against a German trench raiding party, although he did add that on 8 March 1917 the Battalion had a trench strength of just twenty-two officers and 318 other ranks.[36] It is noticeable that the 7th Royal Irish Rifles had the highest number of courts martial in the 47th Brigade in May, June and July 1917 and, indeed, one of the worst discipli- nary records of any Service battalion in the 16th (Irish) Division.

Meanwhile, Captain O. L. Beater noted in November 1916, 'the [7th] Royal Irish Rifles, from whom we are taking over had left the dugout, and in fact everything else in a rotten state. They have not got a very good reputation for keeping trenches in good repair, in fact I consider them a dashed lazy lot.'[37] In January 1917 Beater, when relieving the 7th Royal Irish Rifles in the trenches, found one of their majors, 'gloriously drunk, quite incoherent, and almost incapable of movement'.[38]

There may also have been a more obvious political influence on discipline which led to the disbandment of the 7th Royal Irish Rifles. Major Denys Reitz, who was posted to the Battalion in August 1917, stated,

> I do not know whether it was one more ramification of Irish poli- tics, but Colonel Francis was transferred to the command of a brigade, and the 7th. [Royal] Irish Rifles were broken up. I heard it said that there were too many Sinn Feiners among us. The men certainly talked a lot of politics, and even my friend Freeney [Reitz's batman] waxed hot on occasion, but, coming as I did from a country [South Africa] where everyone talks politics, I paid little attention to their frequent wranglings. Whatever the cause, we were disbanded.[39]

The 7th Royal Irish Rifles had a relatively small number of courts martial in August to November 1917. However, this is somewhat misleading; while during this period only 8 men of the battalion were tried by courts martial, 5 were tried for deser- tion, 4 of whom were found guilty. In addition to this, the fate of the 7th Royal Irish Rifles itself does something to bear out Reitz's comments. When the unit was disbanded, its men were drafted to battalions of the Royal Irish Rifles serving in the 36th (Ulster) Division, which would have been viewed as more immune to Sinn Fein infiltration than the 16th (Irish) Division.

There is also some evidence to suggest that the 9th Royal Dublin Fusiliers faced amalgamation due to disciplinary problems. Captain O. L. Beater noted a catalogue of failings of the officers in his battalion. In November 1916 he noted, 'We have a terrible pair of junior subs in this company, to wit Hawe and Brown[e], who are forever speculating on their chances of being done in by a Trench Mortar, asphyxiated by gas shells, or done to death while on their way home to their dugout, by some brutal sniper. They are invariably late for breakfast, and incidentally for parade. They are nearly always bemoaning their fate, and bewailing the fact of ever having joined the army.'[40]

Later in November, Beater suggested that Captain Long of 'A' Company had 'lost his nerve' and faked illness to be sent home.[41] He was even more condemnatory of Captain Greene, who in January 1917 was recovering at a rest camp following a breakdown, stating, 'Green[e] is a most accomplished lead-swinger and manages to work these little stunts to perfection.'[42] The situation had further deteriorated by February 1917, when Beater noted, 'Captain Shine who is acting C.O. during the temporary absence of Colonel Thackerary is laid up in bed: unkind people say it is the over indulgence in John Jameson [whiskey] which has laid him low.'[43]

In terms of NCOs the 9th Royal Dublin Fusiliers also had serious problems. In March 1917 their RSM was reduced to corporal and transferred to the 8th Battalion, for drunkenness.[44] In September 1917, Acting RSM McCullagh was reduced to sergeant for being absent and breaking out of camp. Also, in September 1917, Hon. Lieutenant and Quartermaster J. Merry was found guilty of an offence under Section 40 of the Army Act and received a reprimand and forfeiture of seniority. The fact that two key members of the Battalion were convicted by courts martial in July 1917 suggests that it is no coincidence that this battalion was disbanded in October 1917.

However, disciplinary records were by no means solely responsible for deciding which units should be amalgamated or disbanded. The 6th Connaught Rangers, for example, had a relatively poor disciplinary record over this period, yet survived until August 1918. This is particularly surprising when we consider that the Battalion experienced two mutinies, of a sort, during this period and that there was a serious personality clash between the CO and Second in Command.

The two mutinies in this unit are really of a very minor

nature. Captain C. A. Brett recalled that at some point in the winter of 1916/17 there 'was a near mutiny in the Battalion when one day we had served up to us boiled chestnuts instead of potatoes, which naturally evoked so much furious protest from an Irish Regiment that the powers that be never again (in my experience) tried it on'.[45] The second mutiny occurred in November 1916 and was in essence an officers' protest. When Lieutenant Colonel Rowland Feilding ordered the arrest of Captain Lambert on a charge of drunkenness, most of the other officers in the Battalion joined Lambert in his room and removed their Sam Browne belts (the removal of this article of equipment denoted that an officer was under open arrest).[46]

What exactly this officers' mutiny was about is unclear. In September 1916 Feilding[47] had taken over command of the 6th Connaught Rangers following the death of its popular CO, Lieutenant Colonel John Lenox-Conyngham at the Battle of Guillemont. As a Coldstream Guards officer, Feilding was something of an outsider, which made it doubly difficult for him to replace Lenox-Conyngham. Feilding, receiving a promoted sergeant of the Coldstream Guards as a second lieutenant shortly after the Battle of Ginchy, appointed him Adjutant and set him to teaching the officers of the Battalion how to salute properly.[48] This latter measure would appear to account for the protest.

This situation was exacerbated in March 1917 when Major H. F. N. Jourdain, who had been the CO of the 5th Connaught Rangers and commanded, temporarily, a brigade of the 10th (Irish) Division, became acting CO of the 6th Connaught Rangers while Feilding was on leave. Jourdain was far from pleased with his new command; following an inspection on 13 March he noted,

> The men were very young indeed, and were disgracefully dressed and equipped, their clothes were worn out and dirty beyond words, and their bearing was good, but they were too inexperienced. The officers were good as far as I could see but the Battalion was not at all fit for service in an offensive. I was much depressed by the knocked about appearance of all ranks. What a change from my 5th. Battalion at Salonika!
> The shirts worn by the men were almost black, and their caps and putties were long worn out.

I saw nearly all the men, but was not struck with the demeanour of the N.C.O.s and men.[49]

Three days later, Jourdain applied for some cavalry recruits, 'to stiffen up the Batt.[allion]',[50] and, by 22 March 1917 he stated that Major General Hickie believed that there had been 'a tremendous improvement in the Battalion'.[51]

There does appear to be some truth in Jourdain's comments; however, we should be aware that Jourdain was trying to replace Feilding as the CO of the 6th Connaught Rangers and was, possibly, painting a rather too negative picture of the discipline in the Battalion. Jourdain noted that Feilding's return from leave saw the return of 'the unsatisfactory state of affairs'.[52] When Feilding was CO and Jourdain his Second in Command, the situation became unbearable. Jourdain appears to have turned most of the officers against Feilding, while Feilding mobilised the NCOs against Jourdain. By 23 April 1917 Jourdain had applied to transfer and was given a staff post in the 47th Brigade.[53]

The rights and wrongs of this dispute are difficult to assess. Jourdain, an officer in the Connaught Rangers of twenty-four years' standing, had some justification in thinking that he should replace a Coldstream Guards officer as CO of the Battalion. Also, Jourdain appears to have uncovered some irregularities in the battalion accounts.[54] Feilding, whose selection of a commissioned Coldstream Guards sergeant as Adjutant was tactless, nevertheless appears to have become a popular CO. Captain C. A. Brett noted, 'Colonel Feilding – Snowball he was known by the men (he was about 40 but his hair was quite white) was always at hand in any difficult or dangerous situation.'[55] Even the then Second Lieutenant F. W. S. Jourdain (Colonel H. F. N. Jourdain's nephew) seems to have approved of Feilding, although he did, waspishly, suggest that Feilding had been sent to the 6th Connaught Rangers simply because he was a Roman Catholic.[56]

Jourdain was presumably not seen as a particularly effective CO. In August 1914 he was a Major and, in a war in which promotion was unusually fast, he had only reached the rank of Lieutenant Colonel by November 1918. Also, Captain C. A. Brett, who served in the 3rd Connaught Rangers in 1917, stated,

'Our Colonel was then Colonel Jourdain, a Regular, who had been second in command of the 6th. Battalion in France while I was there. I knew him well and we got on well together, he was a good and just man but not a great Commanding Officer.'[57] Nevertheless, the rivalry between Jourdain and Feilding appears to have had a serious impact on the 6th Connaught Rangers and therefore it is difficult to explain why this battalion survived the February 1918 disbandments while the apparently more disciplined 7th Leinster Regiment was broken up.

Amalgamations of Service battalions appear to have had very little impact on morale in the units concerned. Second Lieutenant T. H. Witherow showed no resentment at the creation of the 8/9th Royal Irish Rifles,[58] while Captain E. A. Godson's only complaint regarding the transfer of men of the North Irish Horse into the 9th Royal Irish Fusiliers was that with eleven new officers, some of them senior captains, joining the Battalion, his chances of becoming Adjutant were very small.[59] Perhaps many officers and men shared the sentiments of the historian of the Leinster Regiment who noted,

> The failure of recruiting in Ireland had rendered it impossible to maintain all the Irish battalions at full strength, and very wisely the authorities decided so far as possible to amalgamate existing Irish formations instead of endeavouring to keep them all alive by watering them down with alien stock ... This system of allowing the Regular Irish battalions to absorb their Service ones had the outstanding merit that nationality and regimental *esprit de corps* were preserved.'[60]

This is, perhaps, to over state the case. While amalgamations seem, largely, to have been viewed as necessary measures, the actual disbandment of units was unpopular. Writing about the 7th Leinster Regiment, J. H. M. Staniforth commented, 'The old Battalion was simply disbanded – not amalgamated at all: a big proportion of officers and men was absorbed into the regular B[attalio]n., the remainder went to form, of all things – a new Entrenching Battalion. (I was offered the post of senior captain in this – but not for this kid, thank you).'[61] Lieutenant Witherow, who had little difficulty in accepting the amalgamation of the 8th and 9th Royal Irish Rifles, was mortified at the disbandment of the Battalion,

> That day the 6th. February [1918] I will always remember as one
> of the most depressing that I have ever come through. We had
> received orders to join the 2nd. Battalion Royal Irish Rifles which
> had some time previous come into our Division ... We were such
> a happy crowd that it is difficult to realise the feeling of depres-
> sion that settled down on everybody at the prospect of parting ...
> We were looked upon as strangers by most of the officers who
> were not originally Ulster Division officers at all and who were
> not inclined to look at things from the Ulster point of view. They
> were most careful to distribute us all over the battalion so that we
> could not collect together in a clan.[62]

In an attempt to retain the 'Irishness' of the 16th (Irish) and
36th (Ulster) Divisions, most regular Irish battalions serving on
the Western Front were drafted into them. This would appear to
have adversely affected morale in most of the units concerned.
When the 2nd Royal Irish Rifles was transferred to the 36th
(Ulster) Division, Second Lieutenant John Lucy, with the
support of most of the other officers of this unit, issued men of
the Battalion with green flags so that they could show their
disgust at being sent to this 'poisonously loyal' formation.[63]
Father Henry Gill, the chaplain of the 2nd Royal Irish Rifles
noted,

> We were to be transferred to the 36th. (Ulster) Division. This
> news came as a surprise and disagreeable shock to almost every-
> one in the 25th. Division where we had a well established place in
> the esteem and good will of all. We were the only Irish battalion
> in the Division, and had an excellent reputation and were on
> good terms with our English neighbours. The prospect of a
> change into a political division was not pleasant, nor did the
> outlook appear very bright. Everything possible was done to
> have the decision changed, but without success.[64]

In a similar vein, Captain A. J. Trousdell, writing of the transfer of the 1st Royal Irish Fusiliers to the 36th (Ulster) Division,
stated, 'The 87th. [i.e. 1st Royal Irish Fusiliers] has been ordered
off to join the Ulster men and they are all mud sick about it.'[65] In
only one case does there appear to have been any enthusiasm
over the transfer of a regular battalion to one of the Irish New
Army divisions. Major Guy Nightingale of the 2nd Royal
Munster Fusiliers wrote in January 1918, 'we are off again + this
time we are going to join the 16th. Div.[ision] ... The men are

awfully pleased + in many ways I think it will be a good thing, though we have now been 6 years into the 1st. Division ... It will be the first time the 1st. + 2nd. B[attalio]ns. have been together since S.[outh] Africa.'[66] However, it is significant that Nightingale favoured the transfer as it would reunite the two regular battalions of his regiment, rather than as a move to the 16th (Irish) Division *per se*.

The proposal to amalgamate the 16th (Irish) and 36th (Ulster) Divisions produced the effect of both formations serving in the same corps. Members of the IPP were very much in favour of this policy as a purely political demonstration that men from all parts of Ireland could work together. Speaking to Captain W. T. Colyer shortly after the Battle of the Somme, Major William Redmond explained his political vision,

> I do want to see a united Ireland. As you know, there is a big gulf between South and North between Catholic and Protestant. Catholic as I am, I want that gulf to be bridged over, and I believe it can be. I have worked for it all my life. Out here is a golden opportunity. Here we have two whole Divisions, the 16th. Irish Division, representing the Catholic, and the 36th. Ulster Division. At present these two Divisions are kept severely apart, on the traditional assumption that they would fight each other like wild cats if they came into contact. Well, I am exerting the utmost political pressure to bring them together, because I believe they would do no such thing if they were fighting side by side against a common foe. It would be the first step towards the ideal. Then – well, if only I could get amongst these Irish lads in the trenches, if only I could see for myself Ulster shaking hands with County Cork, I should feel that I have not striven in vain.[67]

Meanwhile, Captain Stephen Gwynn, MP was writing, 'we are alongside of the Ulster division + making great friends with them – which is well.'[68] However, it appears that relationships between men of the 16th (Irish) and 36th (Ulster) Divisions were not all that satisfactory. Lieutenant Colonel Feilding noted that, while the divisions played football against each other in front of crowds of 3,000 spectators, 'a wag on the Ulster side was heard to say, "I wonder if we shall get into trouble for fraternising with the enemy."'[69] Denys Reitz related how he, as the CO of the 7th Royal Irish Rifles, prevented a major outbreak of violence between the divisions,

In the course of the evening I sent a fatigue party to fetch supplies for our canteen from the Ulster depot. Soon after their return I heard a violent commotion in the marquee tent where we kept our stores. There was the sound of breaking crockery, mingled with oaths and shouts, and, rushing up to enquire, I found that the men were busy wrecking the place. When I demanded the reason, several of them angrily flourished bottles in my face, to the accompaniment of threats and curses against the bloody Orangemen. To me the bottles seemed harmless, for they contained only soda-water, but, when I asked for enlightenment, it appeared that the root of the trouble was the labels, which bore the title 'Boyne Water'. The men started off in a body for the Ulster Division, to avenge what they considered a mortal insult. I had heard of the Battle of the Boyne, but it conveyed no political implications and I thought the men had gone crazy. Fortunately, I was able to telephone through to the Ulster headquarters, who hastily turned out several hundred men to surround the malcontents; and with the tactful assistance of our Adjutant, young Hartery, who understood Irish politics, we managed to get our men back to camp without bloodshed.[70]

At a more basic level, Lieutenant Witherow, an officer of the 8th Royal Irish Rifles, was arrested by a sentry when he strayed into the 16th (Irish) Divisional area. It took the intervention of Captain Stephen Gwynn, MP, to release him.[71] Likewise, officers of the 2nd Royal Dublin Fusiliers felt that bringing the two Irish divisions together in this way would damage the men's morale.[72] Therefore, it appears that while the joint service of the 16th (Irish) and 36th (Ulster) Divisions provided good political propaganda for the IPP, its effect on discipline and morale in these formations was, in many cases, a negative one.

The actual battlefield performance of Irish units during this period demonstrates very few problems in discipline and morale. Certainly morale in both the 16th (Irish) and 36th (Ulster) Divisions was adversely affected by the botched action at Langemarck late in 1917, especially as this followed the highly successful action at Messines. Indeed, at least one staff officer felt that the 16th (Irish) Division was too tired to carry out this attack.[73]

In terms of front-line discipline, it would appear that there were two unofficial truces carried out by Irish units in this period. The most serious of these took place in the 6th

Connaught Rangers in February 1917, when, following a trench raid, a ceasefire was organised to evacuate the wounded. Apparently Major General W. B. Hickie established a Court of Inquiry to look into this affair.[74] Also, in February 1917 the 9th Royal Irish Fusiliers allowed the Germans to rescue some of their wounded after the Germans erected a notice which read 'Let save two wounded Kamerards'.[75]

Having considered the whole issue of amalgamations, disbandments and breaches of front-line discipline, it is worth making some comments about the differences in discipline in Irish regular and Service battalions. Even by this stage of the war, there were marked differences between regular and Service battalions, as demonstrated in table 5.1. For example drunkenness was noticeably higher in regular infantry battalions than their Service equivalents. It is noticeable that the number of courts martial in some units had changed little in the October 1916 to February 1918 period compared to October 1915 to September 1916, even allowing for the different timescales involved. The 6th Connaught Rangers, with 60 men tried by courts martial in the first period had 57 in the latter, while similar figures for the 2nd Royal Dublin Fusiliers were 93 and 95. Units which received large drafts of English conscripts such as the 14th Royal Irish Rifles appear to have seen a small, though not excessive, rise in their courts martial rate. It is also noticeable that the number of men tried for drunkenness rose sharply in the October 1916 to February 1918 period: in the 9th Royal Irish Rifles, the numbers rose from 7 to 12, while in the 2nd Royal Dublin Fusiliers it was from 19 to 43. A final point worth stressing in regard to courts martial figures is that battalions of the 36th (Ulster) Division generally had fewer men tried by courts martial than their counterparts in the 16th (Irish) Division.

David Englander has suggested that 1917 saw a tightening of the British courts martial system, with harsher punishments being awarded, most notably in September 1917 when twenty men were executed, the most for any month of the war.[76] A consideration of courts martial in Irish units over this period demonstrates that indiscipline was not escalating in 1917. Most offenders were still sentenced to periods of field punishment number one, with executions and periods of penal servitude being imposed very rarely, as demonstrated in table 5.2. Only in

Table 5.1. Offences for which men serving in sample Irish battalions were tried by courts martial, 1 October 1916 to 28 February 1918

Offence	5Lancers	1RInnsF	8RInnsF	10RInnsF	2RIRifs	9RIRifs	14RIRifs	6CR	2RDF	8RDF
War Treason	0	0	0	0	0	0	0	0	0	0
DORA	0	0	0	0	0	0	0	0	0	0
Offence against an inhabitant	0	0	0	1	0	0	0	0	0	1
Mutiny	0	0	0	0	0	0	0	1	0	0
Cowardice	1	0	0	0	0	0	0	1	0	0
Desertion	1	12	5	4	2	2	0	0	11	4
Absence	0	0	0	0	0	0	0	0	0	0
Striking or violence	0	0	1	0	0	0	0	0	1	0
Insubordination	3	0	3	0	0	1	0	1	2	1
Disobedience	0	4	3	0	2	0	1	3	9	4
Quitting post	0	0	0	0	1	1	0	3	0	0
Drunkenness	1	15	3	4	9	7	4	12	19	4
Injuring property	0	0	0	0	0	0	0	1	0	0
Loss of property	0	0	0	0	0	0	0	0	0	0
Theft	0	1	0	0	2	0	0	2	2	2
Indecency	0	0	0	0	0	0	0	0	0	0
Resisting escort	0	0	0	0	0	0	0	0	0	0
Escaping confinement	0	0	1	0	0	0	0	0	0	0
Miscellaneous and multiple offences	3	31	12	15	38	7	14	36	49	30
Miscellaneous civil offences	0	0	0	0	0	0	0	0	0	0
Self-inflicted wound	0	0	0	0	0	0	0	0	0	0
Fraudulent enlistment	0	0	0	0	0	0	0	0	0	0
Enlisting after discharge	0	0	0	0	0	0	0	0	0	0
False answer	0	0	0	0	0	0	0	0	0	0
Neglect	0	0	0	0	0	0	0	0	0	0
Fraud	0	0	0	0	0	0	0	0	0	0
Totals	9	63	28	24	54	18	19	60	93	46

the 2nd Royal Dublin Fusiliers is any significant change in this direction clear, as the number of men sentenced to hard labour increased from seven during the October 1915 to September 1916 period, to thirteen in the October 1916 to February 1918 period. Another point worthy of note is that in the latter period a much higher number of NCOs of the 1st Royal Inniskilling Fusiliers were reduced following trial by courts martial.

Finally in this chapter, some brief comments must be made regarding morale and discipline in the BEF as a whole in 1917. Historians have generally found this a difficult issue to examine. David Englander and James Osborne commented, 'The Russian armies collapsed, the Italians deserted, the French mutinied: the British soldier however, apparently did little more than curse his fate.'[77] This sort of approach has led to some rather bleak portraits of British discipline and morale in 1917. The presumption of some historians appears to be that as there were serious problems in other European armies, then there must have been equally forceful pressures on British soldiers. After concluding that the Fifth Army did not suffer from major disciplinary problems in late 1917 and early 1918, David Englander has argued, 'It had been a close run thing. How close is still a matter for speculation. Whether there was a mutiny in the making which, but for the March offensive, would have issued in a spectacular conflagration comparable with those in other armies is an intriguing possibility ... The British army, like others, became deeply depressed during 1917–18.'[78] Of course, Englander's views are based on some inescapable facts: 1917 witnessed the largest mutiny in the BEF during the Great War, namely that at Etaples Base Camp; the High Command was concerned about Socialist and Pacifist political pressure on British troops;[79] and, of course, the BEF now contained a large number of conscripts.

Table 5.2. Sentences imposed on men serving in sample Irish units tried by courts martial, 1 October 1916 to 28 February 1918

Sentence	5Lancers	1RInnsF	8RInnsF	10RInnsF	2RIRifs	9RIRifs	14RIRifs	6CR	2RDF	8RDF
Death	0	1	0	0	1	0	0	0	0	0
Penal servitude	1	0	2	0	1	1	0	1	2	0
Hard labour	0	3	3	4	3	3	0	7	13	4
Imprisonment	0	0	0	0	0	0	0	0	0	0
Detention	0	0	0	0	0	0	0	0	0	0
FP1	4	22	14	11	32	8	7	26	43	22
FP2	0	3	1	3	4	0	0	4	1	4
Discharged with ignominy/cashiered	0	0	0	0	0	0	1	0	0	0
Reduced/reprimanded	0	13	2	2	5	3	2	4	12	2
Stoppages, fines, etc.	0	2	0	0	1	1	4	1	2	2
Quashed/not confirmed	1	4	0	0	0	0	1	1	2	0
Suspended sentence	0	12	3	0	4	1	0	1	8	6
Not guilty, acquitted, etc.	3	3	3	4	3	1	4	15	10	6
Totals	9	63	28	24	54	18	19	60	93	46

Before considering these issues in more detail, the point must be made that the British army was, in many respects, different from other European armies in 1917. Firstly, British losses, while high, were comparatively low in European terms. For example, in the French case, casualties in the first fifteen months of the war almost equalled those of the next three years.[80] Related to this point is the fact that Britain, entering the war with a small, volunteer, regular army did not reach its maximum effort on the Western Front until 1916.[81] Thirdly, there was still consent for the war in Britain, which was certainly no longer the case in Russia or Italy.[82] Fourthly, the British army did not face the serious ethnic tensions faced by the Austro-Hungarian, or even German armies, in 1917–18.[83] Finally, the point must be made that some armies which 'collapsed' in 1917 were actually able to take the field again.[84]

To return to disciplinary and morale problems in the BEF in 1917, it is clear that a number of these have been overstated. The Etaples mutiny was, in many ways, a disaster waiting to happen and was also a very atypical mutiny. Colonel Seymour Jourdain who, as a second lieutenant, served at Etaples in mid-1916 was shocked by the 'brutal N.C.O.s', slack organisation and pointless bayonet practice which took place there.[85] Captain C. C. Miller, of the Royal Inniskilling Fusiliers who served at Etaples during the mutiny commented that the camp 'was a matter of constant nagging and petty irritation combined with rotten rations and wretched organisation', and, indeed, after the mutiny he refused to identify ringleaders.[86] There was, therefore, some sympathy from officers for the plight of other ranks at Etaples and, indeed, those targeted by the mutineers were military policemen rather than officers.[87] However, Etaples was by no means the only mutiny which occurred in the BEF during the Great War and given that it involved troops in reserve, it was, arguably, not the most serious. Mutinies were a constant, if infrequent, aspect of British military life.[88]

Concerns about Socialist and Pacifist influence on British soldiers were largely unfounded. Attempts by some socialists to create soldiers' councils in imitation of Russian soviets were almost totally unsuccessful.[89] Nevertheless the British High Command reacted relatively quickly to this perceived threat. By January 1918 a lecture series on current affairs had been approved for use in all BEF formations with a view to providing both education in citizenship and to provide men with useful skills for their return to civilian life.[90] Due to the return of open warfare in March 1918 this lecture programme was largely abandoned. Nevertheless, it is perhaps significant that one of the earliest of these citizenship lectures, entitled 'America and the War', was delivered to the 16th (Irish) Division in October 1917.[91]

The assimilation of conscripts into the British army appears to have caused relatively few disciplinary problems. In the sample of non-Irish units, indiscipline did not greatly increase over this period. Equally, as Englander and Osborne point out, indiscipline in the Royal Navy was much more likely to occur amongst regulars than conscripts and the fact that most regular soldiers had been killed by 1917 meant that there was little serious indiscipline in the BEF.[92]

Finally, surviving censorship reports suggest that the BEF was suffering from relatively few morale problems. One such report stated, 'The Morale of the Army is sound. In spite of increasing references to peace which occupy much space in the newspapers, in spite of the Russian debacle and the Italian set back there is ample ground for the belief that the British army is firmly convinced, not only of its ability to defeat the enemy and its superiority man to man, but also of the dangers of a premature peace.'[93]

It would appear that, contrary to the scenario outlined by some historians, the British army did not suffer from a major crisis of morale in 1917. David Englander's findings that there were no serious disciplinary problems in the Fifth Army appear to be borne out by the study of the court martial records for the sample of non-Irish units. The situation with regard to Irish units is rather more complex. Sinn Fein, unlike previous Republican groups, did not seek to infiltrate Irish units in the British army, and there is no evidence to suggest that Irish battalions serving on the Western Front were subverted during this period. However, the decision to remove Irish Special Reserve battalions from Ireland in late 1917 and early 1918, discussed in more detail in chapter 7, does demonstrate that there were some doubts regarding the reliability of Irish soldiers.

While the decision to amalgamate and disband Irish Service battalions was inspired purely by recruiting difficulties, it is noticeable that in practice this was used in a disciplinary fashion. While, when the decision was taken to reduce British divisions from thirteen to ten battalions, the most junior battalions were disbanded, this was not the case with Irish battalions. Thus, for example, the 7th Royal Irish Rifles and 9th Royal Dublin Fusiliers were disbanded before their more junior sister battalions, due to disciplinary problems.

Notes

1 PRO, WO163/21, 'Minutes of the Proceedings of, and Precis Prepared for, the Army Council for the Years 1915 and 1916', PRO, pp. 23–4.
2 *Ibid.*, p. 55.
3 N. Perry, 'Nationality in the Irish Infantry Regiments in the First World War', *War and Society*, XII, 1, 1994, p. 81.
4 PRO, WO163/21, 'Minutes of the Proceedings of, and Precis Prepared for, the Army Council for the Years 1915 and 1916', PRO, p. 26.
5 NLI, Ms.15,189, Redmond papers, letter, David Lloyd George to John Redmond, 29 September 1916.
6 NLI, Ms.15,205/2, Redmond papers, letter, John Redmond to General Sir Nevil Macready, 31 October 1916.
7 PRONI, D.1507/A/19/16, Farren Connell papers, letter, Major General Oliver Nugent to (Macready ?), 6 October 1916.
8 *Ibid.*
9 Perry, 'Nationality in the Irish Infantry Regiments', pp. 82–3; NLI, Ms.15,205/2, Redmond papers, letter Macready to Redmond; and PRO, WO95/26, Adjutant General's war diary, entry for the 26 October 1916.
10 N. Perry, 'Maintaining Regimental Identity in the Great War: The Case of the Irish Infantry Regiments', *Stand To*, 52, 1998, p. 8.
11 NLI, Ms.15,205/2, Redmond papers, letter, Redmond to Macready, 26 October 1916.
12 NLI, Ms.15,205/2, Redmond papers, letter, Macready to Redmond, 15 November 1916.
13 J. E. Nelson, 'Irish Soldiers in the Great War: Some Personal Experiences', *The Irish Sword*, XI, 1974, p. 173.
14 *Ibid.*, pp. 173–4.
15 I. F. W. Beckett, 'The Real Unknown Army: British Conscripts, 1916–19', in J. J. Becker and S. Audoin-Rouzeau (eds.), *Les Sociétiés*

Europeénnes et la Guerre de 1914–18 (Universite de Paris X, Nanterre, Paris), 1990, pp. 340–1.

16 Sir Barclay Nihill, 'Turning Point 1918', *The Tablet*, 30 March 1968, p. 1. Copy of manuscript version in NAM, 7603–69–2, Lieutenant Colonel Holt's papers.

17 Royal Ulster Rifles Museum, Anon., 'Service with the 14th Battalion, Royal Irish Rifles (Young Citizen Volunteers), 1914–18 War', p. 253.

18 IWMSA, 9547/1, interview with Edward Bowyer-Green.

19 IWM, 76/51/1, W. T. Colyer, 'War Impressions of a Temporary Soldier', unpaginated.

20 NLI, Ms.21,278, Parsons papers, letter, Lieutenant Colonel G. A. M. Buckley to Lieutenant General Sir Lawrence Parsons, 15 August 1917.

21 Letter, PRONI, Farren Connell papers, Nugent to his wife, 21 September 1916, cited Perry, 'Maintaining Regimental Identity', p. 7.

22 F. W. Perry, *The Commonwealth Armies: Manpower and Organisation in Two World Wars* (Manchester University Press, 1988), p. 24.

23 E. A. James, *British Regiments, 1914–18* (Samson Books, London, 1978), p. 110.

24 Perry, 'Nationality in the Irish Infantry Regiments' and Perry, 'Maintaining Regimental Identity'.

25 Perry, *The Commonwealth Armies*, p. 28.

26 I. F. W. Beckett, *The Amateur Military Tradition, 1558–1945* (Manchester University Press, 1991), p. 233.

27 P. Morris, 'Leeds and the Amateur Military Tradition: the Leeds Rifles and their Antecedents, 1859–1918', unpublished PhD thesis, University of Leeds, 1983, pp. 960 and 999.

28 PRONI, MIC/571/10, Farren Connell papers, letter, Nugent to James Johnston, Lord Mayor of Belfast, 28 February 1918.

29 Indeed, there is a copy of this correspondence in PRONI, D.961/8, the papers of Lieutenant A. N. Anderson, 14th Royal Irish Rifles. This suggests that some officers expected political pressure to be applied to prevent the disbandment of their battalions.

30 PRONI, MIC/571/10, Farren Connell papers, letter, Nugent to Johnston, 28 February 1918.

31 PRONI, MIC/571/10, Farren Connell papers, letter, Nugent to the Adjutant General, 11 December 1917.

32 Perry, 'Maintaining Regimental Identity', p. 10.

33 C. Falls, *The History of the 36th (Ulster) Division* (Constable, London, 1996. First published by McCaw, Stevenson and Orr, Belfast, 1922), pp. 117–18.

34 LC, J. MacRoberts papers, p. 204.

35 Falls, *The History of the 36th (Ulster) Division*, p. 132.

36 PRO, WO95/1955, war diary of 16th Divisional General Staff, report by Hickie to IV Corps relating to enemy raids, 16th Divisional Front, 8/9 March 1917, dated 10 March 1917.

37 IWM, 86/65/1, Captain O. L. Beater's diaries, entry for 26 November 1916.

38 *Ibid.*, entry for 20 January 1917.

39 D. Reitz, *Trekking On* (Faber and Faber, London, 1933), pp. 184–5.

40 IWM, 86/65/1, Captain O. L. Beater's diaries, entry for 4 November 1916.

41 *Ibid.*, 14 November 1916.

42 *Ibid.*, 19 January 1917.

43 *Ibid.*, 9 February 1917.

44 *Ibid.*, 9 February 1917. I have found no mention of this case in the court martial registers. However, under certain circumstances a CO could reduce an NCO without reference to a court martial, War Office, *Manual of Military Law* (HMSO, London, 1914), pp. 32–3.

45 NAM, 7608–40, C. A. Brett, 'Recollections', p. 15.

46 IWMSA, 11214/4, interview with Colonel F. W. S. Jourdain.

47 There are no adverse comments about Feilding in his personal file, see PRO, WO339/48941, the personal file of Colonel Rowland Feilding.

48 IWMSA, 11214/4, interview with Colonel F. W. S. Jourdain.

49 NAM, 5603–12–1, diaries of Colonel H. F. N. Jourdain, entry for 13 March 1917.

50 *Ibid.*, entry for 16 March 1917.

51 *Ibid.*, entry for 22 March 1917.

52 *Ibid.*, entry for 21 April 1917.

53 *Ibid.*, entries for 22–24 April 1917.

54 *Ibid.*, entries for 16 March 1917 to 24 April 1917.

55 NAM, 7608–40, C. A. Brett, 'Recollections', p. 24.

56 IWMSA, 11214/3, interview with Colonel F. W. S. Jourdain.

57 NAM, 7608–40, Captain C. A. Brett, 'Recollections', p. 36.

58 LC, T. H. Witherow, 'Personal Recollections of the Great War', p. 21.

59 IWM, P.446, Captain E. A. Godson diaries, p. 10.

60 F. E. Whitton, *The History of the Prince of Wales' Leinster Regiment (Royal Canadians)*, vol. II (Gale and Polden, London, no date (1926?)), p. 442.

61 IWM, 67/41/3, letter from Staniforth to his parents, 28 February 1918.

62 LC, T. H. Witherow, 'Personal Recollections of the Great War', pp. 34–5.

63 J. F. Lucy, *There's a Devil in the Drum* (Faber and Faber, London, 1938), pp. 378–9.

64 JAD, H. V. Gill, 'As seen by a Chaplain with the 2nd Battalion, Royal Irish Rifles', pp. 154–5.

65 LC, A. J. Trousdell, Journal for 1916–17, p. 34.

66 PRO, PRO30/71/3, Nightingale papers, letter, Nightingale to his mother, 30 January 1918.

67 IWM, 76/51/1, W. T. Colyer, 'War Impressions of a Temporary Soldier', unpaginated, but chapter 12.

68 PRONI, D.2912/1/19, letter, Gwynn to his cousin, Amelia, 26 December 1916.

69 R. Feilding, *War Letters to a Wife: France and Flanders, 1915–1919* (The Medici Society, London, 1929), p. 170.

70 Reitz, *Trekking On*, p. 182.

71 LC, The papers of Second Lieutenant (sic.) T. H. Witherow, p. 5.

72 IWM, 76/65/1, W. T. Colyer, 'War Impressions of a Temporary Soldier', unpublished manuscript, unpaginated, but chapter 23.

73 LC, tape 430, interview with Major General Sir N. Holmes.

74 Feilding, *War Letters to a Wife*, pp. 154–9.

75 IWM, P.446, Captain E. A. Godson diaries, p. 13.

76 D. Englander, 'Discipline and Morale in the British Army, 1917–18', in J. Horne (ed.), *State, Society and Mobilization in Europe during the First World War* (Cambridge University Press, 1997).

77 D. Englander and J. Osbourne, 'Jack, Tommy and Henry Dubb: The Armed Forces and the Working Class', *Historical Journal*, XXI, 3, 1978, p. 594.

78 Englander, 'Discipline and Morale in the British Army, 1917–1918', p. 141.

79 G. Dallas and D. Gill, *The Unknown Army: Mutinies in the British Army in World War I* (Verso, London, 1985), p. 77; and N. Macready, *Annals of An Active Life* (Hutchinson, London, 1924), vol. I, p. 277.

80 D. Porch, 'The French Army and the Spirit of the Offensive, 1900–14', in B. Bond and I. Roy (eds.), *War and Society: A Yearbook of Military History* (Croom Helm, London, 1975), p. 117.

81 I. F. W. Beckett, 'The Nation in Arms, 1914–18', in I. F. W. Beckett and K. Simpson (eds.), *A Nation in Arms: A Social Study of the British Army in the First World War* (Manchester University Press, 1985), p. 12.

82 See, R. Service, 'The Industrial Workers', in R. Service (ed.), *Society and Politics in the Russian Revolution* (Macmillan, London, 1992), p. 154; and G. Procacci, 'A "Latecomer" in War: The Case of Italy', in F. Coetzee and M. Shevin-Coetzee (eds.), *Authority, Identity and the Social History of the Great War* (Berghahn Books, Oxford, 1995), pp. 3–26.

83 M. Cornwall, 'Morale and Patriotism in the Austro–Hungarian

Army, 1914–18', in J. Horne (ed.), *State, Society and Mobilization in Europe*, pp. 175–7; G. Wawro, 'Morale in the Austro–Hungarian Army: The Evidence of Hapsburg Army Campaign Reports and Allied Intelligence Officers', in H. Cecil and P. H. Liddle (eds.), *Facing Armageddon: The First World War Experienced* (Leo Cooper, London, 1996), pp. 401–3; H. Strachan, 'The Morale of the German Army 1917–18', in *Ibid.*, pp. 386–8; and A. Kramer, 'Wackes at War: Alsace-Lorraine and the Failure of German National Mobilization, 1914–18', in Horne (ed.), *State, Society and Mobilization in Europe*, pp. 110–14.

84 On the reformation of the French army following the mutinies of 1917, see, L. V. Smith, *Between Mutiny and Obedience: The Case of the French Fifth Infantry Division During World War I* (Princeton University Press, 1994), pp. 215–43.

85 IWMSA, 11214/2, interview with Colonel F. W. S. Jourdain.

86 IWM, 83/3/1, C. C. Miller, 'A letter from India to my daughters in England', pp. 25–7.

87 D. Gill and G. Dallas, 'Mutiny at Etaples Base in 1917', *Past and Present*, 69, 1975, p. 92.

88 On this issue, see J. Putkowski, *British Army mutineers 1914–1922* (Francis Boutle Publishers, London, 1998).

89 Englander and Osbourne, 'Jack, Tommy and Henry Dubb', pp. 604–5; and L. James, *Mutiny in the British and Commonwealth Forces, 1797–1956* (Buchan and Enright Publishers, London, 1987), pp. 96–7.

90 S. P. Mackenzie, *Politics and Military Morale: Current Affairs and Citizenship Education in the British Army, 1914–1950* (Clarendon Press, Oxford, 1992), p. 12.

91 PRO, WO95/1957, Adjutant and Quarter Master General's war diary, 16th (Irish) Division, entry for 12 October 1917.

92 Englander and Osborne, 'Jack, Tommy and Henry Dubb', p. 602.

93 PRO, WO106/401, censor's report on morale, c. January 1918(?).

6

The final phase

The period March to November 1918 raises a number of important issues relating to the discipline and morale of Irish units serving on the Western Front. Firstly, the German Spring Offensive almost destroyed both the 16th (Irish) and 36th (Ulster) Divisions, and it is worth considering just how well these units reacted to this onslaught. Secondly, when the 10th (Irish) Division was Indianised in the Middle East, its Irish infantry units were mostly sent to France. These Service battalions, along with Irish regular battalions on the Western Front, provided more than enough manpower to reform the 16th (Irish) Division, yet this formation was re-established as a non-Irish division. Thirdly, the aftermath of the Spring Offensive saw a number of Irish garrison battalions converted to Service units and sent to the Western Front, and it is worth considering how well these units performed in action. Finally, an underlying theme in the consideration of discipline and morale in Irish units over this period must be the changing view of the High Command towards the loyalty of Irish soldiers, especially in the aftermath of the conscription crisis in Ireland and the mutiny in the 16th (Irish) Division in April 1918.

In broader terms, this period of the war is being radically re-assessed by historians of the British army. Richard Holmes, summing up historical thinking on the BEF in 1918 just nine years ago stated, 'One British officer reckoned that the instinct of self-preservation reached very great proportions: there developed a new spirit of taking care of one's self amongst the men, which ended, in late 1918, in few rifles being fired, and would, in a few weeks, have meant the cessation of the war, by the front line troops not refusing but quietly omitting to do duty.'[1] More recent work on the British army in 1918, especially in the so-called '100 days' from 8 August to 11 November 1918, has reached very different conclusions. Peter Simkins suggests that, not only did morale remain high in the BEF, but by the last three months of the war weapons systems, small unit tactics and junior leadership had all improved.[2] Bill Rawling's work on the Canadian Expeditionary Force during the Great War has come to similar conclusions. Indeed, Rawling stresses that the CEF in the last three months of the war was much better equipped and trained than in 1915.[3] An analysis of court martial statistics for this period suggests that Simkins and Rawling's conclusions are accurate, and can be applied to Irish units serving on the Western Front.

Both the 16th (Irish) and 36th (Ulster) Divisions were serving in Fifth Army when the German Spring Offensive began on 21 March 1918. The 16th (Irish) Division came in for much criticism from contemporaries for its seemingly poor performance in this action. Writing to the official historian in 1927, Lieutenant General Sir Walter Congreve, formerly the GOC, VII Corps, stated, 'You have been kind in your remarks on the 16th. Division, for the real truth is that their reserve Brigade did not fight at all and their right Brigade very indifferently, but there are excuses to be made for them in length of time they had been in the line and in a late reorganisation of units, and in any case no use to wash dirty linen in public now.'[4] General Sir Hubert Gough, the former commander of Fifth Army, suggested that problems were even more serious in the 16th (Irish) Division, noting,

> I was aware (pre-March 1918) that the (16th.) Division was not of the highest standard, and [Lieutenant General H. E.] Watts [G. O. C., XIX Corps] was equally aware of this fact.
> Later on, in March 1918 – [Lieutenant General W.] Congreve commanding the VII Corps in which the 16th. Division was serving – wrote me a private note expressing his anxiety on the reliability of this division, and saying that its morale was being undermined by political propaganda. I consider that a commander is fully justified in expressing his opinion of the conduct of his troops, however adverse such an opinion may be.[5]

Finally, Field Marshal Sir Douglas Haig commented, 'Our 16th. (Irish) Division which was on the right of the VII Corps and lost Ronssay Village is said not to be so full of fight as the others. In fact, certain Irish units did very badly, and gave way immediately the enemy showed.'[6]

However, not all officers felt that the 16th (Irish) Division had reacted badly to the German offensive. Major General C. P. A. Hull, who had replaced Hickie as GOC, 16th (Irish) Division on 10 February 1918, stated,

1 I understand that rumours are being circulated at home that the infantry of this division have not fought well since the attack commenced.

2 I desire most emphatically to contradict this. I have only been in command of this division for a short time and therefore may be considered as unbiased in any way.

3 On the first day the enemy broke in to the south of the division in the fog and the first thing that the garrison of Ronssay knew of the actual attack was that the enemy were in their rear, this affected the whole line but it held for some considerable time and the fighting was very bitter.

4 On March 23rd. when the withdrawal from the GREEN line was ordered, it was carried out under difficult conditions in a perfectly orderly manner, units retiring and supporting each other with their fire.

5 On March 30th. they were holding a portion of the line south of the SOMME about HAMEL when a determined attack was made by a fresh German division. The line was penetrated in places but immediate counterattacks drove the enemy out and our troops held their ground inflicting heavy casualties on the enemy. The Corps commander sent his personal congratulations on the fighting at this period ...

6 I shall be glad if this letter be forwarded to G. H. Q. so that steps may be taken to contradict these rumours.[7]

Clearly Hull felt that his division had been unfairly maligned and most historians have agreed with this analysis.[8] The massive restructuring of the 16th (Irish) Division between November 1917 and February 1918, inefficient staff intelligence work, and the fact that the Division was defending a salient, all contributed to the German success on 21 March.[9] In addition, while the average trench strength of a battalion in the Third and Fifth Armies on 17 March 1918 was 42 officers and 950 other ranks, many Irish battalions were well below this. The 2nd Royal Irish Regiment had just 18 officers and 514 other ranks and the 2nd Royal Munster Fusiliers, 22 officers and 629 other ranks.[10]

One of the main factors in the collapse of the 16th (Irish) Division on 21 March 1918 was its poor dispositions and these partially explain Gough's and Congreve's adverse comments. Congreve, as Corps Commander, ordered five of the 16th (Irish) Division battalions to occupy the forward zone, believing that the division was liable to a surprise attack. Major General Hull protested that this policy would make defence in depth impossible; however, Gough backed Congreve.[11] This left the 16th (Irish) Division with a defensive scheme which was, effectively, useless. Although having noted this, it is worth considering Tim Travers's view that the BEF was actually unable to operate the defence in depth system at all, as many units were unclear whether they should hold the front or supporting lines in depth and, as many second- and third-line trenches had not actually been completed by the time of the German Spring Offensive.[12]

Certainly contemporary accounts, or indeed the courts martial figures for units of 16th (Irish) Division in March and April 1918 considered later in this chapter, give the impression that morale and discipline was preserved in the 16th (Irish) Division in March 1918. The 6th Connaught Rangers, for example, carried out a counter-attack, unsupported by artillery, with heavy losses.[13] Meanwhile, Major Guy Nightingale of the 1st Royal Munster Fusiliers noted, 'The whole Division fought every inch + were splendid.'[14]

However, following the Spring Offensive the 16th (Irish) Division was effectively disbanded. Irish units were posted to other divisions and the Division was eventually reformed with only one Irish battalion, the 5th Royal Irish Fusiliers.[15] This treatment of 16th (Irish) Division was, of course, not unique. The 14th, 25th, 30th, 39th, 40th, 50th, 59th and 66th Divisions were all 'reduced and reconstituted' post March 1918.[16] However, the reduction of the 16th (Irish) Division has been seen as a policy adopted by the War Office to break up a 'disloyal' formation. As Denman notes, 'It is not clear whether a deliberate policy was followed by allowing the 16th. Division to wither away as a distinct Irish formation, but it seems likely.'[17]

The decision to break up the 16th (Irish) Division appears to have had mixed results. The 49th Brigade, or at least a large number of men in it, mutinied in April 1918.[18] None of the case transcripts for these trials survive, one of the largest of the war in the BEF. It would seem that this mutiny had little to do with the conscription crisis in Ireland. As discussed in the previous chapters, few Irish soldiers appear to have been influenced by Sinn Fein. Likewise, few soldiers on active service would have exhibited much sympathy in support of those then campaigning against the extension of conscription to Ireland.[19]

This mutiny appears, like most mutinies, to have been caused by military, rather than political grievances. Indeed, the lenient sentences passed by the courts martial (no man was sentenced to more than ten years penal servitude, and all sentences were suspended) suggests that this mutiny was of the nature of a pre-war strike. This mutiny would appear to have occurred as on 16 April 1918 the 7th Royal Irish Regiment and 7/8th Royal Inniskilling Fusiliers were to be reduced to training staffs.[20] Presumably brigade and battalion loyalty reacted to this measure, which would, effectively, have seen the disbandment of these battalions. The mutiny appears to have had its desired effect, as while the brigade was broken up the two Service battalions serving in it, the 7th Royal Irish Regiment and 7/8th Royal Inniskilling Fusiliers survived until the end of the war, serving in the 30th Division.[21]

That peculiar and imprecise Northern Irish activity of trying to ascertain where someone comes from by using their surname, further suggests that this mutiny had military rather than political roots. Of the 116 men charged with mutiny, only twenty-five had obviously 'Irish' surnames. While, of course, many people in twentieth-century Ireland had 'non-Irish' surnames, this very high concentration of English and Scots surnames does suggest that by April 1918 English drafts accounted for a large proportion of the men involved in this mutiny. If so this further demonstrates the extent to which men could develop a firm loyalty to a unit from outside their own locality.

Another point which should be made regarding this mutiny is that two of the units involved, namely the 7th Royal Irish Regiment and 7/8th Royal Inniskilling Fusiliers had already faced significant changes. The 7th Royal Irish Regiment could, uniquely amongst Irish Service battalions, trace its history back to at least 1902, as it had been formed in September 1917 from the South Irish Horse. The 7/8th Royal Inniskilling Fusiliers did not have such a long history, however, having been formed from the amalgamation of the 7th and 8th Battalions; men in this unit perhaps felt that this sacrifice should have been enough to insure the survival of one Service battalion of the Regiment. This mutiny in the 49th Brigade appears to have much in common with the mutinies of the 25th, 37th, 54th and 56th Battalions, Australian Imperial Force, in September 1918. While the military authorities planned to break up these units, to provide drafts for other Australian Imperial Force battalions, men in these battalions refused to fall out on parade, thus, technically mutinying.[22]

The decision to break up the 16th (Irish) Division, had been made before the mutiny in the 49th Brigade and was not only because of the perceived poor performance of the Division in March 1918. Presumably it was felt that, with falling recruitment in Ireland, there was no way in which this formation could be maintained. Another point worth emphasising is that by March 1918 the 16th (Irish) Division was a regular division in all but name, with only three surviving Service battalions. Post March 1918 the War Office may have felt that it was a mistake to concentrate so much regular experience in one, supposedly New Army, division. Indeed, when Irish units were posted to other formations, it is noticeable that many went to divisions, such as the 30th, 50th and 57th Divisions[23] which were certainly not regarded as elite formations. Not all members of the 16th (Irish) Division were depressed at its reconstitution. Major Nightingale of the 1st Royal Munster Fusiliers noted, 'We like our new Division [57th] very much + now they have got to know us, I think they are very pleased to have us, especially a line B[attalio]n. I'm glad we've left the 16th. Div.[ision]. It was a rotten staff + it was entirely due to their bad staff work that Haig didn't mention the Div.[ision] more in his communiqués.'[24]

While the 16th (Irish) Division was seen as performing poorly on 21 March 1918, the experience of the 36th (Ulster) Division was little better. Neither Gough, nor Haig, made any adverse comments regarding the 36th (Ulster) Division's actions during the German Spring Offensive. However, historians have been more critical. Terence Denman suggests that the 36th (Ulster)

Division 'arguably had not fought as well as its sister [16th] division'.[25] Meanwhile, Martin Samuels stresses the 'patchy' nature of defence in the 36th (Ulster) Division. For example, while 'C' Company of the 1st Royal Irish Rifles carried out a suicidal counter-attack, the 12th Royal Irish Rifles fled at the sight of German tanks, Lieutenant Colonel Lord Farnham surrendered 11 officers and 241 men of the 2nd Royal Inniskilling Fusiliers after a token defence, and a captain and 30 men of the same battalion surrendered to a single German NCO.[26]

Before painting too bleak a picture of the 36th (Ulster) Division's actions on 21 March 1918, it should be stressed that the Division, like the 16th (Irish) Division, had just completed a major reorganisation; the divisional reserves (2nd Royal Irish Rifles and 9th Royal Inniskilling Fusiliers) were committed very late in the day and the Division was attacked in the rear.[27] Units in the 36th (Ulster) Division, like their counterparts in the 16th (Irish) Division, faced serious manpower shortages.[28] Defences in the 36th (Ulster) Divisional zone were poor. As Captain C. C. Miller of the 2nd Royal Inniskilling Fusiliers recounted, 'instead of [strong points] being deeply dug and strongly revetted and wired it was quite obvious that when the moment came to use them the strong points would hardly be strong enough to keep out a well aimed snowball'.[29]

Nevertheless, there is evidence to suggest that Major General Oliver Nugent was decidedly unimpressed with the performance of the 36th (Ulster) Division. There appears to have been an enquiry held into the actions of Lieutenant Colonel J. N. Crawford, DSO, the CO of the 1st Royal Inniskilling Fusiliers. His battalion appears to have retreated in some disarray around noon on 22 March. Both of the witnesses interviewed by Nugent (Sergeant A. Rice and Private Magee, both of the 1st Royal Inniskilling Fusiliers) stated that Crawford had initially ordered wounded men who could do so, to get away, but had later said that any men who thought they could evade capture by the Germans could leave the Battalion.[30]

Lieutenant Colonel Cole Hamilton, the CO of the 15th Royal Irish Rifles, felt moved, while a POW in Germany, to explain why he had surrendered his battalion. According to Cole Hamilton, visibility on 21 March was down to ten yards. Shelling started at 4.15 a.m. and by 9.30 a.m. all communications had been cut and, finally, at 5.15 p.m. a conference of senior officers was held, and break-out being impossible and the position being heavily shelled by *minenwerfers*, the battalion officers decided to surrender at 5.35 p.m. He continued,

> It was a bitter moment, but I do not think we could have done more. The Officer in command of the Battalion who captured us told me he had taken over command as his C. O. had been killed, that a Battalion had been attacking us all day and a second had been sent up to help them or had been engaged for some time, so I think we did what we could to help the cause. I had only about 30 men left unwounded – only 60 all told were able to walk away and this included various oddments – Trench Mortar and Machine Gun Teams ... every Officer, N. C. O. and man under my command did their damnedest and I am proud to have had the honour to have commanded such men ... I met some of my front line Company Officers and men since and they all agree that the front line was not attacked from the front at all, but from the rear.[31]

Lieutenant Colonel Lord Farnham, holding an unofficial enquiry into the collapse of the 2nd Royal Inniskilling Fusiliers, while a POW in Karlsruhe Camp, came to different conclusions. Only the headquarters staff and one company of his unit had been able to put up any real defence, and Farnham attributed this to the weakness of the 'strong-points' which his battalion had manned.[32]

Nevertheless, while the performance of the 36th (Ulster) Division on 21 March 1918 was variable, it would be wrong to attribute this to a collapse in morale or discipline. Major Montgomery, relating his experiences during the German Spring Offensive, demonstrated that, even when their battalions ceased to exist, a number of men in the Division continued to fight,

> The Division wasn't surrounded – not quite – but it has been badly cut up + undoubtedly many of the missing are in the hands of the enemy. At the time the enemy attacked the Division had 3 battalions in the Forward Area. That is holding outposts, front line, counterattack positions + passive resistance positions. These three Batt[alions] were 2nd. Enniskillings [Royal Inniskilling Fusiliers], 15th. R.[oyal] I.[rish] R.[ifles], 12th. R.[oyal] I.[rish] R.[ifles]. These three Battalions were entirely overrun by the

enemy ... It may interest you to know that in 56 hours your son
formed a composite Batt.[alion] of the details of the 3 Batt[alion]s.
washed out in [the] Forward Area, did an Advance guard, took
up a position, formed a flank guard, covered the blowing up of
bridges + then finished up by fighting no less than 5 rearguard
actions.[33]

On 23 March, when Lieutenant Witherow rejoined the 36th
(Ulster) Division from a platoon commanders' course, he was
posted to a scratch force, commanded by Lieutenant Colonel
Peacocke and Major Montgomery, which he found to consist of
about 200 men, mainly from the 9th Royal Inniskilling Fusiliers,
but also including such oddments as butchers, pioneers and
Army Service Corps personnel.[34]

Following the German Spring Offensive, the 36th (Ulster)
Division was reorganised and its battalions brought up to
strength. However, there were a number of changes in the
commands of the Division, which appear more than coincidental. Brigadier General Withycombe was removed from his
command of 107th Brigade on 30 April 1918, Brigadier General
Griffith, GOC, 108th Brigade was relieved on 21 May 1918 and,
crucially, Major General Nugent, the GOC of the 36th (Ulster)
Division was relieved of his command on 6 May. Significantly,
none of these officers held another command in France,
although Nugent did see further service in India.[35]

It would appear that these changes occurred with justification. An officer of the 61st Brigade, allocated as a reserve
formation to the 36th (Ulster) Division, stated, 'On the evening
of the 21st. [March] I saw the 36th. Division commander at
Ollezy. I never saw him again during these operations, nor did I
ever see one of his Staff Officers, nor did I receive any assistance
of any kind from Divisional Headquarters.'[36] Therefore, while
the poor performance of the 16th (Irish) Division was ascribed to
poor morale, in an attempt to absolve Gough and Congreve
from any blame over the dispositions of this division, the less
than excellent showing of the 36th (Ulster) Division appears to
have been attributed largely to the failure of Nugent and his
senior officers to provide effective leadership.

Following the German Spring Offensive, the need for
manpower on the Western Front saw the 'Indianisation' of the
10th (Irish) Division, serving in the Middle East. Effectively this

meant that six Irish battalions were released for service on the Western Front. Irish Nationalists at the time, and historians subsequently, have suggested that this was due to a misplaced concern over the discipline and morale of these units.[37] However, as in the decision not to reform the 16th (Irish) Division as an 'Irish' formation, there were some more practical concerns. Firstly, these battalions were very experienced, and possibly the closest thing which the British army had to pre-1914 regular battalions. For example, when it was proposed that the 5th Royal Irish Fusiliers be broken up to provide drafts for other units, 'The Corps Commander Lieutenant General Peyton, seeing that this was a Battalion still very largely composed of men of the First Hundred Thousand, and of men of the pre-war Regular Army, all veteran soldiers with three years and more continuous service in the field, brimful of *esprit de corps* and retaining their old smartness and appearance, reported against this, preferring that the unit be kept intact for the more strenuous days ahead.'[38] It was perhaps felt, as in the case of Irish regular battalions, that the experience of the Service battalions of 10th (Irish) Division should be spread throughout other formations.

The second practical problem which called for the 10th (Irish) Division to be split up was malaria. Captain N. E. Drury, of the 6th Royal Dublin Fusiliers, certainly believed that the 10th (Irish) Division was to be broken up purely so that the men could become acclimatised.[39] Private G. T. Nevell noted that malaria was a serious problem in the 7th Royal Dublin Fusiliers, while in the 5th Royal Irish Fusiliers 'several hundred' men had to be treated for this disease over a period of ten days.[40] Obviously, concentrating so many men with malaria in one division could have lead to that division being unfit for action on an almost permanent basis. Lastly, bereft of political allies and in a situation where the BEF generally was facing serious manpower problems, it is not surprising that the 10th (Irish) Division was broken up, rather than other formations transferred from the Middle East to the Western Front.

The quality of drafts being sent to Irish units on the Western Front was relatively poor during this period. Lieutenant Witherow noted that, while after 21 March 1918 the 2nd Royal Irish Rifles received some experienced men from the disbanded

10th and 14th Royal Irish Rifles, 'The men from home were mere boys of 18 years of age and under who had been rushed out during the crisis from the home training battalions.'[41] Of even worse physique were 'B1' men of the Irish Home Service and Garrison units sent to the Western Front, when their units were hastily converted into Service battalions.[42] Some of these new Service units in Irish regiments had nothing to do with Ireland, for example the 11th Garrison Guard Battalion became the 13th Royal Inniskilling Fusiliers on 13 July 1918.[43] Others had firmer Irish connections; the 11th Royal Irish Fusiliers was formed on 1 June 1918 from the cadre of the 7th Royal Dublin Fusiliers and men of the 3rd Royal Irish Fusiliers,[44] while the 8th Royal Irish Regiment was formed on 25 May 1918, when the 2nd Garrison Guard Battalion, Royal Irish Regiment was converted to a Service battalion.[45] Information on these units is sparse, with few primary sources relating to them having been found during this research. However, courts martial statistics for these units are surprisingly good. This may suggest that men prevented by their 'B1' medical status from seeing active service earlier in the war actually relished service in France.

Certainly the dispersion of Irish battalions throughout the BEF in 1918, despite its practical considerations, does appear to suggest that Irish units were increasingly distrusted by the military authorities. This dispersion should not be overstated. Irish battalions were concentrated in just nine divisions: namely the Guards, 16th, 29th, 30th, 36th (Ulster), 50th (Northumbrian), 57th (2nd West Lancashire), 63rd (Royal Naval) and 66th (2nd East Lancashire) Divisions, and there were four Irish battalions in both the 50th and 66th Divisions.[46] While there is no evidence of a deliberate policy of dispersion, some soldiers serving in Irish battalions were certain that their loyalty was viewed with suspicion. Major Guy Nightingale wrote of the 1st Royal Munster Fusiliers, in April 1918,

> The Brigadier ... says we could knock spots out of any B[attalio]n. in the [57th] Div.[ision] already though we've only been reorganised three days. That's the hardest part of the whole show, to feel we've been through a pretty rotten battle and wherever we go it's always – 'There go the Sinn Feiners' ... I'm glad I'm an Englishman in an Irish regiment, as I can go unprejudiced to these outside fellows and tell them straight that though I'm not

an Irishman I would sooner be in an Irish regiment with Irish soldiers behind me in a scrap than any English or Scotch troops they would like to produce.[47]

Mistrust of Irish soldiers during this period must have been shaped not only by the perceived poor performance of the 16th (Irish) Division in March 1918, but by the conscription crisis in Ireland. Since 1916 conscription had been a major political issue in Ireland, and, with relevance to discipline and morale, politicians and military officers disagreed amongst themselves on the usefulness of the proposed conscripts. In broad terms, the only political grouping in Ireland in favour of conscription was the Irish Unionist Alliance.[48] Even within Unionism there were divisions. Belfast Unionists, for example, as early as August 1916 felt that they had contributed more than their fair share of men. Their public support of conscription concealed their private views that only rural Ulster and Southern Ireland would actually provide conscripts.[49] Likewise, while one leading Southern Unionist, Lord Midleton, backed conscription in Ireland with reservations, another, James O'Connor, the Attorney-General for Ireland, opposed it, believing (correctly) that an attempt to introduce conscription would merely bring Nationalists and Republicans together.[50] Other leading Unionists, such as Sir Edward Carson and Sir James Campbell, the Lord Chief Justice of Ireland, believed that 'the price in disorder for a number of unreliable men would be unacceptable unless Irish conscription was absolutely necessary to secure further conscription in Britain'.[51]

Despite the lack of support for conscription the British army's desperate need for manpower meant that, in April 1918, attempts were made to extend this to Ireland. If this was not a practical political measure, there were also doubts about the military efficiency of Irish conscripts. Field Marshal Viscount French believed that if Irish conscripts were shipped to France for training 'where extreme penalties could be inflicted for serious breaches of discipline, these men could be made into soldiers'.[52] In contrast, H. E. Duke, the Chief Secretary for Ireland, felt that 'Irish conscripts would be as useful as conscripted Germans.'[53] Significantly, the politically astute GOC in Chief in Ireland, Lieutenant General Sir Bryan Mahon, was determined, if ordered to introduce conscription, to implement a version of the Derby Scheme.[54]

Of course, conscription was never introduced into Ireland, a one-day General Strike on 18 April 1918 uniting Sinn Fein, Nationalists, organised Labour and the Catholic Church against this measure. For the purposes of this work, the failure to introduce conscription in Ireland had two important outcomes. Firstly, it demonstrated the views of senior military and political figures that Irish conscripts would not be entirely reliable soldiers. It is not assuming too much to suggest that similar views must have been held about Irish soldiers in general by this time. Secondly, the conscription crisis made it very clear to senior military and political figures that there had been a sea change in Irish public opinion. If Irish civilians had so quickly embraced Republicanism, there must have been fears that Irish military personnel would behave in a similar fashion.

Such fears appear to have been unfounded. While there was a mutiny in the 49th Brigade, 16th (Irish) Division in April 1918, as already discussed, this appears to have been over military rather than political matters. In more general terms, the decision to break up the 10th (Irish) Division appears to have been unpopular. As Captain N. E. Drury stated, 'It is an enormous pity that the good old 10th. Division could not have come over complete and with our own Staffs, whom we know and who know us.'[55] However, this disappointment was tempered by the embarkation of the 6th Royal Dublin Fusiliers for France, on which Drury commented, 'I think we are all glad we are to see a bit of the French front as everyone tells us that we have seen no proper fighting up to this and that now they'll show us what fine fellows they are in France. Well, that's as may be, but I bet our hardy lads will give a good account of themselves, and the "Blue Caps" will be called on when someone wants to be helped out of a mess.'[56] It is difficult to generalise on Drury's comments. However, discipline in the 5th Royal Irish Fusiliers, 5th Connaught Rangers and 6th Royal Dublin Fusiliers all improved when these battalions were serving in France from June 1918. This suggests that morale improved when men were fighting against German, rather than Bulgarian or Turkish troops.

In the Irish units as a whole courts martial rates fell drastically in most battalions during this period and were especially low in the last three months of the war, as demonstrated in table 6.1. It is noticeable that, even during this final phase of the war,

Table 6.1. The number of men tried by courts martial, while serving in Irish units on the Western Front, 1 March to 11 November 1918[a]

Unit	Mar.	Apr.	May	June	July	Aug.	Sept.	Oct.	Nov.	Total
4th RIDG	0	0	0	0	0	0	0	0	0	0
6th Inniskilling Dragoons	1	0	3	1	0	2	3	1	1	12
8th Hussars	0	0	1	0	1	0	0	0	0	2
5th Lancers	0	0	0	1	0	0	0	1	0	2
NIH	3	2	1	0	0	0	0	0	0	6
SIH	0	0	0	1	0	0	0	0	0	1
1st Irish Guards	5	10	5	4	6	0	1	4	0	35
2nd Irish Guards	2	2	5	1	1	1	1	3	1	17
2nd Royal Irish Regiment	2	19	5	5	1	0	2	1	0	35
5th Royal Irish Regiment	–	–	–	–	1	2	3	6	0	12
7th Royal Irish Regiment	0	31	1	0	0	2	1	2	0	37
8th Royal Irish Regiment	0	0	0	0	0	1	3	2	0	6
1st Royal Inniskilling Fusiliers	4	0	2	5	7	6	8	1	1	34
2nd Royal Inniskilling Fusiliers	3	5	2	6	2	3	2	0	0	23
5th Royal Inniskilling Fusiliers	–	–	–	–	4	0	0	0	0	4
6th Royal Inniskilling Fusiliers	–	–	–	4	4	6	12	6	0	32
7/8th Royal Inniskilling Fusiliers	0	66	0	0	3	3	1	4	2	79
9th Royal Inniskilling Fusiliers	4	2	2	4	1	0	2	0	0	15
13th Royal Inniskilling Fusiliers	–	–	–	–	1	4	7	8	4	24
1st Royal Irish Rifles	7	4	5	1	6	0	22	2	0	47
2nd Royal Irish Rifles	3	1	4	5	8	4	3	0	1	29
12th Royal Irish Rifles	2	1	2	5	2	7	3	1	1	24
15th Royal Irish Rifles	4	2	1	3	3	1	2	0	0	16
16th Royal Irish Rifles	2	2	1	4	2	0	7	2	1	21
1st Royal Irish Fusiliers	5	2	3	0	2	3	5	1	0	21
5th Royal Irish Fusiliers	–	–	–	4	1	2	3	2	0	12
9th Royal Irish Fusiliers	0	1	2	5	1	5	3	0	0	17
11th Royal Irish Fusiliers	–	–	–	–	–	4	1	0	0	5
5th Connaught Rangers	–	–	–	–	2	2	3	2	1	10
6th Connaught Rangers	2	2	2	0	0	0	–	–	–	6
2nd Leinster Regiment	1	2	7	6	8	5	10	2	5	46
6th Leinster Regiment	–	–	–	–	1	0	3	0	0	4
1st Royal Munster Fusiliers	1	1	4	5	2	2	1	0	4	20
2nd Royal Munster Fusiliers	1	0	0	1	1	9	9	1	0	22
1st Royal Dublin Fusiliers	1	1	5	6	4	7	11	0	1	36
2nd Royal Dublin Fusiliers	2	0	0	2	5	2	15	2	1	29
6th Royal Dublin Fusiliers	–	–	–	–	1	6	0	5	1	13
Totals	55	156	63	79	81	89	147	59	25	754

[a]For periods where dashes are entered, the unit was either serving in another theatre of war or had been disbanded.

there was a marked difference between regular and New Army units. For example, while the 1st Royal Dublin Fusiliers had 23 courts martial between 1 July and 11 November 1918, the 6th Royal Dublin Fusiliers (which, ironically, saw itself as a regular battalion in all but name[57]) had just 13. Likewise, while from the 1 March to 11 November 1918, the 1st Royal Irish Rifles had 47 men tried by court martial, the 12th Royal Irish Rifles had just 24, the 15th Royal Irish Rifles, 16 and the 16th Royal Irish Rifles, 21. The number of courts martial held in Irish cavalry regiments remained very low. Another point worth emphasising is the excellent disciplinary record in new Service battalions, converted from former garrison units. The 8th Royal Irish Regiment, 13th Royal Inniskilling Fusiliers and 11th Royal Irish Fusiliers all had relatively low numbers of courts martial, with 6, 24 and 5 cases respectively.

Miscellaneous and multiple offences still provided the bulk of courts martial cases in this period. However, drunkenness was accounting for significantly fewer courts martial cases post February 1918. Levels of insubordination and, with the exception of the 1st Royal Irish Rifles, disobedience, also fell after February 1918. Instances of cowardice also appear to have fallen. These statistics all suggest that, if anything, Irish units in the BEF were better disciplined in the March to November 1918 period than October 1916 to February 1918. This certainly suggests that discipline in the Irish units was not close to breaking point in November 1918.

There was no tightening in discipline post February 1918; sentences designed to deter potential offenders, i.e. death, penal servitude and hard labour were infrequently used, accounting for just eighteen of the 388 sentences passed in Irish units. The majority of sentences (121) consisted of field punishment number one. In the Irish units, the numbers of suspended (136) and not guilty (51) sentences were relatively high. These figures suggest that both officers sitting on courts martial and the High Command perceived no imminent breakdown of discipline and were, in most cases, prepared to award lenient sentences.

If these are the conclusions which can be drawn regarding discipline in Irish units post February 1918, it is much more difficult to assess morale. Certainly some of the Irish Service battalions were a shadow of their former selves. Captain C. A.

Brett, rejoining the 6th Connaught Rangers in August 1918 stated, 'I must say that we, in the then 6th. Battalion, were a very poor lot compared with the 6th. Battalion as I had known it. I expect one who had been in it before the massacre of Guillemont and Guinchy [sic.] in 1916 (before I joined it) felt much the same on rejoining it six months after.'[58] Not surprisingly, given this situation, this battalion was disbanded in August 1918, some of its personnel being sent to the 5th Connaught Rangers.[59]

The situation in other Irish battalions was much better. Major Guy Nightingale writing of the 1st Royal Munster Fusiliers stated, 'The men are full of delight ... Everyone is very cheery, but if only we could get recruits ourselves + the Gov[ernmen]t. allow the few Irish, who are fighting to be allowed a share in some of the praise, everything would be tophole.'[60] Likewise, in October 1918 Captain N. E. Drury felt that there were no morale problems in the 6th Royal Dublin Fusiliers, noting, 'the General (Hunter) came round to have a decko [look] round and seemed rather surprised to see all the men shaving and washing and togging [dressing?] up a bit after the shelling last night. Seemed to think our morale was pretty good and so it is. It's a good thing to boast a little on suitable occasions, and we told him he would have to be up very early to catch the Blue Caps dirty or unshaved.'[61]

Comments on the reaction of soldiers in Irish units to news of the Armistice suggests that morale remained high in these battalions up to the very end of the war. Captain Drury wrote that his CO informed him of the Armistice stating, 'I don't know what I feel, but somehow its like when one heard of the death of a friend – a sort of forlorn feeling. I went along and read out the order to the men, but they just stared at me and showed no enthusiasm at all. One or two just muttered "We were just getting a bit of our own back." They all had the look of hounds whipped off just as they were about to kill.'[62] Nightingale encountered a similar reaction in the 1st Royal Munster Fusiliers, 'Nothing happened. We had parades till 12.30 as usual + then came back to dinners + there was no excitement.'[63] There was a similar reaction in the 1st Royal Dublin Fusiliers, where, 'the announcement that the war was really over was received by the battalion with extraordinary calm.'[64] In the 2nd Leinster Regiment there was also little rejoicing at the news of the

Armistice, as Captain Hitchcock remembered, 'we all felt as if a great weight had been lifted off our shoulders', most men in the Battalion merely discussed their dead comrades and the likelihood of the Battalion being sent to India.[65] In the 36th (Ulster) Division there appears to have been more excitement over the Armistice. The 1st Royal Irish Fusiliers celebrated with a rugby match, while the fife and drum bands of the 9th Royal Irish Fusiliers played and fireworks were set off.[66] These responses, while varied, suggest that morale in battalions of the Irish regiments remained high until the Armistice.

The broader picture appears to suggest that the experience of the Irish units is not atypical of that of the BEF as a whole. From 1 March to 11 November 1918 the sample of eleven non-Irish battalions had an average of 16.6 men tried by courts martial. These figures are somewhat skewed by the inclusion of the 1st AIF which had sixty-nine cases and the 1st Border Regiment which had thirty cases. The number of courts martial cases was particularly low during the so-called '100 days' immediately proceeding the Armistice, only seventy-two of the 183 cases occuring over this period. There may, of course, be purely practical reasons for this, namely that with the return of open warfare, it was more difficult to convene a court martial. Also, the prospect of victory may have meant that many officers were unwilling to bring charges against men, especially wartime volunteers or conscripts, who would be demobilised shortly after hostilities ceased. Even more surprising are the figures for men tried by courts martial on the Western Front while serving in the reconstituted 16th Division. Between 1 August (when the Division 'returned' to the Western Front) and 11 November 1918, the Division had a total of only seventeen courts martial cases. Three of the battalions, the 9th Black Watch, 14th Leicestershire Regiment and 34th London Regiment had no courts martial over this period and the 5th Royal Irish Fusiliers, with the worst record in the Division, had a mere seven cases. This demonstrates that British infantry battalions retained high levels of discipline and morale, even when transferred from one formation to another. It also demonstrates that, perhaps, divisional loyalty was never as strong as battalion or regimental loyalty, given that only one battalion in the reformed 16th Division (the 11th Hampshire Regiment) had served in it before March 1918.

These high levels of discipline and morale in Irish and, indeed, BEF units generally are even more surprising when we consider that, as discussed in chapter one, methods planned by the army to maintain morale could not be put into effect due to the re-emergence of open warfare. That is not to say that the government or high command did not entertain fears regarding troop morale. In June 1918 the Director of Personnel Services at the War Office was expressing concern regarding trades union activity in the BEF[67] There was also concern, at least in Fourth Army, that the German 'peace offensive', 'may partly achieve its object of diverting the attention of officers and men from their task of defeating the enemy'.[68]

However, even without activities organised by the High Command, regimental, brigade and divisional games remained to boost morale. For example, 1 Royal Munster Fusiliers had a regimental boxing match on 1 May 1918,[69] while the 6th Royal Dublin Fusiliers organised an officers versus sergeants soccer match in July 1918.[70] Likewise, the 86th Brigade held a boxing match on 16 July and the 29th Division organised a horse show and football match on 9 July 1918.[71] There is also some evidence to suggest that paternalism survived throughout the war, which may have helped to boost morale. For example, in June 1918, Major Guy Nightingale asked his mother to send him hockey sticks and shorts for the men under his command.[72]

The Irish regiments and the BEF as a whole appear to have suffered from few serious disciplinary or morale problems during March to November 1918. The performance of the 16th (Irish) and 36th (Ulster) Divisions on 21 March 1918 was not excellent, but compares favourably with that of other divisions in the Fifth Army. The mutiny in the 49th Brigade, 16th (Irish) Division in April 1918 must, of course, be seen as a breakdown in discipline. However, the causes of this mutiny do not appear to have been inspired by political motives. Indeed, this mutiny, apparently opposing the disbandment of battalions in the 49th Brigade, actually demonstrated high *esprit de corps*. The lenient sentences awarded to the mutineers and the survival of the 7th Royal Irish Regiment and 7/8th Royal Inniskilling Fusiliers until the end of the war, suggest that this mutiny had its desired effect.

Discipline in the entire BEF does not seem to have been facing serious problems. Indeed, during the '100 days' when British casualties were appallingly high, discipline appears to have improved. Morale is, of course, much more difficult to assess; however, reactions of soldiers serving in Irish regiments to the Armistice suggest that, in some cases, men felt cheated of victory and, indeed, would have been prepared to fight on.

Perhaps the most surprising aspect of this period is that, not only did units decimated in March 1918 reform successfully, but that units hastily transferred from Home Service and the Middle East, actually appear to have relished service in France. The reformed 16th Division, with obviously no divisional loyalties to play on, and composed of battalions from throughout the United Kingdom, had a commendable disciplinary record while serving on the Western Front from August to November 1918.

Notes

1 R. Holmes, *Firing Line* (Pimlico, London, 1994), p. 319.

2 P. Simkins, 'Co-Stars or Supporting Cast? British Divisions in the "Hundred Days", 1918', in P. Griffith (ed.), *British Fighting Methods in the Great War* (Frank Cass, London, 1996), pp. 60–2.

3 B. Rawling, *Surviving Trench Warfare: Technology and the Canadian Corps, 1914–1918* (University of Toronto Press, London, 1992), especially, pp. 216–17.

4 PRO, CAB45/192, letter, Congreve to Edmonds, 6 January 1927.

5 PRO, CAB45/140, letter, Gough to Edmonds, 3 May 1944.

6 R. Blake (ed.), *The Private Papers of Douglas Haig, 1914–19* (Eyre and Spottiswoode, London, 1952), p. 296.

7 PRO, WO95/1956, war diary of the General Staff, 16th (Irish) Division, report to XVIII Corps by Major General C. P. A. Hull, 5 April 1918.

8 T. Johnstone, *Orange, Green and Khaki: The Story of the Irish Regiments in the Great War, 1914–18* (Gill and Macmillan, Dublin, 1992), p. 371; T. Denman, *Ireland's Unknown Soldiers: The 16th (Irish) Division in the Great War, 1914–1918* (Irish Academic Press, Dublin, 1992), pp. 153–70; and L. S. Lemisko, 'Politics, Performance and Morale: 16th (Irish) Division, 1914–18', unpublished MA thesis, University of Calgary, Canada, 1992, p. 118.

9 Denman, *Ireland's Unknown Soldiers*, pp. 154–7.

10 Lemisko, 'Politics, Performance and Morale', p. 118.

11 Denman, *Ireland's Unknown Soldiers*, p. 157; Lemisko, 'Politics, Performance and Morale', p. 120; M. Middlebrook, *The Kaiser's Battle, 21 March 1918: The First Day of the German Spring Offensive* (Penguin, London, 1978), p. 200.

12 T. Travers, *How the War was Won: Command and Technology in the British Army on the Western Front, 1917–1918* (Routledge, London, 1992), pp. 56–60. See also, I. F. W. Beckett, 'Hubert Gough, Neill Malcolm and Command on the Western Front', in B. Bond (ed.), *'Look to your Front': Studies in the First World War* (Spellmount, Staplehurst, 1999), p. 9.

13 NAM, 7707–12, 'Statement by Desmond MacWeeney, M.C., of the 6th Batt[allio]n. The Connaught Rangers on the events of 21st March, 1918' and R. Feilding, *War Letters to a Wife: France and Flanders, 1915–19* (The Medici Society, London, 1929), p. 266.

14 PRO, PRO30/71/3, Major Guy Nightingale papers, letter, Nightingale to his mother, 22 March 1918.

15 Denman, *Ireland's Unknown Soldiers*, p. 172.

16 I. F. W. Beckett and K. Simpson (eds.), *A Nation in Arms: A Social Study of the British Army in the First World War* (Manchester University Press, 1985), pp. 235–6.

17 Denman, *Ireland's Unknown Soldiers*, p. 172.

18 Altogether 116 men of the 2nd and 7th Royal Irish Regiment, 7/8th Royal Inniskilling Fusiliers and 49th Company, Machine Gun Corps were charged with mutiny, of whom ten were found not guilty. These men were tried on 13 to 15 April 1918, suggesting that this mutiny occurred in early April 1918.

19 For example, Major Nightingale believed that the 1st Royal Munster Fusiliers, 'would do grandly', if conscription was introduced in Ireland. PRO, PRO30/71/3, Nightingale papers, letter, Nightingale to his mother, 7 September 1918.

20 PRO, WO95/1957, A. A. Q. M. G. 16th (Irish) Division, war diary, entry for 16 April 1918.

21 Johnstone, *Orange, Green and Khaki*, p. 399.

22 P. Adam-Smith, *The ANZACS* (Hamish Hamilton, London, 1978), pp. 320–1.

23 Johnstone, *Orange, Green and Khaki*, p. 394.

24 PRO, PRO30/71/3, Nightingale papers, letter, Nightingale to his mother, 24 April 1918.

25 Denman, *Ireland's Unknown Soldiers*, p. 166.

26 M. Samuels, *Command or Control? Command, Training and Tactics in the British and German Armies, 1888–1918* (Frank Cass, London, 1995), pp. 255–62.

27 *Ibid.*, p. 267; and C. Falls, *The History of the 36th (Ulster) Division*

(Constable, London, 1996. McCaw, Stevenson and Orr, Belfast, 1922), p. 195.

28 N. Perry, 'Maintaining Regimental Identity in the Great War: The Case of the Irish Infantry Regiments', *Stand To*, 52, 1998, p. 8.

29 IWM, 83/3/1, Captain C. C. Miller, 'A Letter from India to my daughters in England', pp. 30–1.

30 PRONI, MIC/571/11, Farren Connell papers, statements by Sergeant A. Rice and Private Magee, relating to 21 and 22 March 1918.

31 IWM, MISC.124/item 1918, Report by Lieutenant Colonel Cole Hamilton, Karlsruhe Camp, 31 March 1918.

32 IWM, 83/3/1, Captain C. C. Miller, 'A Letter from India', p. 37.

33 PRONI, D.2794/1/1/34, letter, Montgomery to his parents, 1 April 1918.

34 LC, T. H. Witherow, 'Personal Recollections of the Great War', pp. 38–40.

35 Falls, *The 36th (Ulster) Division*, pp. 244–5 and 305–9.

36 PRO, CAB45/192, letter, N. Cochrane to Edmonds, 16 April 19?, cited in T. Travers, *How the War was Won*, p. 55.

37 Denman, *Ireland's Unknown Soldiers*, p. 172; Johnstone, *Orange, Green and Khaki*, p. 395; and Perry, 'Maintaining Regimental Identity', p. 9.

38 Anon., *A Short Record of the Services and Experiences of the 5th Battalion, Royal Irish Fusiliers in the Great War* (Helys Ltd., Dublin, 1919), p. 36.

39 NAM, 7607/69/5A, Captain Drury's diaries, entry for 20 July 1918.

40 LC, recollections of Private G. T. Nevell, pp. 2–3; and Anon., *A Short Record of the Services and Experiences of the 5th Battalion, Royal Irish Fusiliers*, p. 36.

41 LC, T. H. Witherow, 'Personal Recollections of the Great War', p. 44.

42 K. Grieves, *The Politics of Manpower, 1914–18* (Manchester University Press, 1988), p. 196.

43 E. A. James, *British Regiments, 1914–18* (Samson Books, London, 1978), p. 71.

44 *Ibid.*, p. 107.

45 *Ibid.*, p. 61 and S. Geoghegan, *The Campaigns and History of the Royal Irish Regiment, vol. II, From 1900 to 1922* (William Blackwood & Sons Ltd., Edinburgh and London, 1927), p. 127.

46 Johnstone, *Orange, Green and Khaki*, p. 394.

47 PRO, PRO30/71/3, Nightingale papers, letter, Nightingale to his mother, 24 April 1918.

48 D. Fitzpatrick, *Politics and Irish Life, 1913–21: Provincial Experience of War and Revolution* (Gill and Macmillan, Dublin, 1977), p. 65.

49 E. Mercer, 'For King, Country and a Shilling a Day: Recruitment in

Belfast during the Great War, 1914–18', unpublished MA dissertation, The Queens University of Belfast, 1998, p. 35.

50 The Earl of Middleton, *Records and Reactions, 1856–1939* (John Murray, London, 1939), p. 250; and Grieves, *The Politics of Manpower*, p. 191.

51 A. J. Ward, 'Lloyd George and the 1918 Irish Conscription Crisis', *Historical Journal*, XVII, 1, 1974, p. 111.

52 CAB23/5/75, cited in R. J. Q. Adams and P. P. Poirer, *The Conscription Controversy in Great Britain 1900–18* (State University Press, Ohio, 1987), p. 283.

53 *Ibid.*, p. 283.

54 PRO, WO32/9556, cited in Grieves, *The Politics of Manpower*, p. 191.

55 NAM, 7607–69–4, Captain N. E. Drury diaries, entry for 15 July 1918.

56 NAM, 7607–69–5A, Captain N. E. Drury diaries, entry for 12 July 1918.

57 For example, Captain Drury consistently referred to the 6th Royal Dublin Fusiliers as the 'Blue Caps', a term associated with the 1st Royal Dublin Fusiliers. NAM, 7607–69–4, Drury diaries, entry for 11 October 1918.

58 NAM, 7608–40, C. A. Brett, 'Recollections', p. 37.

59 *Ibid.*, p. 37 and James, *British Regiments, 1914–18*, p. 107.

60 PRO, PRO30/71/3, Nightingale papers, letter, Nightingale to his mother, 7 September 1918.

61 NAM, 7607–69–4, Drury diaries, entry for 11 October 1918.

62 NAM, 7607–69–4, Drury diaries, entry for 11 November 1918.

63 PRO, PRO30/71/3, Nightingale papers, letter, Nightingale to his mother, 18 November 1918.

64 H. C. Wylly, *Neill's 'Blue Caps': The History of the First Battalion, Royal Dublin Fusiliers vol. III, 1914–22* (Gale and Polden, Aldershot, 1925), p. 123.

65 F. C. Hitchcock, *'Stand To', A Diary of the Trenches, 1915–18* (Hurst and Blackett, London, 1937. Reprinted by Gliddon Books, London, 1988), p. 314.

66 M. Cunliffe, *The Royal Irish Fusiliers, 1793–1950* (Oxford University Press, 1952), p. 361.

67 PRO, WO83/31, letter, Judge Advocate General to Director of Personnel Services, 21 June 1918, pp. 669–70.

68 NAM, 7607–69–4, Drury diaries, entry of 21 to 31 October 1918, citing a confidential letter of 8 October.

69 PRO, PRO30/71/3, Nightingale papers, letter, Nightingale to his mother, 1 May 1918.

70 NAM, 7607–69–5A, Drury diaries, entry for 27 July 1918.

71 PRO, WO95/2301, war diary of the 1st Royal Dublin Fusiliers, entries for 9 July 1918 and 16 July 1918, war diary of the 1st Royal Dublin Fusiliers.

72 PRO, PRO30/71/3, Nightingale papers, letters of the 3 June 1918 and 11 June 1918 from Nightingale to his mother.

7

Irish units
on Home Service

It seems quite fashionable to refer to elements of the British army in the Great War as 'unknown'[1] and with justification this term could also be applied to the Irish Special and General Reserve battalions during the conflict. The neglect of these units is somewhat understandable. Most soldiers or officers writing their memoirs saw service in a reserve battalion as the prelude to more exciting, or at least purposeful, service in a regular or Service battalion, or as an unhappy interlude between being discharged from hospital and rejoining their own unit.[2] Some officers also resented the bizarre mess traditions in these units and, in some cases, the obvious incompetents who commanded them. As the war went on, reserve battalions increasingly became dumping grounds for officers who were too old, sick or incompetent to be allowed to command units on active service.

That many soldiers were not enamoured with their time in such units should not surprise us. The Special Reserve itself was a fairly botched compromise, especially in Ireland, resulting from the Haldane Reforms.[3] The decision not to establish Territorial Force units in Ireland meant that Irish regiments had a larger number of Special Reserve battalions than their counterparts in Great Britain, twenty in all. The original intention was that the senior Special Reserve battalions would carry out the somewhat contradictory roles of draft finding and coastal defence, while the junior battalions would serve overseas as complete units, to relieve colonial garrisons.[4] The situation was further complicated as the two Irish Yeomanry regiments, the

North and South Irish Horse were designated as Special Reserve units under the 1908 reforms, but with a clear role as reconnaissance troops for the original expeditionary force.[5]

The role of the Special Reserve battalions at the beginning of the war was unclear. Elaborate plans to garrison Ireland with Territorial troops, from the East and West Lancashire Divisions, during the war were set aside and the Special Reserve battalions were all allocated to home defence and training roles.[6] In August 1914, of the twenty Irish Special Reserve battalions, only two, the 4th and 5th Royal Dublin Fusiliers, were detailed for duty outside Ireland, in Sittingbourne, England.[7] However, in October 1914 plans emerged to convert Special Reserve battalions into Service battalions in the 4th New Army, although nothing actually came of these.[8] While in September 1914 some Special Reserve battalions were ordered to send twenty regular privates, suitable as drill instructors, to New Army divisions, an unusual request given the demand for instructors in Special Reserve battalions themselves. Despite early indecision over the role of reserve battalions they did perform a valuable service during the war in providing trained drafts for overseas service. Cyril Falls notes that during the entire war, the 3rd Royal Irish Rifles sent 8,069 men overseas, the 4th Royal Irish Rifles, 2,188 and the 5th Royal Irish Rifles, 1,934.[9] General Reserve battalions were formed from the depot companies of Service battalions in 1915 and performed broadly similar roles to Special Reserve battalions.

During the war, reserve battalions both had ill-defined and, at times, pointless roles in officer training. Men who had already passed through Sandhurst, or Officer Cadet battalions, were often sent to reserve battalions for a few months before being posted to a unit overseas. Those going through this process only appear to have learnt anything from it if they suceeded in being sent to specialist (i.e. musketry, machine-gun or signalling) schools.[10] Some reserve units also established what were often misleadingly termed 'cadet companies'. The one in the 3rd Royal Irish Regiment was certainly not an OTC, and seems to have been designed to enable middle-class recruits to enlist and serve together. Certainly Private A. R. Brennan who served in this unit was very shocked at his eventual posting in July 1915,

> In barracks in Dublin we had occupied quarters apart from the
> other companies [of the 3rd Royal Irish Regiment] and we had an
> idea that this practice would be followed even in France. On
> arrival at Acheux, however, our Company was broken up and we
> were drafted to different Companies. I suppose this was
> inevitable, but we were new to the Army then and some of us
> thought that it was a breech of faith.[11]

However, a similar 'Cadet Company' in the 17th Royal Irish
Rifles does seem to have been established as an OTC type unit
and at least four men were commissioned as a result of their
service in it.[12]

Training for other ranks was also deficient in these units, but
this was hardly surprising. The fluctuating size of these units
made training very difficult. For example, the 3rd Connaught
Rangers consisted of 32 officers and 1,194 other ranks in
December 1914, but 67 officers and 2,798 other ranks in July
1915.[13] The problems resulting from this were acknowledged by
Sergeant J. McIlwaine in February 1915, when, having been
wounded with the 2nd Connaught Rangers in France, he was
posted to the 3rd Connaught Rangers as a Company Sergeant
Major: 'I could never make out the Company, it was so big and
in such a condition of fluidity.'[14]

Incompetent, ill or elderly officers were hardly calculated to
turn out first-class soldiers and a number of these seem to have
ended up in reserve battalions. Posted to the 4th Royal Irish
Rifles in January 1916, having been wounded at Gallipoli, the
then Second Lieutenant David Campbell was far from
impressed with at least one of his seniors,

> I did not take very kindly to the life here. The Mess was ruled by
> the senior Subaltern who was also Mess President. He was a man
> well in his forties, and why he never got promotion was not
> revealed, nor why he was never sent to the front. He was a stick-
> ler for etiquette and discipline in the mess, a regular martinet and
> nothing pleased him more than to be given the opportunity [of]
> telling off some unfortunate who infringed a rule ... I am afraid
> we led a frivolous sort of life. We had practically no duties or
> responsibilities.[15]

Similarly, Second Lieutenant A. M. Jameson, serving in the 5th
Leinster Regiment noted in March 1916, 'There are rumours that

the C.O. is going to resign – I wish he would he [is?] a sly under-
hand old Girl, knows nothing about anything, and altogether a
bluggy [sic] old fool.'[16]

These were by no means isolated examples. When officers
were found incompetent for active service, the easiest course of
action was for their CO to have them reassigned to a reserve
battalion, as this did not require either a court martial or the
officer to be deprived of his commission. As noted in chapter 4
this happened in the case of a number of officers in the 36th
(Ulster) Division. An excellent example of this is the case of
Captain E. R. Kennedy, who Lieutenant Colonel R. T. Pelly of
the 8th Royal Irish Rifles felt to be 'too nervous' for service in the
trenches. Incredibly, the CO of the 17th Royal Irish Rifles,
Lieutenant Colonel H. T. Lyle, who himself had been removed
of the command of the 8th Royal Irish Rifles, actually requested
Kennedy's services for his battalion, stating, 'I have known this
officer since September, 1914. He is painstaking and conscien-
tious in all his work, and he is the stamp of Officer required in a
Reserve Battalion.'[17] A similar example is the case of Captain
J. M. Henderson of the 8th Royal Irish Rifles. Henderson was
found to be suffering from shell shock and in December 1915
was attached to the 17th Royal Irish Rifles. Writing about
Henderson's duties, Brigadier General G. W. Hacket Pain, in
temporary command of the 15th (Ulster) Reserve Infantry
Brigade, stated, '[Captain Henderson] has been placed as second
in command of a Company and is assisting in the interior
economy of that Company. He attends no route marches nor
does he perform any other arduous duties.'[18]

Not surprisingly, officers of this calibre often offered very
poor quality training. In March 1917, Captain Staniforth
commenting on his posting to the 4th Leinster Regiment[19]
stated, 'They've given me B Company to play around with, but
as far as I can see nobody ever dreams of doing any work or
attending any parades whatever, leaving it all to the NCOs. One
subaltern hasn't been on parade yet, and he arrived over six
months ago ... or so he says.'[20] Major General Oliver Nugent
was so dissatisfied at the drafts which the 36th (Ulster) Division
was receiving in late 1917 that he asked one of his staff officers,
while on leave, to inspect the Division's reserve formations.
Nugent wrote to Brigadier General G. W. Hacket Pain,

The gist of Mudie's report was that young officers are not taught their duties as regards their personal responsibility towards their men … I might mention that a number of wounded officers returned to the Division after a tour of duty with the Reserve Brigade to whom I have spoken, make the same comment, viz. that such experience as they have gained out here is not made use of for purposes of instruction at home.[21]

The strengths and weaknesses of the Irish reserve battalions were shown most starkly during the Easter Rising of 1916. All units, to their credit, rapidly mobilised and, indeed, it was the swift action of reserve units, such as the 3rd Royal Irish Rifles and 10th Royal Dublin Fusiliers which contained the rebellion in central Dublin and denied the rebels access to some key buildings, such as the Bank of Ireland, telephone exchange and electricity generating station.[22] These battalions also incurred relatively heavy losses. The 3rd Royal Irish Rifles, which could muster just 200 men at the start of the Rising, lost 1 officer and 6 other ranks killed and 4 officers and 29 other ranks wounded.[23] Outside Dublin, reserve battalions formed mobile columns which supported the RIC in arresting suspected rebels.[24]

The weaknesses of these reserve battalions were clearly demonstrated. Second Lieutenant A. M. Jameson, writing of his experiences in the 5th Leinster Regiment noted, 'You'll hardly believe it, but of myself + 10 men in A [company?], only three of us could shoot at all most of the others were newly joined recruits + had never fired a shot so all my time was taken up with potting.' More seriously, Jameson noted that the men in his piquet took an attack of 'funk' and, 'lossed [sic] off any amount of ammunition at nothing'.[25]

The most glaring weakness of any reserve battalion was shown in the 3rd Royal Irish Rifles. Captain Bowen-Colthurst's murder of four unarmed civilians, most notably the well-known Dublin pacificist, Francis Sheehy Skeffington, and his subsequent court martial and confinement to Broadmoor Criminal Lunatic Asylum was a *cause célèbre* at the time and has been recounted by a number of historians since.[26] Certainly, Bowen-Colthurst's actions were a serious breach of discipline, but what was even more concerning from a disciplinary point of view was that officers in the 3rd Royal Irish Rifles seemed incapable of restraining Bowen-Colthurst. The Royal Commission into the murders, which has, incredibly, been overlooked by most historians of the Rising, came to a number of disturbing conclusions. Most of the officers in the Battalion were young second lieutenants or lieutenants and seemed to be overawed by Bowen-Colthurst, a regular captain who had seen active service. More worryingly, officers of the Battalion seemed unclear what powers a declaration of martial law gave them and condoned Bowen-Colthurst's actions in taking civilian 'hostages' with him on raids. Finally, in the absence of Colonel McCammond, who was seriously ill, command of the Battalion devolved upon Major Rossborough, who seemed unwilling to take action against Bowen-Colthurst as 'Captain Bowen-Colthurst was the senior captain in the barracks, and, although not the equal in rank, was of longer standing and of greater experience in the Army than Major Rosborough.'[27] Unfortunately, such illegal acts may not have been isolated, as General Maxwell noted,

> possibly, some unfortunate incidents which we should regret now may have occurred ... It is even possible that under the horrors of this attack some of [the troops] 'saw red'; that is an unfortunate consequence of a rebellion of this kind. It was allowed to come into being among these people and could not be surpressed by velvet glove methods.[28]

There appear to have been no problems of disloyalty with Irish soldiers during the Rising. Indeed a number of soldiers on leave in Dublin at the time reported to the nearest reserve battalion. Thus Sergeant J. Barror of the 3rd Connaught Rangers attached himself to the 5th Royal Dublin Fusiliers and Sergeant C. Leeson, also of the 3rd Connaught Rangers attached himself to the 3rd Royal Irish Rifles.[29] Similarly, a number of soldiers from different regiments reported for duty at Portobello Barracks.[30] The courts martial records of four reserve battalions examined for this period, namely, the 3rd Royal Irish Regiment, 3rd Royal Irish Rifles, 18th Royal Irish Rifles and 4th Royal Dublin Fusiliers did not rise spectacularly following the Rising, as demonstrated in graph 7.1. The number of courts martial in the 4th Royal Dublin Fusiliers reached a peak of seventeen cases in January 1917 and declined fairly steadily from then until the end of the war, and a similar pattern occurred in the 3rd Royal Irish Regiment. The 3rd Royal Irish Rifles saw a very high

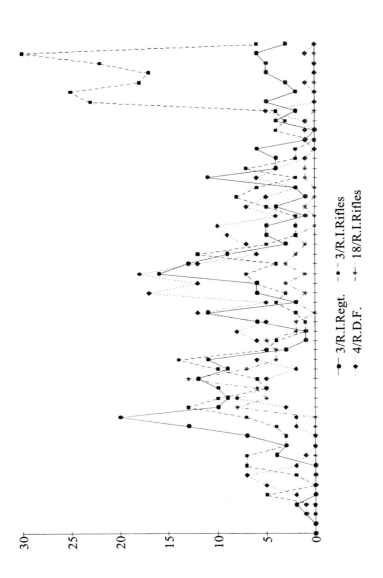

Figure 7.1. The courts martial records of selected Irish reserve battalions, 4 August 1914 to 11 November 1918

3/R.I.Regt. 3/R.I.Rifles
4/R.D.F. 18/R.I.Rifles

number of courts martial post April 1918, reaching a peak of thirty cases in October 1918 alone. It would seem likely that this occurred simply due to the increased strength of the Battalion, following the disbandment of other reserve battalions of the Royal Irish Rifles in early 1918. It is also worth noting, that most cases concerned absence without leave or drunkenness, not cases with any political overtones.

Nevertheless, disciplinary concerns may have accounted for the removal of most of the Southern Irish regiments' Special and General Reserve battalions from Ireland in late 1917. In November 1917 the Special Reserve and General Reserve battalions of the Connaught Rangers, Leinster Regiment, Royal Munster Fusiliers and Royal Dublin Fusiliers were all moved to Great Britain. The Special Reserve battalions of the Royal Irish Regiment, Royal Inniskilling Fusiliers, Royal Irish Rifles and Royal Irish Fusiliers all left Ireland in April 1918.

The removal of all remaining Irish reserve battalions from Ireland in April 1918 is simply explained by the fact that it was not felt helpful to have Irish units enforcing conscription if it was introduced in Ireland.[31] However, the reasons for the move of twelve Irish reserve battalions in November 1917 are more complex. Certainly, at the time, a number of officers believed that disloyalty in Irish units was responsible for the transfer. J. H. M. Staniforth, then serving with the 4th Leinster Regiment, commented, 'All the Irish battalions have been moved out of Ireland and replaced by English troops to prevent Sinn Fein contagion.'[32] Meanwhile, Second Lieutenant P. J. Mansfield, whose unit, the 3rd Cameron Highlanders, had been sent to Ireland in November 1917, noted,

> Without any previous warning, the whole of the troops in Ireland (i.e. Irish troops) were shifted over to Scotland in one night, and all Scottish troops sent over here, the reasons being (1) The increased activity of the Sinn Feiners (2) the proposal to bring conscription into Ireland, in which latter case, the Irish troops were considered by the higher authorities to be unreliable in the case of their being ordered to fire on their own countrymen – hence the importation of Scotchmen to do the dirty work.[33]

However, there appears to be little evidence to suggest that Irish reserve battalions were transferred to Britain due to actual subversion. Indeed, Sergeant J. McIlwaine, then serving with the 3rd Connaught Rangers was dismissive of the reasons for his battalion's move, believing that his superiors had 'Wind up about the Sinn Fein agitation'.[34] Such fears of Sinn Fein infiltration do seem rather baseless and since the outbreak of the war, Irish Republicans had simply opposed recruitment, seeing those who enlisted as at best misguided and at worst traitors. For example, James Connolly referred to Irish recruits as 'these poor misguided brothers of ours [who] have been tricked and deluded into giving battle for England'.[35] Roger Casement suggested that recruits were 'Not Irishmen but English soldiers'.[36] It therefore appears that Sinn Fein, or other advanced nationalist groups, had no concerted policy of attempting to infiltrate Irish units of the British army, seeing men in them as already lost to the Republican cause. In this respect Sinn Fein differed greatly from earlier Republican groups, notably the Fenian movement in the 1860s.[37] More recent fears of 1914 may also have been relived by the military authorities. Between March and July 1914 there was considerable concern that, in the event of Home Rule being implemented, large numbers of Special Reservists would defect to the UVF.[38]

One type of crime which appears to have been increasing in 1917 was the theft of Irish soldiers' rifles by Irish Volunteers.[39] In the 3rd Royal Inniskilling Fusiliers measures were taken to prevent this in November 1917, when a battalion order was introduced which meant that all rifles had to be returned to store rooms by 5 p.m. each day and that each store room would be guarded by one NCO and three privates.[40] The worst example of rifle stealing occurred in November 1917, in Longford, when 200 rifles were stolen from the 11th Royal Dublin Fusiliers.[41] How exactly this theft occurred is unclear. Captain Terence Poulter, a former officer in the Battalion, wrote sixty-seven years after the event that men of the Longford IRA had infiltrated the Battalion.[42] Nevertheless, it appears unlikely that infiltration was on anything but a very small scale, as in a report to the War Cabinet,

> Lord French reported that, in regard to the unit most concerned with the recent loss of rifles [11th Royal Dublin Fusiliers] this unit had paraded for embarkation with only two absentees, which pointed to the fact that the loyalty and discipline of the unit were

not seriously affected, and the loss of arms could not be attributed to treacherous or seditious action.[43]

Violence against Irish soldiers also appears to have been on the increase in 1917. J. H. M. Staniforth, writing of the situation in Limerick, noted, 'This town in particular is a nest of Sinn Feinery, and our men won't go through the riverside streets after dark unless there are two or three of them together.'[44] The situation in Dublin was little better; Lieutenant General Sir Bryan Mahon, the GOC in Ireland noted in June 1917, 'In addition to many other unsatisfactory indications, several cases have recently been reported to me of abuse and hostile demonstrations being levelled against the Troops in Dublin when proceeding on their normal duties through the streets.'[45] It appears that soldiers in Cork were also being attacked on a frequent basis.[46]

The poor quality of training in Irish reserve battalions may have partially accounted for the move to England. While most barracks in Ireland were small and widely dispersed, when the Irish reserve battalions were moved to England they were concentrated at Oswestry, a large camp with good facilities, where more uniform training could be carried out. More importantly, the point must be made that the downturn in Irish recruiting removed one of the *raisons d'être* for Irish reserve battalions staying in Ireland. Rifleman Hutchinson, serving in the 18th Royal Irish Rifles in 1917 and 1918, noted that many of his comrades were English or Scottish conscripts.[47] When a number of Irish reserve units were disbanded in England, this appears to have simply been in response to recruiting difficulties. Cyril Falls noted that the 17th, 18th and 19th Royal Irish Rifles were disbanded and their personnel sent to the 3rd Royal Irish Rifles in April 1918 as 'There were no longer anything like the number of Irish recruits to fill the ranks of so many battalions.'[48]

Therefore, as with Irish battalions on overseas service, there is little to suggest that reserve battalions exhibited Sinn Fein sympathies. The courts martial record of reserve units was broadly in line with that of other Irish units. The disciplinary problems in reserve units had more to do with incompetent officers and the high turnover of personnel than the work of

Republican agitators, and the move of these units to Great Britain in late 1917 and early 1918 was based more on recruiting problems and training needs, than fears of Sinn Fein infiltration.

Notes

1 I. F. W. Beckett, 'The Real Unknown Army: British Conscripts, 1916–19', in J. J. Becker and S. Audoin-Rouzeau (eds.), *Les Sociétiés Européennes et la Guerre de 1914–18* (Université de Paris X-Nanterre, Paris, 1990); G. Dallas and D. Gill, *The Unknown Army: Mutinies in the British Army in World War I* (Verso, London, 1985); and T. Denman, *Ireland's Unknown Soldiers: The 16th (Irish) Division in the Great War, 1914–18* (Irish Academic Press, Dublin, 1992).

2 See, for examples, LC, Second Lieutenant T. H Witherow, 'Personal Reflections of the Great War', p. 1; and IWM, 83/3/1, Captain C. C. Miller, 'A Letter from India to my daughters in England', p. 17.

3 R. Williams, *Defending the Empire: The Conservative Party and British Defence Policy 1899–1915* (Yale University Press, London, 1991), pp. 112–14.

4 J. K. Dunlop, *The Development of the British Army 1899–1914: From the Eve of the South African War to the Eve of the Great War, with Special Reference to the Territorial Force* (Methuen, London, 1938), p. 274.

5 E. M. Dorman, 'The North Irish Horse', *Army Review*, III, 1913.

6 PRO, WO32/7110, 'Mobilization of the Territorial Division allotted to Ireland'.

7 PRO, WO162/3, 'Allocation of Extra and Special Reserve Battalions to Defended Ports, etc., December 1914'.

8 PRO, WO162/3, 'New Armies Organisation, 1914 + 1915', letter War Office to GOC in Commands, 25 October 1914.

9 C. Falls, *The History of the First Seven Battalions, Royal Irish Rifles (Now the Royal Ulster Rifles) in the Great War* (Gale and Polden, Aldershot, 1925), p. 186.

10 IWMSA, 11214/1, interview with Colonel F. W. S. Jourdain.

11 IWM, P.262, diary of Private A. R. Brennan, entry for 1 August 1915.

12 LC, Second Lieutenant T. H. Witherow, 'Personal Reflections of the Great War', p. 1; PRO, WO339/44458, personal file of Second Lieutenant J. S. McMaster; PRO, WO339/45658, personal file of Second Lieutenant Samuel Mercer; PRO, WO339/57731, personal file of Captain H. G. Morrow; and PRO, WO339/67962, personal file of Second Lieutenant T. A. Valentine. I would like to thank Mr James Taylor for bringing these files to my attention.

13 PRO, WO79/40, 'Records of 3rd Connaught Rangers', entries for 31

December 1914 and 31 July 1915.

14 IWM, 96/29/1, diary of J. McIlwaine, 20 February 1915.

15 LC, diaries of Captain David Campbell, p. 29.

16 IWM, 98/13/1, papers of Second Lieutenant A. M. Jameson, letter, Jameson to his mother, 18[?] March 1916.

17 PRO, WO339/14322, personal file of Captain E. R. Kennedy, letters, Lieutenant Colonel R. T. Pelly to Staff Captain, 107th Brigade, 15 January 1916 and Lieutenant Colonel H. T. Lyle to Brigade Major, 15th (Ulster) Reserve Infantry Brigade, 10 July 1916.

18 PRO, WO339/14318, personal file of Captain J. M. Henderson, letter Brigadier General G. Hacket Pain to Secretary, War Office, 17 February 1916.

19 Staniforth had been invalided to Britain from the 7th Leinster Regiment, as he required extensive dental treatment, PRO, WO339/23115, personal file on Lieutenant [sic.] J. H. M. Staniforth.

20 IWM, 67/41/1, letter, Staniforth to his parents, 4 March 1917, cited, J. H. M. Staniforth, 'Kitchener's Soldier', p. 192.

21 PRONI, MIC/571/10, Farren Connel papers, undated letter (November 1917?) Nugent to Hacket Pain.

22 A brief account of the actions of the 3rd Royal Irish Rifles during the rebellion is given in *Standing Orders of the 3rd Battalion, Royal Irish Rifles* (Thomas Brough and Cox, Belfast, 1917), p. 13.

23 *Ibid.*, p. 14.

24 PRO, WO79/40, 'Records of 3rd Connaught Rangers', entries for 26 April 1916 to 26 May 1916.

25 IWM, 98/13/1, letter, Jameson to Fairdee, 2 May 1916.

26 F. Vane, *Agin the Governments* (Samson Low and Marston, London, 1928), pp. 262–8; M. T. Foy and B. Barton, *The Easter Rising* (Sutton Publishing, Stroud, 1999), pp. 190–2; and M. Caulfield, *The Easter Rebellion* (Gill and Macmillan, Dublin, 1995), pp. 161–2.

27 *The Report of the Royal Commission on the Arrest and Subsequent Treatment of Mr. Francis Sheehy Skeffington, Mr. Thomas Dickson and Mr. Patrick James McIntyre*, HMSO, London, 1916, Cmd.8376, especially pp. 11–12.

28 Cited in Barton and Foy, *Easter Rising*, p. 121.

29 PRO, WO79/40, 'Records of 3rd Connaught Rangers', entries for 26 April 1916 to 26 May 1916.

30 *The Report of the Royal Commission on the Arrest and Subsequent Treatment of Mr. Francis Sheehy Skeffington, Mr. Thomas Dickson and Mr. Patrick James McIntyre*, p. 11.

31 D. Fitzpatrick, *Politics and Irish Life, 1913–1921: Provincial Experience of War and Revolution* (Gill and Macmillan, Dublin, 1977), p. 26.

32 IWM, 67/41/3, letter, Staniforth to his parents, 7 December 1917.

33 PRO, WO83/30, Judge Advocate General's papers, letter, Second Lieutenant P. J. Mansfield to Dr B. O. A. Mansfield, 21 November 1917, p. 793.

34 IWM, 96/29/1, diary of J. McIlwaine, entry for 3 November 1917.

35 J. Connolly, 'The Slums and The Trenches', in J. Connolly, *Collected Works* (New Books Publications, Dublin, 1988), vol. II, p. 147.

36 T. P. Dooley, *Irishmen or English Soldiers? The Times and World of a Southern Catholic Irish Man (1876–1916) Enlisting in the British Army during the First World War* (Liverpool University Press, Liverpool, 1995), p. 1.

37 A. J. Semple, 'The Fenian Infiltration of the British Army', *Journal of the Society of Army Historical Research*, 52, 1974, p. 160.

38 PRO, WO141/4, 'Memo. on the situation in Ireland on the 31st March 1914 prepared in the Intelligence Section of the General Staff at Head Quarters, Irish Command', pp. 13–14 and PRO, WO141/26, extract from Inspector General's summary of Police Reports to 24 July 1913.

39 National Archives, Dublin, Chief Secretary's Office Registered Papers, 1917, entries 19147 and 25012.

40 Royal Inniskilling Fusiliers Museum, 'Battalion Orders for 3rd Royal Inniskilling Fusiliers', entry for 26 October 1917.

41 P. Callan, 'Voluntary Recruiting for the British Army in Ireland during the First World War' (PhD thesis, University College Dublin, 1984), p. 267.

42 *Irish Times*, 24 April 1984, cited, *ibid.*, p. 267.

43 PRO, WO32/9507, extract from War Cabinet 267, 9 November 1917, included in 'Measures to be taken with regard to unauthorized drilling of parties in Ireland'.

44 IWM, 67/41/1, letter, Staniforth to his parents, 14 March 1917, cited J. H. M. Staniforth, 'Kitchener's Soldier', p. 195.

45 PRO, WO32/9513, 'Report by Commander in Chief on the Situation in Ireland, 1917'.

46 National Archives, Dublin, Chief Secretary's Office Registered Papers, 1917, 28936. While this file entry is included in the catalogue of the Chief Secretary's Office it is not available, apparently having been destroyed at some stage in 1921–22.

47 PRONI, D.3804, J. Hutchinson, 'The Early Reminiscences of a Royal Irish Rifleman, 1917–19', pp. 19 and 24.

48 Falls, *The History of the First Seven Battalions, The Royal Irish Rifles*, p. 162.

Conclusion

This study of discipline and morale in the Irish regiments between 1914 and 1918 has shown that during the Great War, Irish soldiers committed a large number of disciplinary offences. This, in turn, questions the conclusions of some previous works on this subject.[1] In general terms, it appears that the number of men tried by courts martial was generally higher in Irish than in English, Scots or Welsh units. It appears that Irish soldiers were more likely to be involved in crimes involving drunkenness or serious indiscipline (which, of course, could be closely inter-related) and the number of mutinies committed in Irish units during the Great War appears to be out of proportion to the number of Irish units in the British army.

While the numbers of soldiers tried by courts martial in Irish units was generally higher than that in other British units, this does not necessarily mean that discipline was generally worse in Irish units. British army officers did see the Irish soldier as being distinct from his English counterpart and it does seem likely that Irish soldiers were tried by courts martial for offences where an English soldier would simply have appeared before his CO. On more specific issues attention must be given to the operation of British military law during the Great War, the differences between discipline in regular and New Army units, the political and manning pressures on Irish regiments, the differences between Irish units serving on the Western Front and in other theatres of war and, finally, the attempts made to maintain morale in Irish units during the Great War.

The operation of military law in the British army during the Great War was rather more just than some historians have allowed. This study has shown that most British soldiers appearing before courts martial during 1914 to 1918 were sentenced to nothing more severe than short terms of field punishment and executions were an unusual but at times necessary aspect of life in the Irish regiments during the Great War. On the rare occasions when executions were carried out 'for the sake of example', there is some evidence to suggest that this had the intended impact; for example, in the 107th Brigade of the 36th (Ulster) Division in early 1916.

During the entire war there was generally a clear distinction between regular and New Army battalions in disciplinary terms. Regular battalions largely had higher numbers of men tried by court martial than their New Army counterparts. Of course, there are exceptions to this rule, for example the 6th Connaught Rangers had a courts martial pattern which was similar to regular, rather than New Army, trends. In the early years of the war, this does seem to be easily explained. Many regular soldiers had committed offences in peacetime and thus were tried by courts martial when they re-offended on active service. By contrast, men serving in New Army units normally began the war with unblemished records and were initially punished by their CO rather than being referred to a court martial.

As the war went on, it is more difficult to account for this differentiation between regular and New Army battalions, especially as post 1916 both were receiving replacements from exactly the same sources. However, the initial attitude of New Army battalion COs may account for this difference. Many COs, especially in the 36th (Ulster) Division, recognised that they were dealing with 'temporary soldiers' and made allowances for this. For example, in the 14th Royal Irish Rifles, Lieutenant Colonel Chichester always referred to his men as 'Young Citizens' and the original Adjutant refused to have men tried by courts martial for desertion.[2] However, this recognition of 'citizen soldiers' was by no means universal. The high courts martial record in the 6th Connaught Rangers is directly attributable to the fact that this battalion's first CO, Lieutenant Colonel John Lenox-Conyngham, ran it like a regular battalion.[3]

This differentiation between New Army units merits some further comment. Lenox-Conyngham's methods appear to have been, at least initially, unpopular. No less than three mutinies occurred during the 6th Connaught Rangers' training period in Ireland. Nevertheless, Lenox-Conyngham was seen as an efficient CO by his subordinate officers,[4] and he survived the purge of senior officers in the 16th (Irish) Division in late 1915, presumably by Major General Hickie, the then GOC of the Division. Also, the 6th Connaught Rangers had an enviable combat record in France, their disbandment in 1918 being one of the last of Irish Service battalions and largely due to recruiting problems in Ireland. By contrast, the 14th Royal Irish Rifles, whose original CO took a more lenient view of indiscipline amongst his 'citizen soldiers', was not a successful combat unit. A good courts martial record in this battalion disguised a large number of leadership problems and when this unit was disbanded in 1917, Major General Oliver Nugent, GOC of the 36th (Ulster) Division, made it quite clear that this was due to its poor performance in action.[5]

An important point which has emerged from this study is that each battalion has its own distinctive courts martial record. When discussing morale and discipline in Irish units on the Western Front, the careers of fifty-six separate infantry battalions and six cavalry regiments are being examined, not one homogeneous body.

Social composition may also have affected discipline in New Army battalions. For example, in the 36th (Ulster) Division, the 14th Royal Irish Rifles was seen as socially superior to the other Belfast-raised battalions in this formation: the 8th, 9th, 10th and 15th Royal Irish Rifles.[6] This may, at least partially, account for the differing courts martial records in these units. It is also noticeable that commanders still prized Irish rural rather than urban recruits,[7] which may also have accounted for the varying court martial rates within divisions.

Political pressure was present in Irish units from the beginning of the war, and proved to be a very mixed blessing. Ulster Unionist support for the 36th (Ulster) Division did see this formation supplied with equipment, arms and some trained officers long before its sister divisions in 'K6'. However, this political support came at a high price. Many officers who were not fit for active service commands were appointed to the division more on the basis of their political contacts than their military capabilities. Two leading examples of this political jobbery are the appointments of Colonel Couchman, who had been the Belfast UVF commander, as the GOC of the 107th Brigade and Captain James Craig, MP as the Division's Assistant Adjutant and Quartermaster General, with the rank of Lieutenant Colonel. Couchman was removed from his command shortly after the 107th Brigade arrived in France due to the poor standard of training in this formation.[8] Meanwhile, Lieutenant Colonel James Craig was ill during most of 1915 and early 1916 and therefore unable to fulfill his duties in the 36th (Ulster) Division.[9] The politicisation of the 36th (Ulster) Division had other serious side-effects. The identification of the Division with the UVF meant that recruiting was hampered as Catholic recruits were reluctant to join this formation. Likewise the proposal that units in the Division should wear UVF style badges seemed to threaten the entire regimental system, which British army officers saw as essential in maintaining morale.

IPP influence on the 16th (Irish) Division was considerably less than that exerted by the Ulster Unionists on the 36th (Ulster) Division; however, it too led to problems. With the 47th Brigade being dubbed the 'Irish brigade' and appealing for recruits from the INV, the regimental recruiting system was thrown into chaos. While 600 INV from Belfast joined the 6th Connaught Rangers, the 7th Royal Irish Rifles, a Belfast-based unit in the less politically favoured 48th Brigade, was starved of recruits. Lieutenant General Sir Lawrence Parsons spent a considerable amount of time dealing with political issues such as to what units recruits were being posted, where officers came from and the badges used by the 16th (Irish) Division. This time could have been much better spent by Parsons in drawing up a proper training schedule for his division.

Post 1916 events in Ireland appear to have soured attitudes to Irish soldiers. While there is little evidence to suggest that soldiers in Irish units felt any sympathy for the Sinn Fein movement, Irish battalions were treated with mistrust by other units. This may partly account for the black propaganda campaign surrounding the retreat of the 16th (Irish) Division in March 1918. Certainly the removal of Irish Special Reserve battalions from Ireland in 1917 and 1918 and the almost indecent haste with which some Irish Service battalions were disbanded, does suggest that the War Office was concerned about Sinn Fein infiltration into Irish units, however little basis this had in reality.

During the Great War, Irish units, like most units of the BEF, faced serious manning problems. However, the decision not to introduce conscription in Ireland greatly exacerbated this problem. The impact of this was that many Irish Service battalions were reinforced with drafts from Great Britain and, then Irish regular battalions had to resort to a policy of 'cannibalising' their Service battalions for men. The effect of this on the disciplinary record of the Irish units is difficult to assess. Certainly, there was no drastic change in the courts martial patterns in Irish Service battalions when they received non-Irish drafts. Conversely, many officers and men in Service battalions resented the disbandment of their units. This resentment appears to have found expression in the mutiny of a large number of men in the 2nd and 7th Royal Irish Regiment, the 7/8th Royal Inniskilling Fusiliers and the 49th Company, Machine Gun Corps in April 1918 when their units were due to be reduced.

While in other regiments of the British army, the most junior battalions were disbanded first in the face of increasing manpower problems, this was not the case in Irish battalions. A number of Irish units appear to have been disbanded due to disciplinary, rather than recruiting problems. Thus, the 7th Royal Irish Rifles, the most senior Royal Irish Rifles Service battalion in France, was the first to be disbanded, largely due to disciplinary problems and feared Sinn Fein infiltration. By contrast, the 16th Royal Irish Rifles, the most junior service battalion of the Regiment in France, survived until the Armistice.

As examined in chapters 6 and 7 it appears, based on the sample of Irish units used, that troops serving in the United Kingdom or in other theatres of war were generally worse disciplined than those serving on the Western Front. Indeed, discipline drastically improved in battalions of the 10th (Irish) Division when they were transferred from the Middle East to France in 1918.

Troops serving in the United Kingdom appear to have had higher military crime rates for very good reasons. The closeness of home and familiarity with the area in which a unit was stationed meant that absence and desertion were more prevalent in reserve battalions. Soldiers must have been aware that the sentence for desertion while their unit was based in the United Kingdom would be much less harsh than when they were on active service.

With regard to soldiers serving in other theatres of war, the situation is more complicated. It does seem more than coincidental that Irish regular battalions, with good disciplinary records in France, were transferred to other theatres. Such units appear to have maintained good disciplinary records when serving elsewhere. By contrast, Irish Service battalions serving at Gallipoli, Salonika and in the Middle East appear to have, generally, experienced worse courts martial records than their sister Service battalions serving in France. One can only suppose that the extreme weather conditions, endemic malaria in Salonika and the feeling amongst troops that by fighting Turks and Bulgarians, they were not fighting the 'real' enemy, led to low morale which manifested itself in high levels of indiscipline.

As has been demonstrated, no concerted attempts were made by the High Command to address the issue of troop morale in the BEF. In the Irish regiments, a mixture of regimental traditions and battalion sports were utilised to improve morale. A number of officers procured gifts for their men and battalion chaplains aided morale, not only through the spiritual comfort which they afforded men, but also in more practical ways.

At the divisional level attempts were also made to improve morale. Both the 16th (Irish) and 36th (Ulster) Divisions, like other units of the BEF, organised divisional baths. The 36th (Ulster) Division had its own comforts fund and portable cinema. Divisional sports proved popular, while both divisions issued their own gallantry certificates to deserving officers and other ranks. To modern eyes, these measures may appear far from innovative; however, they generally seem to have been successful in maintaining morale in Irish units.

One must address the question of what the experience of the Irish units on the Western Front tells us about the experience of the BEF as a whole? The answer may well be very little. This study has demonstrated that discipline and morale varied at the battalion, let alone the brigade or divisional level. It would appear that, generally, Irish units had worse courts martial records than their English, Scottish or Welsh counterparts. Certainly, the number of mutinies which occurred in Irish units is out of all proportion to their number in the British army.

This study also suggests that morale remained high in the BEF throughout the war questioning the views of other historians that crises of morale occurred in the BEF during the winters of 1914/15 and 1917/18 and during and immediately after the German Spring Offensive of 1918. The introduction of conscription in Britain led to few disciplinary problems in the BEF; courts martial rates were much higher in 1914–15 than 1917–18.

In terms of morale, it is worth quoting the view of Major W. A. Montgomery, 9th Royal Irish Rifles, in August 1917, 'Morale. I have heard of it. It is taught. Thank God it just IS anywhere I have had to do with men up to now.'[10] It appears that Montgomery's comment could have been applied to almost any Irish unit serving on the Western Front at any point of the war. The unique British regimental system, officer–man relations in the British army, and the fact that the BEF did not reach its peak strength on the Western Front until 1916, all help to explain why the BEF, unlike most European armies during the Great War, did not face serious morale problems.

Notes

1 T. Denman, 'The Catholic Irish Soldier in the First World War: The "Racial Environment"', *Irish Historical Studies*, XXVII, 108, 1991, p. 360.
2 Royal Ulster Rifles Museum, Anon, 'Service with the 14th Battalion, Royal Irish Rifles (Young Citizen Volunteers), 1914–18 War', p. 42.
3 IWMSA, 11214/2, interview with Colonel F. W. S. Jourdain.
4 See Captain Stephen Gwynn's comments in, M. Lenox-Conyngham, *An Old Ulster House and the People who Lived in it* (Dundalgan Press, Dundalk, 1946), pp. 225–6.
5 PRONI, MIC/571/10, Farren Connell papers, letter, Nugent to the Adjutant General, 11 December 1917.
6 E. Mercer, 'For King, Country and a Shilling a Day: Recruitment in Belfast during the Great War, 1914–18', unpublished MA dissertation, Queen's University of Belfast, 1998, p. 10.
7 Letter, Lieutenant General Sir Lawrence Parsons to Mr Crilly

(undated but c.1915) cited, D. Gwynn, *The Life of John Redmond* (George G. Harrap & Co. Ltd., London, 1932), p. 400.

8 PRONI, D.3835/E/2/5/8, Farren Connell papers, letter, Nugent to his wife, 10 October 1915.

9 PRO, WO339/3792, personal file of Lieutenant Colonel James Craig.

10 PRONI, D.2794/1/1/30, letter, Major W. A. Montgomery to his parents, 17 August 1917.

Select bibliography

Primary sources

Archives

The Guildhall Library
Ms.17,684 and Ms. 17,686 papers relating to the Inns of Court OTC.

The House of Lords Record Office
David Lloyd George papers.

The Imperial War Museum
Armstrong papers; Beater papers; Brennan papers; Brett papers; Butterworth papers; Campbell papers; Carden-Roe papers; Cole-Hamilton papers; Colyer papers; Daubeny papers; Dobbyn papers; Doran papers; Fitzroy papers; Ford papers; French papers; Glanville papers; Godson papers; Kirkpatrick papers; Knott papers; Lake papers; Lynas papers; Lyons papers; McCarthy papers; MacDonnell papers; McElwaine papers; McIlwaine papers; McKay papers; McPeake papers; de Margry papers; May papers; Miller papers; Nicol papers; Nixon papers; O' Sullivan papers; Roser papers; Roworth papers; Staniforth papers; Starrett papers; Stewart-Moore papers; Sulman papers; Trefusis papers; Verschoyle papers; Weldon papers; Westmacott papers; Williams papers; Wood papers; Woodley papers; Woodroffe papers; Woods papers.

Imperial War Museum Sound Archives
Interviews with: Private Hugh James Adams; Private Edward Bowyer-Green; Private Walter Edward Collins; Private E. J. Furlong; Captain (?)

Sir Derrick Gunston; Private Harold Joseph Hayward; Colonel F. W. S. Jourdain; Private Victor Packer; Private Douglas Arthur Riddle; Major Terence Verschoyle.

Irish Labour History Museum and Archives
Cathal O'Shannon papers.

Jesuit Archives, Dublin
Father F. M. Browne papers; Father W. J. Farley papers; Father H. V. Gill papers; Father J. Gwynn papers; Father J. Wrafter papers.

Liddell Hart Centre for Military Archives
Jeffries papers; Lewis papers; Parsons papers.

Liddle Collection, University of Leeds
Brierly papers; D. Campbell papers; J. Campbell papers; Cripps papers; Downs papers; Faithful papers; Grange papers; Hobday papers; MacRoberts papers; Trousdell papers; Verschoyle papers; Witherow papers.
Interviews conducted by Peter H. Liddle with Major V. Holland, VC, tape 248; Major General Sir N. Holmes, tape 430; Private M. Kane, tape 579; Major Verschoyle.

Liverpool Record Office
Derby papers.

The National Army Museum
Ahern papers; Brett papers; Drury papers; Foster papers; Harrison papers; Holt papers; Jourdain papers; McConville papers; McPeake papers; Maconchy papers; MacWeeney papers; Mathews papers; Rawlinson papers; Rice papers; Richardson papers.

The National Library of Ireland
Kilmainham papers; Berkeley papers; Art O'Brien papers; Hickie papers; Moore papers; Parsons papers; Redmond papers.

The Public Record Office
Dublin Castle papers: CO 904; Kitchener papers: PRO 30/57; War Office papers: WO32, WO33, WO35, WO68, WO71, WO76, WO79, WO81, WO83, WO84, WO86, WO90, WO92, WO93, WO95, WO138, WO141, WO154, WO158, WO159, WO162, WO213, WO339; Midleton papers, PRO30/67; Nightingale papers, PRO30/71.

The Public Record Office of Northern Ireland
Adams papers; Anderson papers; Carrothers papers; Carson papers; Davidson papers; Farren Connell papers; Granard papers; Gwynn papers; Herdman papers; Hill papers; Hutchinson papers; Kelso papers; Kerr papers; McCrory papers; Maxwell papers; Montgomery papers; Nugent papers; Penrose papers; Richardson papers; Shaw papers; Spender papers; Stitt papers; Young Citizen Volunteers of Belfast papers; Young papers.

The Royal Inniskilling Fusiliers Museum
Battalion orders for the 3rd Royal Inniskilling Fusiliers; Armstrong papers; McCarter papers; McCrory papers; Ricardo papers; Wilson papers.

The Royal Irish Fusiliers Museum
Burrows papers; Warnock Armstrong papers.

The Royal Ulster Rifles Museum
Anon., 'Historical Records of the 13th Service Battalion of the Royal Irish Rifles'; Anon., 'Service with the 14th Battalion, Royal Irish Rifles (Young Citizen Volunteers), 1914–18 War'; Membership roll for 14th Royal Irish Rifles, 1914–15.

The Somme Heritage Centre, Newtownards
Collins papers, Johnstone papers, Smith papers.

Official publications

The General Annual Reports on the British Army (including the Territorial Force) for the period from 1 October 1913 to 30 September 1919, Cmd. 1193 (1921).

The Report of the Committee constituted by the Army Council to enquire into the Laws and Rules of Procedure Regulating Military Courts Martial, HMSO, Cmd. 428 (1919).

The Report on Men of Military Age in Ireland, Cmd. 8390 (1916).

The Report on the Rebellion in Ireland, Cmd. 8311 (1916).

The Report on Recruiting compiled by the Earl of Derby, Cmd. 8149 (1914–16).

The Report on Recruiting in Ireland, Cmd. 8168 (1914–16)

The Report of the Royal Commission on the Arrest and Subsequent Treatment of Mr. Francis Sheehy Skeffington, Mr. Thomas Dickson and Mr. Patrick James McIntyre, Cmd. 8376 (1916).

The Report of the Royal Commission on Capital Punishment, 1949–53, Cmd. 8932 (1953).

The Report of the War Office Committee of Enquiry into Shell Shock, Cmd. 1734 (1922).
War Office, *Statistics of the Military Effort of the British Empire during the Great War* (HMSO, London, 1922).
War Office, *Manual of Military Law, 1914* (HMSO, London, 1914).

Newspapers

Belfast Evening Telegraph
Belfast Newsletter
County Down Spectator and Ulster Standard
Freeman's Journal
The Incinerator (troop journal compiled by the 14th Royal Irish Rifles)
Irish News and Belfast Morning News
Irish Times
Northern Whig
The Times

Secondary sources

Books

Adams, R. J. Q. and Poirer, P. P., *The Conscription Controversy in Great Britain 1900–18* (State University Press, Ohio, 1987).
Adam-Smith, P., *The Anzacs* (Hamish Hamilton, London, 1978).
Addison, P. and Calder, A. (eds.), *Time to Kill: The Soldier's Experience of War in the West 1939–1945* (Pimlico, London, 1997).
Anon., *A Short Record of the Services and Experiences of the 5th Battalion Royal Irish Fusiliers in the Great War* (Hely's Ltd., Dublin, 1919).
Anon. (A. P. I. S. and D. G. S.), *With the Ulster Division in France: A Story of the 11th Battalion Royal Irish Rifles (South Antrim Volunteers) from Bordon to Thiepval* (William Mullan and Son, Belfast, n.d. [1918?]).
Ashworth, T., *Trench Warfare, 1914–18: The Live and Let Live System* (Macmillan, London, 1980).
Babington, A., *For the Sake of Example: Capital Courts Martial 1914–18, The Truth* (Leo Cooper, London, 1983).
Barnes, B. S., *This Righteous War* (Richard Netherwood, Huddersfield, 1990).
Barry, T., *Guerilla Days in Ireland* (Anvil Books, Dublin, 1981).
Bartlett, F. C., *Psychology and the Soldier* (Cambridge University Press, 1927).

Bartlett, T. and Jeffery, K. (eds.), *A Military History of Ireland* (Cambridge University Press, 1996).

Baynes, J., *Morale: A Study of Men and Courage: The Second Scottish Rifles at the Battle of Neuve Chapelle, 1915* (Leo Cooper, London, 1987. First published by Cassell, London, 1967).

Beckett, I. F. W, *The Amateur Military Tradition, 1558–1945* (Manchester University Press, 1991).

Beckett, I. F. W., *The Great War 1914–1918* (Longman, London, 2001).

Beckett, I. F. W. (ed.), *The Army and the Curragh Incident, 1914* (Bodley Head for the Army Record Society, London, 1986).

Beckett, I. F. W. and Gooch J. (eds.), *Politicians and Defence* (Manchester University Press, 1981).

Beckett, I. F. W. and Simpson, K. (eds.), *A Nation in Arms: A Social Study of the British Army in the First World War* (Manchester University Press, 1985).

Benson, J., *The Working Class in Britain, 1850–1939* (Longman, London, 1989).

Bew, P, *Ideology and the Irish Question: Ulster Unionism and Irish Nationalism, 1912–1916* (Clarendon Press, Oxford, 1994).

Bew, P., *John Redmond* (Historical Association of Ireland, Dundalk, 1996).

Bithrey, J., *A Great Irish Chaplain, Father John Gwynn, S.J.* (privately published, Dublin, 1915).

Blake, R. (ed.), *The Private Papers of Douglas Haig, 1914–19* (Eyre and Spottiswoode, London, 1952).

Bond, B. (ed.), *'Look to your Front': Studies in the First World War* (Spellmount, Staplehurst, 1999).

Bond, B. and Roy, I. (eds.), *War and Society: A Yearbook of Military History* (Croom Helm, London, 1975).

Bond, B. (ed.), *The First World War and British Military History* (Clarendon Press, Oxford, 1991).

Bourne, J. M., *Britain and the Great War, 1914–18* (Edward Arnold, London, 1989).

Boyce, D. G., *The Sure Confusing Drum: Ireland and the First World War* (University College of Swansea, 1993).

Brereton, J. M., *The British Soldier: A Social History from 1661 to the Present Day* (The Bodley Head, London, 1986).

Bridges, G. T. M., *Alarms and Excursions: Reminiscences of a Soldier* (Longmans, Green and Co., London, 1938).

Brown, M. and Seaton, S., *Christmas Truce: The Western Front, December 1914* (Papermac, London, 1994).

Buckland, P., *Irish Unionism 1: The Anglo–Irish and the New Ireland, 1885 to 1922* (Gill and Macmillan, Dublin, 1972).

Buckland, P., *Irish Unionism 2: Ulster Unionism and the Origins of Northern Ireland, 1886–1922* (Gill and Macmillan, Dublin, 1973).

Buckland, P., *James Craig* (Gill and Macmillan, Dublin, 1980).

Campbell, C., *Emergency Law in Ireland, 1918–1925* (Clarendon Press, Oxford, 1994).

Canning, W. J., *Ballyshannon, Belcoo, Bertincourt: The History of the 11th Battalion, The Royal Inniskilling Fusiliers (Donegal and Fermanagh Volunteers) in World War One* (privately published by W. J. Canning, Antrim, 1996).

Caulfield, M., *The Easter Rebellion* (Gill and Macmillan, Dublin, 1995).

Cecil, H. and Liddle, P. H. (eds.), *Facing Armageddon: The First World War Experienced* (Leo Cooper, London, 1996).

Chandler, D. and Beckett, I. F. W. (eds.), *The Oxford Illustrated History of the British Army* (Oxford University Press, 1994).

Childs, B. E. W., *Episodes and Reflections, Being Some Records from the Life of Major General Sir Wyndham Childs* (Cassell, London, 1930).

Coetzee, F. and Shevin-Coetzee, M. (eds.), *Authority, Identity and the Social History of the Great War* (Berghahn Books, Oxford, 1995).

Colvin, I., *The Life of Lord Carson* (Victor Gallancz, London, 1936).

Connolly, J., *Collected Works* (New Books Publications, Dublin, 1987–88).

Cooper, A. M. (ed.), *We Who Knew: The Journal of an Infantry Subaltern during the Great War* (The Book Guild, Lewes, 1994).

Cooper, B., *The Tenth (Irish) Division in Gallipoli* (Irish Academic Press, Dublin, 1993. First published by Herbert Jenkins, London, 1918).

Cooper Walker, G. A., *The Book of the 7th Service Battalion, the Royal Inniskilling Fusiliers: From Tipperary to Ypres* (Brindley and Son Printers, Dublin, 1920).

Corbally, M. J. P. M., *The Royal Ulster Rifles, 1793–1960* (Royal Ulster Rifles Regimental Association, Belfast, 1960).

Corns C. and Hughes-Wilson, J., *Blindfold and Alone: British Military Executions in the Great War* (Cassell, London, 2001).

Costello, C., *A Most Delightful Station: The British Army on the Curragh of Kildare, Ireland, 1855–1922* (The Collins Press, Cork, 1996).

Crang, J. A., *The British Army and the People's War 1939–1945* (Manchester University Press, 2000).

Crozier, F. P., *A Brass Hat in No-Man's Land* (Cedric Chivers, Bath, 1968. First published by Cape, London, 1930).

Crozier, F. P., *The Men I Killed* (Michael Joseph, Plymouth, 1937).

Cunliffe, M., *The Royal Irish Fusiliers, 1793–1950* (Oxford University Press, 1952).

Curtis, L. P., *Apes and Angels: The Irishman in Victorian Caricature* (David and Charles Ltd., London, 1971).

Dallas, G. and Gill, D., *The Unknown Army: Mutinies in the British Army in World War I* (Verso, London, 1985).

Dalton, C., *With the Dublin Brigade, 1917–21* (Peter Davies, London, 1929).

Davison, C. (ed.), *The Burgoyne Diaries* (Thomas Harmsworth Publishing, London, 1985).

Denman, T., *Ireland's Unknown Soldiers: The 16th (Irish) Division in the Great War, 1914–18* (Irish Academic Press, Dublin, 1992).

Denman, T., *A Lonely Grave: The Life and Death of William Redmond* (Irish Academic Press, Dublin, 1995).

Dennis, P., *The Territorial Army, 1906–1940* (The Royal Historical Society and The Boydell Press, Woodbridge, Suffolk, 1987).

Dockrill, M. and French, D., (eds.), *Strategy and Intelligence: British Policy during the First World War* (The Hambledon Press, London, 1996).

Dooley, T. P., *Irishmen or English Soldiers? The Times and World of a Southern Catholic Irish Man (1876–1916) Enlisting in the British Army during the First World War* (Liverpool University Press, 1995).

Dungan, M., *Irish Voices from the Great War* (Irish Academic Press, Dublin, 1995).

Dungan, M., *They Shall Grow Not Old: Irish Soldiers and the Great War* (Four Courts Press, Dublin, 1997).

Dunlop, J. K., *The Development of the British Army 1899–1914: From the Eve of the South African War to the Eve of the Great War, with Special Reference to the Territorial Force* (Methuen, London, 1938).

Enloe, C. H., *Ethnic Soldiers* (Penguin Books, Harmondsworth, 1980).

Ervine, St J., *Craigavon: Ulsterman* (George Allen and Unwin, London, 1949).

Evans, M. and Lunn, K. (eds.), *War and Memory in the Twentieth Century* (Berg, Oxford, 1997).

Falls, C., *The History of the 36th (Ulster) Division* (Constable, London, 1996. First published by McCaw, Stevenson and Orr, Belfast, 1922).

Falls, C., *The History of the First Seven Battalions, Royal Irish Rifles (Now the Royal Ulster Rifles) in the Great War* (Gale and Polden, Aldershot, 1925).

Feilding, R., *War Letters to a Wife: France and Flanders, 1915–1919* (The Medici Society, London, 1929).

Fitzpatrick, D., *Politics and Irish Life, 1913–1921: Provincial Experience of War and Revolution* (Gill and Macmillan, Dublin, 1977).

Fitzpatrick, D., *The Two Irelands, 1912–1939* (OPUS, Oxford, 1998).

Fitzpatrick, D. (ed.), *Ireland and the First World War* (Lilliput Press and Trinity History Workshop, Dublin, 1988).

Fox, F., *The Royal Inniskilling Fusiliers in the World War* (Constable and Co. Ltd., London, 1928).

Foy, M. and Barton, B., *The Easter Rising* (Sutton Publishing, Stroud, 1999).

Fraser, T. G. and Jeffery, K. (eds.), *Men, Women and War* (Lilliput Press, Dublin, 1993).

French, D., *Raising Churchill's Army: The British Army and the War against Germany 1919–1945* (Oxford University Press, 2000).

Fuller, J., *Troop Morale and Popular Culture in the British and Dominion Armies, 1914–18* (Clarendon Press, Oxford, 1990).

Gatrell, V. A. C., Lenman, B. and Parker, G. (eds.), *Crime and the Law: The Social History of Crime in Western Europe since 1500* (Europa Publications, London, 1980).

Grieves, K., *The Politics of Manpower, 1914–18* (Manchester University Press, 1988).

Griffith, P. (ed.), *British Fighting Methods in the Great War* (Frank Cass, London, 1996).

Gwynn, D., *The Life of John Redmond* (George G. Harrap, London, 1932).

Gywnn, S., *John Redmond's Last Years* (Edward Arnold, London, 1919).

Hanna, H., *The Pals at Suvla Bay: Being the Record of 'D' Company of the 7th Royal Dublin Fusiliers* (Ponsonby, Dublin, 1916).

Harries-Jenkins, G., *The Army in Victorian Society* (Routledge and Kegan Paul, London, 1977).

Harris, H. E. D., *The Irish Regiments in the Great War* (Mercier Press, Cork, 1968).

Harris, R. G., *The Irish Regiments: A Pictorial History, 1683–1987* (Nutshell Publishing, Tunbridge Wells, 1988).

Harvey, J. R., *History of the 5th (Royal Irish) Regiment of Dragoons from 1689 to 1799, Afterwards the 5th Royal Irish Lancers from 1858 to 1921* (Gale and Polden, Aldershot, 1923).

Hennessey, T., *Dividing Ireland: World War I and Partition* (Routledge, London, 1998).

Hitchcock, F. C., *'Stand To', A Diary of the Trenches, 1915–18* (Hurst and Blackett, London,1937. Reprinted by Gliddon Books, London, 1988).

Holmes, R., *The Little Field Marshal: Sir John French* (Jonathan Cape, London, 1981).

Holmes, R., *Firing Line* (Pimlico, London, 1994).

Horne, J. (ed.), *State, Society and Mobilization in Europe during the First World War* (Cambridge University Press, 1997).

Hughes, C., *Mametz: Lloyd George's 'Welsh Army' at the Battle of the Somme* (Gliddon Books, London, 1990).

Inglis, B., *Roger Casement* (Hodder and Stoughton, London, 1973).

Jackson, A., *Sir Edward Carson* (Historical Association of Ireland, Dublin, 1993).

James, E. A., *British Regiments, 1914–18* (Samson Books, London, 1978).

Jeffery, K., *Ireland and the Great War* (Cambridge University Press, 2000).

Jeffery, K. (ed.), *'An Irish Empire'? Aspects of Ireland and the British Empire* (Manchester University Press, 1996).

Jervis, H. S., *The 2nd Munsters in France* (Gale and Polden, Aldershot, 1922).

Johnstone, T., *Orange, Green and Khaki: The Story of the Irish Regiments in the Great War, 1914–18* (Gill and Macmillan, Dublin, 1992).

Jourdain, H. F. N., *Record of the 5th (S.) Battalion the Connaught Rangers* (Oxford University Press, 1916).

Jourdain, H. F. N., *The Connaught Rangers* (Royal United Services Institution, London, 1924–28).

Jourdain, H. F. N., *Ranging Memories* (Oxford University Press, 1934).

Kerr, S. P., *What the Irish Regiments Have Done* (Unwin, London, 1916).

Kipling, R., *The Irish Guards in the Great War* (Macmillan, London, 1923).

Kirkpatrick, I., *The Inner Circle: Memoirs of Ivone Kirkpatrick* (Macmillan, London, 1959).

Lavery, F. (ed.), *Irish Heroes in the War* (Everett, London, 1917).

Lavery, F. (ed.), *Great Irishmen in War and Politics* (Andrew Melrose, London, 1920).

Lenox-Conyngham, M., *An Old Ulster House and the People who Lived in it* (Dundalgan Press, Dundalk, 1946).

Liddle, P. H. (ed.), *Home Fires and Foreign Fields* (Brasseys, London, 1985).

Liddle, P. H. (ed.), *Passchendaele in Perspective, The Third Battle of Ypres* (Leo Cooper, London, 1997).

Lucy, J. F., *There's a Devil in the Drum* (Faber and Faber, London, 1938. Reprinted by the Naval and Military Press, London, 1992).

Lyons, J. B., *The Enigma of Tom Kettle: Irish Patriot, Essayist, Poet, British Soldier, 1880–1916* (The Glendale Press, Dublin, 1983).

McCance, S., *The History of the Royal Munster Fusiliers, vol. II, From 1861 to 1922 (Disbandment)* (Gale and Polden, Aldershot, 1927).

MacDonagh, M., *The Irish at the Front* (Hodder and Stoughton, London, 1916).

MacDonagh, M., *The Irish on the Somme* (Hodder and Stoughton, London, 1918).

Mackenzie, S. P., *Politics and Military Morale: Current Affairs and Citizenship Education in the British Army, 1914–50* (Clarendon Press, Oxford, 1992).

Macready, C. F. N., *Annals of an Active Life* (Hutchinson, London, 1924).

Manchester, A. H., *A Modern Legal History of England and Wales, 1750–1950* (Butterworths, London, 1980).

Middlebrook, M., *The Kaiser's Battle, 21 March 1918: The First Day of the German Spring Offensive* (Penguin, London, 1978).

Mitchell, G., *'Three Cheers for the Derrys!': A History of the 10th Royal Inniskilling Fusiliers in the 1914–18 War* (Yes! Publications, Derry, 1991).

Montgomery-Hyde, H., *Carson* (Constable, London, 1987).

Montmorency, H. de, *Sword and Stirrup, Memories of an Adventurous Life* (G. Bell and Sons Ltd., London, 1936).

Moore, W., *The Thin Yellow Line* (Leo Cooper, London, 1974).

Moran, Lord, *The Anatomy of Courage* (Constable, London, 1945).

Muenger, E. A., *The British Military Dilemma in Ireland: Occupation Politics, 1886–1914* (Gill and Macmillan, Dublin, 1991).

Novick, B., *Conceiving Revolution: Irish Nationalist Propaganda during the First World War* (Four Courts Press, Dublin, 2001).

O'Brien, J. V., *'Dear, Dirty Dublin': A City in Distress, 1899–1916* (University of California Press, London, 1982).

O'Halpin, E., *The Decline of the Union: British Government in Ireland 1892–1920* (Gill and Macmillan, Dublin, 1987).

O'Rahilly, A., *Father William Doyle, S. J.* (privately published, London, 1925).

Orr, P., *The Road to the Somme: Men of the Ulster Division Tell Their Story* (Blackstaff Press, Belfast, 1987).

Osburn, A., *Unwilling Passenger* (Faber and Faber, London, 1932).

Perry, F. W., *The Commonwealth Armies: Manpower and Organisation in Two World Wars* (Manchester University Press, 1988).

Philips, D., *Crime and Authority in Victorian England: The Black Country, 1835–1860* (Croom Helm, London, 1977).

Pugsley, C., *On the Fringe of Hell: New Zealanders and Military Discipline in the First World War* (Hodder and Stoughton, Auckland, 1991).

Putkowski, J. and Sykes, J., *Shot at Dawn: Executions in World War One by Authority of the British Army Act* (Leo Cooper, London, 1993).

Rawling, B., *Surviving Trench Warfare: Technology and the Canadian Corps, 1914–18* (University of Toronto Press, London, 1992).

Reitz, D., *Trekking On* (Faber and Faber, London, 1933).

Rickard, L., *Story of the Munsters at Etreux, Festubert, Rue de Bois and Hulloch* (Hodder and Stoughton, London, 1918).

Robertson, N., *Crowned Harp: Memories of the Last Years of the Crown in Ireland* (Allen Figgis, Dublin, 1960).

Samuels, M., *Command or Control? Command, Training and Tactics in the British and German Armies, 1888–1918* (Frank Cass, London, 1995).

Scott, P. T., *'Dishonoured': The 'Colonels' Surrender' at St. Quentin, The Retreat from Mons, August 1914* (Tom Donovan Publishing, London, 1994).

Sellers, L., *For God's Sake Shoot Straight! The Story of the Court Martial and Execution of Sub Lieutenant Edwin Dyett* (Leo Cooper, London, 1995).

Sheffield, G. D., *Leadership in the Trenches: Officer–Man Relations, Morale and Discipline in the British Army in the Era of the First World War* (Macmillan, London, 2000).

Simkins, P., *Kitchener's Army: The Raising of the New Armies, 1914–16* (Manchester University Press, 1988).

Sindall, R., *Street Violence in the Nineteenth Century: Media Panic or Real Danger?* (Leicester University Press, 1990).

Skyrme, T., *History of the Justices of the Peace* (Barry Rose Publishers, Chichester, 1994).

Smith, L. V., *Between Mutiny and Obedience: The Case of the French Fifth Infantry Division During World War I* (Princeton University Press, 1994).

Spiers, E. M., *The Army and Society, 1815–1914* (Longman, London, 1980).

Spiers, E. M., *Haldane: an Army Reformer* (Edinburgh University Press, 1980).

Spiers, E. M., *The Late Victorian Army, 1868–1902* (Manchester University Press, 1992).

Steel, N. and Hart, P., *Defeat at Gallipoli* (Macmillan, London, 1994).

Strachan, H., *The Politics of the British Army* (Clarendon Press, Oxford, 1997).

Swift, R. and Gilley, S. (eds.), *The Irish in Britain 1815–1939* (Pinter Publishers, London, 1989).

Taylor, D., *Crime, Policing and Punishment in England, 1750–1914* (Macmillan, London, 1998).

Tobias, J. J., *Crime and Industrial Society in the Nineteenth Century* (B. T. Batsford, London, 1967).

Townsend, C., *Political Violence in Ireland, Government and Resistance since 1848* (Oxford University Press, 1983).

Travers, T., *The Killing Ground: The British Army, the Western Front and the Emergence of Modern Warfare, 1900–18* (Allen and Unwin, London, 1987).

Travers, T., *How the War was Won: Command and Technology in the British Army on the Western Front, 1917–18* (Routledge, London, 1992).

Turner, J. (ed.), *Britain and the First World War* (Unwin Hyman, London, 1988).

Vane, F., *Agin the Governments* (Samson Low and Marston, London, 1928).

White, S. N., *The Terrors: 16th (Pioneer) Battalion, Royal Irish Rifles, 1914–19* (The Somme Association, Belfast, 1996).

Whitton, F. E., *The History of the Prince of Wales' Leinster Regiment (Royal Canadians)*, vol. II (Gale and Polden, London, n.d. (1926?)).

Williams, R., *Defending the Empire: The Conservative Party and British Defence Policy 1899–1915* (Yale University Press, London, 1991).

Winter, J. M., *The Great War and the British People* (Macmillan, London, 1985).

Woodward, D., *Lloyd George and the Generals* (Associated University Press, London and Toronto, 1983).

Wylly, H. C., *Crown and Company: The Historical Records of the Second Battalion, Royal Dublin Fusiliers, vol. II, 1911–1922* (Gale and Polden, Aldershot, 1922).

Wylly, H. C., *Neill's 'Blue Caps': The History of the First Battalion, Royal Dublin Fusiliers, vol. III, 1914–1922* (Gale and Polden, Aldershot, 1925).

Articles

Beckett, I. F. W., 'The Real Unknown Army: British Conscripts, 1916–19', in J. J. Becker and S. Audoin-Rouzeau (eds.), *Les Societiés Européennes et la Guerre de 1914–18* (Université de Paris X-Nanterre, Paris, 1990).

Bessel, R. and Englander, D., 'Up from the Trenches: Some Recent Writing on the Soldiers of the Great War', *European Studies Review*, XI, 3, 1981.

Bourke, J., ' "Irish Tommies": The Construction of a Martial Manhood, 1914–1918', *Bullán*, III, 2, 1998.

Bowman, T., 'Composing Divisions: The Recruitment of Ulster and National Volunteers into the British Army in 1914', *Causeway Cultural Traditions Journal*, Spring 1995.

Bowman, T., 'The Irish at the Somme', *History Ireland*, 4, 4, 1996.

Bowman, T., 'The Irish Recruiting and Anti-Recruiting Campaigns, 1914–18', in Taithe, B. and Thornton, T. (eds.), *Propaganda: Political Rhetoric and Identity 1300–2000* (Sutton Publishing, Stroud, 1999).

Bowman, T., 'The Ulster Volunteer Force and the Formation of the 36th (Ulster) Division', *Irish Historical Studies*, XXXII, 128, 2001.

Buckley, S., 'The Failure to Resolve the Problem of V.D. among the Troops in Britain during World War One', in Bond, B. and Roy, I. (eds.), *War and Society: A Yearbook of Military History, II* (Croom Helm, London, 1977).

Callan, P., 'The Irish Soldier: A Propaganda Paper for Ireland, September–December 1918', *The Irish Sword*, XV, 59, 1982.

Callan, P., 'Recruiting for the British Army in Ireland during the First World War', *The Irish Sword*, XVII, 66, 1987.

Dallas, G. and Gill, D., 'Mutiny at Etaples Base in 1917', *Past and Present*, 69, 1975.

Denman, T., 'The 10th (Irish) Division, 1914–15: A Study in Military and Political Interaction', *The Irish Sword*, XVII, 66, 1987.

Denman, T., 'Sir Lawrence Parsons and the Raising of the 16th (Irish) Division', *The Irish Sword*, XVII, 67, 1987.

Denman, T., 'An Irish Battalion at War: from the Letters of Captain J. H. M. Staniforth, 7th Leinsters, 1914–18', *The Irish Sword*, XVII, 68, 1989.

Denman, T., '16th (Irish) Division Casualties, 1916–18', *The Irish Sword*, XVII, 68, 1989.

Denman, T., 'The 16th (Irish) Division on 21 March 1918: Fight or Flight?', *The Irish Sword*, XVII, 69, 1990.

Denman, T., 'The Catholic Irish Soldier in the First World War: The "Racial Enviroment"', *Irish Historical Studies*, XXVII, 108, 1991.

Denman, T., ' "A Voice from the Lonely Grave": The Death in Action of Major William Redmond, M.P., 7 June 1917', *The Irish Sword*, XVIII, 73, 1992.

Denman, T., ' "The Red Livery of Shame": The Campaign against Army Recruitment in Ireland, 1899–1914', *Irish Historical Studies*, XXIX, 114, 1995.

Denman, T., ' "Ethnic Soldiers Pure and Simple?": The Irish in the Late Victorian British Army', *War in History*, III, 3, 1996.

Dewey, P., 'Military Recruiting and the British Labour Force during the First World War', *Historical Journal*, XXVII, 1, 1984.

Dominy, G., 'More than just a "Drunken Brawl"? The Mystery of the Mutiny of the Inniskilling Fusiliers at Fort Napier, 1887', *South African–Irish Studies*, I, 1991.

Dooley, T. P., 'Politics, Bands and Marketing: Army Recruitment in Waterford city, 1914–15', *The Irish Sword*, XVIII, 72, 1991.

Dooley, T. P., 'Southern Ireland, Historians and the First World War', *Irish Studies Review*, 4, 1993.

Dooley, T. P., 'The Royal Munster Fusiliers', *History Ireland*, VI, 1, 1998.

Dorman, E., 'The North Irish Horse', *Army Review*, III, 1913.

Englander, D. and Osbourne, J., 'Jack, Tommy and Henry Dubb: The Armed Forces and the Working Class', *Historical Journal*, XXI, 3, 1978.

Englander, D., 'Mutiny and Myopia', *Bulletin of the Society for the Study of Labour History*, LII, 1, 1987.

Fitzpatrick, D., 'The Logic of Collective Sacrifice: Ireland and the British Army, 1914–1918', *Historical Journal*, XXXVIII, 4, 1995.

Forde, F., 'The Tyneside Irish Brigade', *The Irish Sword*, XVI, 1984.

Greenhut, J., 'The Imperial Reserve: The Indian Corps on the Western Front, 1914–15', *The Journal of Imperial and Commonwealth History*, XII, 1, 1983.

Howie D. and J., 'Irish Recruiting and the Home Rule Crisis of August–

September 1914', in Dockrill, M. and French, D. (ed.), *Strategy and Intelligence: British Policy during the First World War* (Hambledon Press, London, 1996).

Jackson, A., 'Unionist Myths 1912–1985', *Past and Present*, 136, 1992.

Jeffery, K., 'Irish Culture and the Great War', *Bullán*, I, 2, 1994.

Johnson, D., 'Trial by Jury in Ireland, 1860–1914', *Legal History*, XVII, 3, 1996.

Karsten, P., 'Irish Soldiers in the British Army, 1792–1922: Suborned or Subordinate?', *The Journal of Social History*, XVII, 1983.

Lemisko, L. S., 'Morale in the 16th. (Irish) Division, 1916–18', *Irish Sword*, XX, 81, 1997.

Mackenzie, S. P., 'Morale and the Cause: The Campaign to Shape the Outlook of Soldiers of the British Expeditionary Force, 1914–1918', *Canadian Journal of History*, XXV, 1990.

Nelson, J. E., 'Irish Soldiers in the Great War: Some Personal Experiences', *The Irish Sword*, XI, 44, 1974.

O'Halloran, M., '"A few notes on German treatment": The Diary of Sergeant Charles Mills, Royal Munster Fusiliers, 1918', *The Irish Sword*, XV, 60, 1983.

Parks, E., 'Guernsey's Contribution to the 16th (Irish) Division', *The Irish Sword*, XVIII, 73, 1992.

Perry, N., 'Nationality in the Irish Infantry Regiments in the First World War', *War and Society*, XII, 1, 1994.

Perry, N., 'Maintaining Regimental Identity in the Great War: The Case of the Irish Infantry Regiments', *Stand To*, 52, 1998.

Roth, A., ' "The German Soldier is not Tactful": Sir Roger Casement and the Irish Brigade in Germany during the First World War', *Irish Sword*, XIX, 78, 1995.

Rowe, P., 'Review Article' (relating to courts martial 1914 to date), *Royal United Services Institute Journal*, August, 1994.

Rubin, G. R., 'The Legal Education of British Army Officers, 1860–1923', *Journal of Legal History*, XV, 3, 1994.

Semple, A. J., 'The Fenian Infiltration of the British Army', *Journal of the Society of Army Historical Research*, 52, 1974.

Sheffield, G., 'British Military Police and their Battlefield Role, 1914–18', *Sandhurst Review of Military Studies*, I, 1990.

Staunton, M., 'Ginchy: Nationalist Ireland's Forgotten Battle of the Somme', *An Cosantoir*, XLVI, 1986.

Staunton, M., 'Kilrush, Co. Clare and the Royal Munster Fusiliers: The Experience of an Irish Town in the First World War', *The Irish Sword*, XVI, 65, 1986.

Staunton, M., 'Soldiers Died in the Great War, 1914–19 as Historical Source Material', *Stand To!*, 27, 1989.

Stubbs, J. O., 'The Unionists and Ireland, 1914–18', *Historical Journal*, XXXIII, 4, 1990.

Townsend, C., 'The Suppression of the Easter Rising', *Bullán*, I, 1, 1994.

Travers, T. H. E., 'The Hidden Structural Problem in the British Officer Corps, 1900–1918', *Journal of Contemporary History*, XVII, 3, 1982.

Tucker, A., 'The Issue of Army Reform in the Unionist Government, 1903–5', *Historical Journal*, IX, 1, 1966.

Ward, A. J., 'Lloyd George and the 1918 Irish Conscription Crisis', *Historical Journal*, XVII, 1974.

Woodward, D. R., 'Did Lloyd George Starve the British Army of Men Prior to the German Offensive of 21 March 1918?', *Historical Journal*, XXVII, 1, 1984.

Theses

Brent Wilson, J., 'The Morale and Discipline of the British Expeditionary Force, 1914–18' (MA thesis, University of New Brunswick, Canada, 1978).

Callan, P., 'Voluntary Recruiting for the British Army in Ireland during the First World War' (PhD thesis, University College Dublin, 1984).

Foy, M. T., 'The Ulster Volunteer Force: Its Domestic Development and Political Importance in the Period 1913 to 1920' (PhD thesis, The Queen's University of Belfast, 1986).

Hannon, C., 'The Irish Volunteers and the Concept of Military Service and Defence, 1913–1924' (PhD thesis, University College Dublin, 1989).

Lemisko, L. S., 'Politics, Performance and Morale: The 16th (Irish) Division, 1914–18' (MA thesis, University of Calgary, Canada, 1992).

Maxwell, I. L., 'The Life of Sir Wilfrid Spender, 1876–1960' (PhD thesis, The Queen's University of Belfast, 1991).

Morris, P., 'Leeds and the Amateur Military Tradition: The Leeds Rifles and their Antecedents, 1859–1918' (PhD thesis, University of Leeds, 1983).

Mercer, E., 'For King, Country and a Shilling a Day: Recruitment in Belfast during the Great War, 1914–18' (MA dissertation, The Queen's University of Belfast, 1998).

O' Flanaghan, N., 'Dublin City in an age of War and Revolution' (MA thesis, University College Dublin, 1985).

Sheffield, G. D., 'Officer-man Relations: Morale and Discipline in the British Army, 1902–22' (PhD thesis, London University, 1994).

Staunton, M., 'The Royal Munster Fusiliers in the Great War, 1914–19' (MA thesis, University College Dublin, 1986).

Index

Printed in the United Kingdom
by Lightning Source UK Ltd.
135461UK00001B/91-93/A